Soviet Policy Toward the Middle East Since 1970

Robert O. Freedman

Soviet Policy Toward the Middle East Since 1970

PRAEGER SPECIAL STUDIES IN INTERNATIONAL POLITICS AND GOVERNMENT

Praeger Publishers   New York   Washington   London

Library of Congress Cataloging in Publication Data

Freedman, Robert Owen.
    Soviet policy toward the Middle East since 1970.

    (Praeger special studies in international politics
and government)
    Bibliography: p.
    Includes index.
    1. Russia—Foreign relations—Near East.   2. Near
East—Foreign relations—Russia.   I. Title.
DS63.2.R9F7   327.47'056   74-31504
ISBN 0-275-05920-0
ISBN 0-275-89170-4 (pbk.)

PRAEGER PUBLISHERS
111 Fourth Avenue, New York, N.Y. 10003, U.S.A.

Published in the United States of America in 1975
by Praeger Publishers, Inc.

Printed in the United States of America

To My Mother and
the Memory of My Father

The four-year period between the death of Egyptian President Gamal Nasser and the sudden resignation of United States President Richard Nixon witnessed a number of major upheavals and changes in the always volatile Middle East. The Arab-Israeli conflict again erupted into full-scale war in October 1973, bringing the United States and the Soviet Union to the brink of nuclear confrontation. The war also brought on a five-month oil embargo against the United States and a quadrupling of oil prices. In addition, the period witnessed the failure of a Communist-supported coup d'etat in the Sudan and a major rearrangement of Middle East alliances. Egypt, under its new President Anwar Sadat, moved from a position of hostility towards oil-rich Saudi Arabia to an alignment with it, while simultaneously moving from an alliance with the Soviet Union to a more neutral position between the superpowers following Sadat's expulsion of the Soviet military forces from their Egyptian bases in July 1972. Indeed, by the time of Nixon's resignation it appeared that Egypt was moving toward the United States—despite all the military aid given by the Soviet Union during the October war. Soviet policy-makers struggled to deal with these developments. It will be the purpose of this book to demonstrate how the Soviet leadership sought to cope with Middle Eastern developments that it not only had not planned but also found most difficult to control.

A number of scholars and government officials were kind enough to comment on this manuscript at various stages of its preparation. Special thanks go to Professors Aaron Klieman of Tel-Aviv University, Abdul Said of American University, Melvin Croan of the University of Wisconsin-Madison, and Teresa Rakowska-Harmstone of Carleton University, as well as to Dr. David Albright of *Problems of Communism* and Mr. Norman Anderson of the State Department's Egyptian desk, whose criticisms helped improve the manuscript. In addition, I would like to thank the other members of the State Department's Near East/South Asia section and the diplomats representing Egypt, Jordan, and Israel who were kind enough to grant me interviews during my research. Finally, I would like to thank the large number of American, Israeli, Arab, and Soviet scholars with whom I had long discussions about the Middle East and my students at Marquette University from whom I learned so much. Needless to say, while I am indebted to all these individuals for their assistance, the views in this book are my own and I bear full responsibility for any errors.

I received research support for this study from Marquette University and from the National Endowment for the Humanities. This support enabled me to travel to the Middle East and to the Soviet Union. I would like to thank the personnel of the Zionist Archives in Jerusalem and the library of Radio Liberty in New York who afforded me every courtesy during my research. I would also like to offer my thanks to Ms. Karen Scibilia, who helped me maintain my files on the Middle East, and to Ms. Sandy Feuerabend, who typed the manuscript.

A final word of thanks to my wife, Sharon, without whose support this book never could have been written.

Portions of this study initially appeared in articles that I wrote for *Problems of Communism* and the *Naval War College Review*. I gratefully acknowledge permission to reprint the material.

CONTENTS

Soviet Policy Toward the Middle East Since 1970

Since the death of Stalin in 1953 the Soviet Union has become increasingly active in Middle Eastern affairs; by the time of Egyptian President Gamal Nasser's death in 1970 even Western statesmen had to acknowledge that the USSR had become one of the leading powers in the region. Yet while there has been general agreement that the Soviet Union now plays an important role in the Middle East, no such consensus exists as to the USSR's goals in the region. Some observers have contended that the main Soviet goal is an offensive one—to dominate the Middle East in order to deny its oil, strategic communication routes, and other assets to the United States and its allies. An opposing view holds that the Soviet aim is primarily defensive, to prevent the region from being used as a base for an attack upon the USSR. Other hypotheses place Soviet objectives somewhere between these two extremes.[1] The Soviet leaders themselves have justified their activity in the Middle East both in terms of its proximity to the southern border of the USSR and in terms of their responsibility as leaders of the "world revolutionary" and "national liberation" movements.[2] Whatever the ultimate goal of Soviet policy—and the author sees it basically as an offensive one—it is evident that since Stalin's death the Soviet leadership has been making a determined effort to increase Soviet influence in the Middle East. To this end the USSR has extended large amounts of military assistance, together with economic aid and diplomatic support, to a number of key Middle Eastern states, in an effort to influence the domestic and foreign policies of these states.

Influence, however, is very difficult for statesman (and political scientists) to measure.[3] The leaders of all the great powers want their nations' interests to be considered very seriously by leaders in other nations when decisions are being made. Yet, as both the United States and the Soviet Union have learned over the last two decades, the mere provision of military and economic aid is no guarantee that a client state will do the superpower's bidding in either its foreign or domestic policies, particularly when the client regime's leadership is making decisions of great importance. The spectrum of influence extending between normal and even good diplomatic relations on the one hand and "control" or dominant influence on the other is a very broad one, as the Russians have discovered in their dealings with the nations of the Middle East, particularly in the period since Nasser's

1

death, when the region's complexity and volatility increasingly hampered Soviet policy makers. Indeed, in order to understand fully the nature of the Soviet drive for influence in the Middle East and the regional obstacles facing it, it is first necessary to analyze briefly the nature of and the interrelationships between the nations of the region. Far from being a "vacuum of power," as the ill-fated Eisenhower Doctrine of 1957 characterized it, the Middle East is a highly complex region with numerous power centers and power conflicts, and the region's complexities have provided both opportunities and problems for Soviet policy-makers.

THE CONTEMPORARY MIDDLE EAST: A BRIEF OVERVIEW

From an ethnic, religious, political, and economic standpoint, the Middle East is perhaps the most complex region on earth. Sunni and Shii Moslems, Catholics and Protestants, Jews, Kurds, Copts, Maronites, and Armenians coexist uneasily in a region characterized by unstable and frequently changing governments, and periodically convulsed by fighting between Arabs and Israelis, Iraqis and Kurds, Lebanese Christians and Moslems, Sudanese Arabs and Blacks, Jordanians and Palestinians, North and South Yemenis, and Iranians and Iraqis. Western-style democracies, feudal monarchies, and "Arab Socialist" military dictatorships are all present, along with a number of other forms of government. Adding to the region's complexity is its broad spectrum of economic systems, which range all the way from free-enterprise capitalism to state socialism.[4]

There are basically two forms of monarchy in the Middle East. Some nations, such as Saudi Arabia and the Sheikdoms of the Persian Gulf, can be called feudal monarchies. Others, such as Iran, Jordan, and Morocco, whose rulers have initiated major economic development projects along with social reforms, can be termed "modernizing" monarchies. The democracies in the region are Lebanon and Israel, although these two nations differ sharply in economic structure; Lebanon possesses a free-enterprise economy, while the Israeli economy is basically socialistic.

The Arab military regimes of the Middle East, such as Egypt, Syria, Iraq, Libya, Algeria, South Yemen, and the Sudan, form another major class of Middle Eastern governments. Although all these nations call themselves republics, despite the fact that their leaders came to power through military coups d'etat, they differ in the degree in which they tolerate Islam, foreign investment, and private ownership of land and industry, to mention only a few important categories.

Soviet leaders, in attempting to classify these varied nations according to the doctrines of Marxism-Leninism, have encountered serious difficulties. According to the Marxist-Leninist ideology, which serves to legitimize the rule of the Soviet Communist Party as well as provide a weltanschauung for its leadership, the nations of the Middle East must be somewhere on the long road to Communism. The fact that a nation may be a feudal monarchy one day and proclaim itself an "Arab Socialist Republic" the next, after a coup d'etat, presents a number of difficulties for Soviet ideologists. While usually accepting the anti-imperialist tenet of Marxism-Leninism, the new military leaders have usually rejected such other basic tenets of the Soviet doctrine as the supremacy of the working class, dialectical materialism, and atheism—indeed, the identification of the Soviet Union with atheism has proved to be a major obstacle to the spread of Soviet influence through the predominantly Moslem Middle East where religion plays a major role in every day life.[5]

A more serious problem to the Soviet leaders is the fact that the Communist parties of some of these Arab military republics (which theoretically should be leading them down the path to Communism) remain as suppressed under the new regimes as they were under the old feudal monarchies. The Russians have had to decide whether or not to give military and economic support to non-Communist "bourgeois" nationalist leaders such as Nasser who, although they suppressed the Communist parties of their countries, nevertheless pursued "anti-imperialist" foreign policies often favorable to the Soviet Union.[6]

Even in cases where the Communist party of a Middle Eastern nation has been tolerated, the Soviet leaders have had great difficulty in determining the degree to which the Communist party of that country should try to retain its independence while cooperating with the ruling nationalist party. In addition, some of the Middle Eastern Communist parties have proved uncomfortably independent of Soviet direction; this too has posed serious problems for the Russian leaders.

The numerous conflicts in the Middle East present another serious dilemma for the Russian leaders. While the Arab-Israeli conflict is perhaps the most familar one to Americans, other conflicts of high intensity abound within the region. Iraq and Iran, whose leaders profess different variants of Islam, have been on the verge of war over their Shatt-al-Arab River boundary, and each accuses the other of aiding dissident movements within its borders. Yet another factor embittering relations between the two countries is their struggle for power over the Persian Gulf, a struggle that sharpened in intensity as British forces were withdrawn from the area in 1971. A further complication of the power struggle in the Persian Gulf lies in Saudi Arabia's claims to the area.

Another conflict in the Middle East involves the relations between Syria and her two smaller Arab neighbors, Jordan and Lebanon. Successive Syrian regimes have sought to dominate the two nations and even to incorporate them into a "greater Syria." The Syrians threatened to invade Lebanon during the Lebanese-Palestinian guerrilla conflict in 1969 and actually did invade Jordan during the Jordanian civil war of September 1970. Syrian-Turkish relations have also been strained for a long time; the Syrians remember with great bitterness Turkey's annexation of its Iskenderun region before World War II when France had a mandate over Syria.

One of the major inter-Arab convlicts of the 1960s was the struggle between Egypt and Saudi Arabia over Yemen. This conflict, which almost broke out into full-scale war in 1963, cooled off following the Egyptian withdrawal from Yemen in 1967 after the Six-Day War and has remained dormant in the early 1970s as the new Egyptian President, Anwar Sadat, sought to forge an alliance with King Faisal. Nevertheless, this conflict could erupt again if Egypt tried to restore its influence in Yemen. However, for the time being at least, it has been superseded by the increasingly sharp conflict between North and South Yemen, which reached the stage of a border War in 1972, and by the guerrilla war that South Yemen is supporting in the Dhofar region of neighboring Oman.

Conflict also pervades the relations among the Arab "republics" in the center of the Middle East. The historic competition for power in the region between Iraq and Egypt goes back to biblical days, and the fact that the two countries now have similar governments has not lessened the conflict. In recent years Syria and Algeria have also entered into the competition with claims of their own for Arab leadership.

Other conflicts in the Middle East include the one between Algeria and Morocco (they fought a brief border war in 1963); between Iraq and Kuwait (Iraq tried unsuccessfully to annex Kuwait in 1961 and invaded it in 1973); and between Egypt and Iran, although this conflict has also been subdued since Sadat came to power. Since 1966 there has been a struggle for power in Jordan between the Palestinians and the regime of King Hussein, while at the same time the various Palestinian guerrilla organizations have been struggling among themselves for control of the Palestinian resistance movement.[7] Domestic conflicts with serious international implications include the hostility between Christian and Moslem Arabs in Lebanon, which erupted into civil war in 1958, and which heavily overshadowed the Lebanese government's conflicts with the Palestinian guerrillas in 1969 and 1973; the strife between Arabs and Blacks in the Sudan (the long and bloody civil war between the two groups came to an end in 1972); and the endemic conflict between the Iraqi government and its Kurdish minority, which periodically erupts into full-scale war.

These interstate and intrastate conflicts have been a major obstacle to the Soviet Union's efforts to extend its influence over the entire region. While siding with one side of a regional conflict has given the USSR entree to a regional state, the Soviet action has usually meant alienating the other side and driving it into the arms of the West, as well as enabling the state receiving Soviet aid to exploit Soviet assistance by undertaking actions not necessarily to the liking of the Soviet leadership. There have been a number of cases where a regional client state's goals have differed sharply from Soviet global aims, and the Soviet leaders have therefore run the risk of getting pulled into a Middle East war over an issue of only secondary or tertiary importance to the USSR. Consequently, the Russians have had a difficult time trying to follow an evenhanded policy in such conflicts as the Iranian-Iraqi, North Yemen-South Yemen, and Egyptian-Iraqi, however much the Soviet leadership may have wished to spread the mantle of a "Pax Sovietica" over the region. Even in the case of the Arab-Israeli conflict, where the Soviet leaders sided with the Arabs, they had to limit their aid to the Arab states lest the USSR become involved in a serious confrontation with the United States and thereby jeopardize the economic and strategic benefits flowing to the Soviet Union from the Soviet-American detente.

Another Middle Eastern problem with which the Russians have had to contend is the issue of Arab unity. Despite the numerous conflicts among the Arab states, there has also been a strong psychological drive for unity. Yet even here conflict is present, since the Arabs have been unable to agree on a political structure on which to build their unity. The one serious attempt at a union of Arab states—the Syrian-Egyptian Union—lasted only three years (1958-61), and the confederation of Egypt, Libya, Syria, and the Sudan, which came into being in 1970, and the Libyan-Egyptian union of 1972 soon collapsed because of personality and policy conflicts between the different nations' leaders. The Arab drive for unity has nevertheless posed yet another dilemma for the Soviet leadership, and at one point it brought Khrushchev into an open confrontation with Nasser. Initially opposed to the idea of Arab unity because of its prewar German and postwar British sponsorship, the Soviet leadership vacillated in the 1950s, 1960s, and early 1970s between supporting the idea of Arab unity as part of their emphasis on the unity of all "anti-imperialist" forces in Third World states and regions, and opposing it on the grounds that a unified Arab world might block Soviet penetration of the Middle East.

In addition to these regional obstacles to the extension of Soviet influence, the Soviet leadership has also been beset with nonregional obstacles. First and foremost among these is competition from other powers, particularly the United States, which actively oppose Soviet efforts to secure dominant influence over the Middle East. Capitalizing on the Soviet debacle in the Sudan, where an abortive Communist-supported coup d'etat in July 1971 led to a sharp deterioration in Soviet-Sudanese relations, both the United States and Communist China used the opportunity to improve relations with the once strongly pro-Russian Nimeri regime. Similarly, as Soviet policy clearly began to tilt toward Iraq during its struggle with Iran, the United States moved to consolidate its relations with the Shah and weaken Soviet influence in Iran. For the Soviet leadership, however, the most serious arena of Soviet-American competition for influence in the Middle East has been Egypt, the most populous and militarily powerful of the Arab states in the region. Indeed, the Soviet-American competition for influence in Egypt, which increased sharply after the death of Nasser, is one of the main themes of this book.

While the Soviet Union and the United States have been the main nonregional powers competing for influence in the Middle East, one cannot overlook the activities of a number of West European powers, especially France, which are also active in the region. Although the Soviet leadership was no doubt pleased with the disarray in NATO caused by transatlantic differences in Middle Eastern strategy in the 1956 and 1973 wars, it must have been less happy with the fact that the Europeans were alternate sources of economic and military assistance to the Middle Eastern states, who were able to play off all the nonregional powers against each other, thus limiting the amount of influence any one power, including the USSR, could wield.

Another important factor affecting Soviet policy toward the Middle East is the Sino-Soviet conflict. While China is as yet only tangentially involved in the Middle East, its conflict with the Soviet Union erupted into a much-publicized series of border clashes in March 1969. These clashes underscored Chinese claims to large parts of Soviet Siberia and raised the possiblity that, should the Soviet Union become involved in a major war in the Middle East, the Chinese might avail themselves of the opportunity to move into Siberia. In addition, the Soviet leadership has long been concerned over the establishment of a Sino-American axis aimed against the USSR. The surprise visit to Peking of Henry Kissinger in July 1971 followed by President Nixon's visit in early 1972 must have made a number of Soviet leaders worry that the Sino-American axis was well under way. These concerns with the Chinese challenge have forced Soviet leaders to exercise a certain degree of caution in their Middle Eastern policies, lest the United States, which under Nixon's leadership also seemed willing to provide long-term credits for the ailing Soviet economy, depart from its detente policy and align itself more closely with the Chinese. For this reason, as mentioned above, the Soviet leadership was unwilling to provide all the aid desired by the Arabs in their confrontation with Israel, but this, in turn, was to cause an exasperated Sadat to expel the Soviet forces from their strategically important bases in Egypt in July 1972—two months after the first Nixon-Brezhnev summit.

Another factor affecting Soviet policy that stems from its triangular relationship with the United States and China is the issue of Jewish emigration from the Soviet Union to Israel. In a move to gain support from liberal circles in the United States following Kissinger's visit to Peking, the Soviet leadership decided in late 1971 to increase the emigration quota from 300 to 3,000 per month. While popular in the United States, this decision (which may also have been aimed at expediting Soviet-American trade relations) was decidedly unpopular in the Arab world, which saw the Jewish immigrants to Israel, a number of whom were highly skilled, as increasing Israel's military power in its confrontation with the Arabs.

Thus, the Soviet leadership has been confronted by a number of regional and extraregional obstacles in its efforts to increase Soviet influence in the Middle East. Interestingly enough, the Soviet leaders (and many Western leaders as well) tend to view the Middle East as what political scientists call a "zero-sum game" contest for influence in which where one side wins, the other side must lose an equivalent amount. This is somewhat ironic, since in the absence of the sanction of armed force, the ability of a major power to influence a smaller state is marginal at best. Indeed, the mere provision of economic and military assistance is not enough, as the Soviet leadership discovered in its attempts to change Yugoslav, Albanian, and Chinese policy through manipulation of military and economic assistance.[8]

Given the complexity of the Middle East and the major obstacles facing the Soviet leaders in their attempts to increase Soviet influence in the region, Soviet policy can perhaps best be viewed in the period since Nasser's death as a highly opportunistic one in which the Soviet leaders primarily reacted to and, on occasion, attempted to exploit regional developments and trends which they had not caused but which they nonetheless hoped to manipulate to weaken Western influence in the Middle East. Unfortunately for the Russians, however, Middle East trends did not always go in pro-Soviet directions, as Dmitry Volsky, associate editor of the Soviet foreign policy weekly *New Times*, somewhat ruefully acknowledged when commenting on the anti-Soviet and anti-Communist reaction in the Arab world to the Communist-supported coup d'etat attempt in the Sudan in July 1971:

> It would be difficult indeed to find a spot in the world where the situation is as contradictory as it is in the Middle East. . . . It is not surprising, therefore, that many observers are finding it difficult to establish what the dominant trend in this troubled area is.[9]

Soviet policy toward the Middle East in the post-1970 period, therefore, will be seen primarily as a series of reactions to developments originating within the volatile Middle East—developments that Soviet leaders discovered they often could neither control nor manipulate.

A NOTE ON SOURCES

The primary source for this study is the Soviet press, especially *Pravda* and *Izvestia*, which reflects the official viewpoint of the Soviet government, as does

Radio Moscow, another source utilized extensively. In addition, the Soviet foreign affairs weekly, *New Times*, has been cited frequently because it usually reflects the opinion of the Soviet Foreign Ministry. Among other Soviet journals, only the *World Marxist Review* can be considered a major source for this study, not only because it reflects the thinking of Soviet party leaders, but also because it provides a sounding board for the opinions of nonruling Communist party leaders; and in the period since the 24th Congress of the Communist Party of the Soviet Union (CPSU) in 1971, Arab Communists have utilized the journal to voice their open disagreements with certain aspects of Soviet Middle Eastern policies. The more specialized Soviet journals, such as *Narodi Azii i Afriki, International Affairs*, and *Mirovaia ekonomika i mezhdunarodnaia otnosheniia*, have been cited only occasionally since they tend to reflect the speculative attitudes of Soviet scholars and research institutes, rather than the official policy of the Soviet government.

On the Middle Eastern side, I have depended primarily on statements by national leaders as broadcast over their government radios or printed in the local press or in interviews with Western correspondents. Since I do not have a reading knowledge of Arabic, I have depended on translations of the Arab Press found in the *Record of the Arab World* and the *Middle East Monitor*. When still in existence, the journal *The New Middle East* was an excellent source of information about the region, and the detailed chronology in the *Middle East Journal* has also been of great benefit. For the Israeli point of view, I have relied on the Jerusalem *Post*, which usually reflects government thinking, and *Ha'aretz*, which takes an independent position. I have also had the opportunity to discuss my research with Egyptian, Jordanian, Palestinian Arab, and Israeli officials, American State Department officials, and a number of Arab, Israeli, American, and Soviet scholars working on Middle Eastern problems—all of whom presented useful perspectives in helping me understand the Middle East, a region that presents numerous obstacles not only for outside powers trying to influence developments within the region but also for scholars seeking to understand it.

NOTES

1. For general surveys of the Soviet involvement in the Middle East, see Walter Laqueur, *The Struggle for the Middle East* (New York: Macmillan, 1969); Aaron Klieman, *Soviet Russia and the Middle East* (Baltimore: Johns Hopkins Press, 1970); M. S. Agwani, *Communism in the Arab East* (Bombay: Asia Publishing House, 1969); and George Lenczowski, *Soviet Advances in the Middle East* (Washington, D.C.: American Enterprise Institute, 1972). For a review of the first three books, see the author's "Soviet Dilemmas in the Middle East," *Problems of Communism* 23, no. 3 (May-June 1972); 71-73.

For a general discussion of possible Soviet objectives, see A. S. Becker and A. L. Horelick, "Soviet Policy in the Middle East" (Santa Monica, Cal.: Rand Publication R-504-FF, 1970), pp. 63-64.

For specific studies of the USSR and the October 1973 Arab-Israeli war, see Foy D. Kohler et al., *The Soviet Union and the October 1973 Middle East War* (Miami: Center for Advanced International Studies, 1974); and Walter Laqueur, *Confrontation: The Middle East in World Politics* (New York: Bantam Books, 1974).

2. For a Soviet view of the USSR's policies in the region, see O. M. Gorbatov and L. I. Cherkasskii, *Sotrudnichestvo SSSR so stranami arabskogo vostoka i Afriki* (Moscow: Nauka, 1973).

3. Political science models dealing with the exertion of influence in Soviet foreign policy in general and Soviet foreign policy toward the Middle East in particular are still relatively rare. The interested reader is advised to consult J. David Singer's article, "Inter-Nation Influence: A Formal Model" in the influence theory section of *International Politics and Foreign Policy*, ed. James N. Rosenau (New York: Macmillan, 1969). Singer makes the useful distinction between influence leading to behavior modification in a target state and influence leading to behavior reinforcement. Another useful study, which examines the phenomenon of influence from the perspective of the target state, is Marshall R. Singer, *Weak States in a World of Powers* (New York: Free Press, 1972), especially chapters 6, 7, 8.

See also Richard W. Cottam, *Competitive Interference and Twentieth Century Diplomacy* (Pittsburgh: University of Pittsburgh Press, 1967).

4. For a useful taxonomy of the governments of the Middle East, see J. C. Hurewitz, *Middle East Politics: The Military Dimension* (New York: Praeger, 1969) and Abid A. Al-Marayati, ed., *The Middle East: Its Governments and Politics* (Belmont, Cal.: Duxbury Press, 1972). For an excellent survey of Middle Eastern politics, see Paul Hammond and Sidney Alexander, eds., *Political Dynamics in the Middle East* (New York: Elsevier, 1972).

5. For a recent Soviet view of the role of religion in Third World states, with a special focus on Islam, see B. Gafurov, ed., *Religiia i obshchestvennaia misl' narodov vostoka* (Moscow: Nauka, 1971).

6. In the 1930s the Soviet leadership faced the same dilemma in its relations with Ataturk's regime in Turkey and Chiang Kai-shek's regime in China. In both instances, Russian support was given to the "bourgeois" nationalist regime rather than to the Communists. For an analysis of these events, see Adam Ulam, *Expansion and Coexistence: The History of Soviet Foreign Policy 1917-1967* (New York: Praeger, 1968), pp. 167-181. For an overall analysis of the twists and turns in Soviet ideological formulations about the Third World, see Ishwer C. Ojha, "The Kremlin and Third World Leadership: Closing the Circle?" in *Soviet Policy in Developing Countries*, ed. W. Raymond Duncan (Waltham, Mass.: Ginn-Blaisdell, 1970), pp. 9-28; and R. A. Yellon, "Shifts in Soviet Policies Toward Developing Areas 1964-1968," in the same volume (pp. 225-286). See also Jaan Pennar, *The USSR and the Arabs: The Ideological Dimension (New York: Crane Russak, 1973). For a recent summary of Soviet thinking about the role of the army in underdeveloped states, see R. E. Sevortian, Armiia politicheskom rezhime stran sovremennogo vostoka* (Moscow: Nauka, 1973).

7. For a study of the conflicts within the Palestinian movement, see William B. Quandt et al., *The Politics of Palestinian Nationalism* (Los Angeles: University of California Press, 1973).

8. On this point, see Robert O. Freedman, *Economic Warfare in the Communist Bloc: A Study of Soviet Economic Pressure Against Yugoslavia, Albania and Communist China* (New York: Praeger, 1970).

9. *New Times*, no. 44, 1971, p. 7.

2

FROM WORLD WAR II TO
THE DEATH OF NASSER

In the period since World War II, the Soviet Union has tended to pursue one line of policy toward the two northernmost nations of the Middle East—Iran and Turkey (hereafter called the Northern Tier)—and 'another toward the other Middle Eastern states. The reasons for this may be traced to both geography and history. Iran and Turkey differ sharply from the other nations of the region in three important respects. Both nations have long borders with the Soviet Union, and both have fought numerous wars against invading Russian troops in the last 400 years. As a result, both Iran and Turkey have had a great deal of experience with Russian imperialism, and for this reason the Soviet leadership has had far greater difficulty in extending Soviet influence in these nations than in the other countries of the Middle East, which neither border on the USSR nor possess a long experience in dealing with Russian imperialism. Indeed, all the nations of what we shall call the Southern Tier have had bitter experience with *Western* imperialism—particularly that of Britian and France—which dominated the region from Morocco to the Persian Gulf in the interwar period. It is in this part of the Middle East that the Soviet Union has seen the greatest increase in its influence since the end of World War II, although the Russians have proven unable to expand their influence to the point of actual control in any nation of the area.[1]

THE STALINIST HERITAGE, 1945-53

Stalin's foreign policy toward the Middle East was a relatively uncomplicated one. Immediately after World War II, he demanded that the Turkish government cede to Russia parts of eastern Turkey and grant the Soviet Union a military base in the Turkish straits. In addition, Stalin claimed the right to a trusteeship over Libya and postponed the withdrawal of Soviet occupation forces from Iran until well into 1946. These relatively crude attempts at territorial aggrandizement were counterproductive. Instead of increasing Russia's security through the acquisition of territory (a similar motive governed Soviet policy in Eastern Europe during this period), Stalin's actions served only to drive the nations of the Northern Tier into the arms of the West.[2]

Stalin's policies towards the Southern Tier were scarcely more productive. Viewing the world in terms of two camps, Communist and anti-Communist, Stalin was either unable or unwilling to see that the leaders of the new nations of what we now call the Third World wished to belong to neither camp, but desired to remain neutral. The Soviet press called such leaders as Nasser, Shishakli, and Nehru "lackeys of the imperialists," and described the newly formed Arab League as an "instrument of British imperialism." The Soviet recognition of the state of Israel in 1948 and its diplomatic and military support for it during the first Arab-Israeli conflict (1947-49) seem to have been aimed at weakening Britain's position in the Middle East and depriving it of key military bases.[3] In any case it did not improve the Russian position among the Arab states, while the period of good relations between the USSR and Israel was of a very short duration.[4]

Thus, Soviet policy toward the Middle East under Stalin was unproductive, if not counterproductive, and Russian influence was at a low ebb in both the Northern and Southern Tiers of the region at the time of Stalin's death in March 1953.

THE KHRUSHCHEV ERA IN THE MIDDLE EAST, 1953-64

The death of Stalin brought a fundamental change in Soviet policy toward the Middle East. Although the Russians had begun to take the side of the Arabs in the Arab-Israeli conflict as early as 1954, when Malenkov was still premier, the real change in Soviet policy did not emerge until after Khrushchev ousted Malenkov from the premiership in February 1955. Unlike Stalin, Khrushchev was not afflicted with a two-camp view of the world. Instead, he saw the world as being divided into three main zones or blocs—the socialist bloc, the capitalist bloc, and the Third World, which he hoped to win over to Communism through political support and large doses of economic and military aid.[5] An irony of this development was that the new American Secretary of State, John Foster Dulles, had a two-camp view of the world much like Stalin's, and tended, therefore, to have little patience with the neutralist aspirations of Third World leaders. Hence, when Dulles tried to integrate a number of Arab states into a military alliance aimed against the Soviet Union, he greatly offended their sensibilities, particularly since England, the former colonial overlord of much of the Middle East, was to be a founding member of the alliance. Egypt's Nasser was particularly irritated by this development, since his principal Arab rival, Nuri Said of Iraq, embraced the alliance (The Baghdad Pact)—and the military and economic assistance that went with it. Nasser then turned to the Russians for arms, and the end result of the process was that Nasser, through the now famous arms deal of 1955, actually invited the Russians to participate in the politics of the Middle East.[6] By obtaining large amounts of sophisticated weaponry from the USSR, Nasser clearly demonstrated the Arabs' independence from their former colonial masters; for the Russians, on the other hand, it was a means of gaining influence in the Middle East.

Nonetheless, even in the process of gaining influence in the Middle East through the sale of weapons, the Russians got themselves involved in a dilemma that has persisted until today. Mere provision of weapons to a country, regardless of its need for the weapons, does not give the doner nation control over the policies of the recipient nation. To the contrary, the supply of advanced weaponry may enable the recipient nation to embark on a military adventure that the donor nation considers undesirable. Even worse, such a military adventure might threaten to drag the donor nation itself into a war it does not want. Although the supply of weapons to military regimes may be relatively inexpensive in terms of cost to the Soviet economy, in terms of the risk that the Russians might be involved in a war not to their choosing as a result of such military assistance, the cost of such aid can be very high indeed. The Russians became aware of this danger in 1956 with the outbreak of the Sinai campaign, and found themselves in an even more dangerous predicament with the outbreak of the Six-Day War in June 1967. Heavy arms shipments to Egypt preceded both conflicts,[7] and the Russians were in danger of involvement in both wars.[8]

Besides running the risk of direct involvement in an Arab-Israeli war, the Russians faced yet another dilemma in their dealings with Nasser. While happily accepting large quantities of Soviet economic and military aid, as well as support against the West following the nationalization of the Suez Canal in 1956 and during the subsequent Suez crisis, Nasser declared the Egyptian Communist Party to be illegal and kept its leaders in prison. Indeed, he made it very clear that he differentiated between the Soviet Union as a "great friend" and the Egyptian Communist Party, which he considered a threat to his dictatorship. As early as August 16, 1955, Nasser had stated in an interview in the Lebanese newspaper *Al-Jarida* that "nothing prevents us from strengthening our economic ties with Russia even if we arrest the Communists at home and put them on trial."[9]

Such a situation posed a painful dilemma to Khrushchev, a dilemma that he never really resolved. Nasser was a useful ally in the cold war, regardless of his treatment of the Egyptian Communist Party. Nonetheless, since Khrushchev considered himself the head of the international Communist movement, he felt constrained to try to protect the Communist parties of the Middle East. On several occasions he complained to Nasser about the treatment of the Egyptian Communists, but Nasser denounced such "interference" in Egypt's "internal affairs," and relations between the Soviet Union and Egypt deteriorated as a result.[10]

The role of the Communist Party was to prove a stumbling block in Khrushchev's policies toward Syria and Iraq as well. In 1957, Syria, of all the nations of the Southern Tier, seemed most ripe for a Communist seizure of power. The Syrian Communist Party had grown rapidly since the overthrow of the Shishakli dictatorship in 1954, and the Syrian government was very pro-Russian. the USSR sent a great deal of economic and military aid to Syria in 1957,[11] and Syrian leaders were frequent visitors to the Soviet Union in that year. Yet even as Syria appeared on the brink of "going Communist" (as some U.S. newspapers speculated), an event occurred that could only have shocked and disappointed the Soviet leadership—the union of Syria and Egypt into the United Arab Republic.[12] And just as the Egyptian Communist Party had been banned by Nasser, so too was the Syrian Communist Party, hitherto the strongest in the Arab world. While the official Soviet response to the announcement of the formation of the United Arab Republic was restrained in tone,[13] the event marked a victory for Arab nationalism, as espoused by Nasser, and a defeat for Arab Communism and, to a lesser degree, the USSR.

The conflict between Arab nationalism and Communism (and indirectly the USSR) became even more acute following the overthrow of the pro-Western regime of Nuri Said in Iraq in July 1958. While Nasser, who later flew to Moscow to discuss this event, had high hopes that Arab nationalists who backed him would take power and bring Iraq into the Egyptian-dominated United Arab Republic, it soon transpired that Kassem, who emerged as the leader of the new regime, was an independent Arab nationalist, one who was willing to utilize the Iraqi Communist Party to combat Nasser's followers in Iraq. Indeed, the Iraqi Communist Party was prominently represented in the new Iraqi regime, and the Soviet leaders soon began to give Iraq large amounts of economic and military aid, much as they had done with Egypt and Syria earlier.[14] In addition, however, the Soviet Union came out in support of Kassem in his efforts to keep Iraq independent of Nasser's unity movement.[15] *Pravda* pointedly stated on March 30, 1959:

> It has lately become apparent that some public figures in the Near East mean by Arab nationalism the immediate and mechanical unification of all Arab states by one of them, regardless of whether they want it or not. All who do not agree with this are denounced as Zionists, communists and enemies of the Arab people.[16]

Despite a brief rapproachement with Nasser in 1960, Khrushchev once again clashed with Egyptian leaders in May 1961 during a visit by an Egyptian parliamentary delegation headed by Anwar Sadat, who was then chairman of the United Arab Republic's National Assembly. Khrushchev attacked the Egyptian leaders for opposing Communism and told them, "If you want socialism, you should not oppose Communism" since the one automatically followed the other. He also told the Egyptians, "Arab nationalism is not the zenith of happiness," and "Life itself will impose Communism." The Egyptians retorted angrily and Soviet-Egyptian relations suffered another setback.[17]

Meanwhile, despite Soviet military, economic, and diplomatic support, Kassem had proven to be difficult person for the Soviet leaders to work with. Although he pulled Iraq out of the Baghdad Pact (securing, in the process, a large Soviet loan), he also skillfully played the Communists off against the Nasserites, weakening both, and emerged himself as the dominant force in Iraq.[18] By 1961 the Communists had lost their last positions of power in his regime and Kassem ruled alone—although he tolerated the presence of Communists in Iraq to a limited extent. The Iraqi Communists lost even this tenuous degree of freedom, however, when an avowedly anti-Communist group of army officers overthrew Kassem in 1963 and proceeded to execute hundreds of Iraqi Communists and drive the remainder either underground or into exile. Although this regime was itself overthrown before its anti-Communist policies led to too severe a breach with the USSR, its successor was not much more hospitable toward the Iraqi Communist Party.

By this time, however, Khrushchev had switched his primary interest in the Arab world to yet another country, Algeria. Following the end of the Algerian war of independence with France in 1962, the USSR established close relations with the regime of Ahmed Ben-Bella. Soviet economic and military aid was provided to Ben-Bella, who allowed a number of Algerian Communists to participate, as individuals, in his regime (the party itself remained illegal) while also nationalizing a sizable portion of Algeria's agricultural land and industry. Relations between the two countries grew so warm that Ben-Bella was awarded the Lenin Peace Prize and decorated as a "hero of the Soviet Union" during his visit to Moscow in April 1964, and at the end of the visit the Algerian leader secured a major loan.[19]

These developments in Algeria, coupled with Nasser's nationalization of a large portion of Egyptian industry following the breakup of the union with Syria in the fall of 1961, encouraged Khrushchev to believe that the Arab nationalist leaders were turning toward socialism even without the help of the Communist parties. Indeed, it probably appeared to Khrushchev that his prediction made to Sadat in 1961 was now coming true. By 1963 Soviet ideologists were casting around for an explanation for this behavior, one that would justify increased Soviet support for such regimes. (The support most likely would have come anyway, but a new ideological concept would help justify it, both to suspicious Communists who were suppressed under the Arab nationalist regimes, and to those in Moscow who questioned the wisdom of aiding leaders such as Ben-Bella and Nasser.[20]) Consequently, the terms "noncapitalist path" and revolutionary democracy" were born. By "noncapitalist path" Soviet ideologists meant an intermediate stage between capitalism (or the primitive capitalist economies the nationalist leaders had inherited from the colonial period) and socialism, and the highly optimistic Khrushchev often used the terms "noncapitalist path" and "socialism" synonymously in describing the progress of such regimes as Nasser's and Ben-Bella's. The term "revolutionary democracy" was used to describe those states moving along the noncapitalist path toward socialism without the help of a Communist Party, which according to previous Marxist-Leninist theory was supposed to be the sine qua non of a transition to socialism.[21]

These semantics enabled Khrushchev to attempt to solve his dilemma of dealing with both nationalist leaders like Nasser and the Communist parties of their states, a dilemma that had caused problems for Soviet policy-makers in the past. Arguing that the Egyptian Communist Party would be more effective working from within Nasser's regime to win the Egyptian leader to "scientific socialism," Khrushchev—and his successors—urged the Egyptian Communist Party (a weak and faction-ridden organization) to dissolve officially and join the Arab Socialist Union (ASU), which was Nasser's mass political organization and the only one permitted in Egypt. In another policy innovation, the Soviet leadership moved to establish direct party-to-party relations between the CPSU and the ASU, such as had already been done with Ben-Bella's Front de Liberation Nationale (FLN) in which Communists occupied key positions. In establishing direct party-to-party relations, the Soviet leaders claimed that this would enable the CPSU to directly transmit its revolutionary experience to the one-party regimes of the Arab states and thereby hasten the trip of Egypt and Algeria down the noncapitalist path toward Communism.

As might be expected, a number of Arab Communists took a rather dim view of these developments in Soviet strategy, which many of them saw as the effective end of their political existence. Writing in the *World Marxist Review*, a journal that serves as a sounding board for the world's nonruling Communist parties as well as for the CPSU, several Arab Communists voiced their unhappiness with these Soviet ideological innovations. Thus, Fuad Nasser, Secretary General of the Jordanian Communist Party and generally a strong supporter of Soviet foreign policy (particularly in the Sino-Soviet conflict), stated in the course of a 1964 symposium on Arab socialism and Arab unity:

> Latterly, there has been a great deal of talk about these ex-colonial countries taking the non-capitalist way, although *frankly speaking* we still are not sufficiently clear as to what this means.[22] [emphasis added]

Similarly, Khalid Bakdash, Secretary General of the Syrian Communist Party and perhaps the most prestigious Communist leader in the entire Middle East (and also a staunch supporter of Soviet policy) pointedly stated:

> *Some people say*, and this can be heard in Syria as well, that the communist parties no longer play the role they used to. This is a shortsighted view, to say the least, and to say it would be tantamount to denying the need for the continued existence of the party. . . . This is a shortsighted view because the role of the working class in our cou[n]tries is bound to grow with the development of the national-liberation movement. The stronger the communist parties and the more ground the ideas of scientific socialism gain, the more certain our progress in the future. [23] [emphasis added]

A second area of disagreement that arose during the symposium dealt with the degree of criticism to which the Revolutionary Democratic leaders should be subjected by Arab Communists. Bakdash took the lead in urging that the shortcomings of these regimes should be clearly pointed out, while other Arab Communists argued that only the positive (that is, genuine socialist) aspects of Nasser's and Ben-Bella's programs should be commented upon because the main role of the Arab Communists was to disseminate "scientific socialism" among the masses. Bakdash disagreed with their emphasis, arguing that while it was important for Arab Communists to teach "scientific socialism" and to promote friendship between their countries and the Soviet Union, it was also important to point out the differences between the Communists and the Revolutionary Democrats.[24]

While the Arab Communists debated the advantages and disadvantages of assisting the Revolutionary Democratic leaders, Khrushchev paid a visit to Egypt in May to examine the situation for himself. Although the visit was supposed to demonstrate the rapprochement between the USSR and Egypt, as symbolized by the Aswan Dam, it also illustrated Khrushchev's fundamental inability to understand the major currents in Arab politics. According to an Egyptian account of his visit, the Soviet leader seemed amazed at the popular responses Iraqi President Aref got from the Egyptian crowds when he cited Koranic verses in his speech. In addition, Khrushchev clashed with Ben-Bella, who reportedly told the Soviet leader that he knew nothing about Arab unity or the Arabs. To this Khrushchev is supposed to have replied, "I must admit I don't understand you, for there is only one unity, the unity of the working class."[25] Nonetheless, the visit ended on a positive note, at least for the Egyptians who were the recipients of a $277-million loan, and Nasser became the second Arab leader to be made a "hero of the Soviet Union."[26]

In addition to their activities in Egypt, Syria, Iraq, and Algeria during the Khrushchev period, the Russians also became active in other parts of the Arab world, although to a much smaller degree. The USSR gave military and economic aid to Morocco and Yemen (and were caught in the middle of the Algerian-Moroccan war of 1963) and granted economic assistance to Tunisia and the Sudan.[27] In addition, diplomatic relations were begun with Libya and Jordan, although repeated Soviet efforts to establish diplomatic relations with Saudi Arabia proved unsuccessful.

Khrushchev's policy toward the Northern Tier nations, Turkey and Iran, was far more limited in scope. Since these two nations were military allies of the United States, Khrushchev was not above rattling Soviet rockets at them, much as he periodically did to Britain, France, and West Germany. This, as can be imagined, was not conducive to an improvement of relations. Nonetheless, toward the end of Khrushchev's reign, relations with both countries were moderated. In the case of Iran, this was primarily due to the Shah's announcement in 1962 that no foreign missiles would be permitted on Iranian soil. This led to a major improvement in Soviet-Iranian relations. Leonid Brezhnev made a state visit to Iran in 1963, and the USSR gave Iran a $38.9 million loan in the same year.[28] It should be pointed out, however, that Iran was sorely beset by internal difficulties at the time of the Shah's announcement. The major land reform campaign under way at the time had aroused a great deal of opposition to the Shah's government, and the improvement of relations with the USSR enabled the Shah to concentrate his attention on his internal opposition.[29]

Soviet-Turkish relations during the Khrushchev era were considerably cooler. While the Russians had renounced their territorial demands against Turkey soon after the death of Stalin, Khrushchev had threatened to go to war against Turkey in 1957 over an alleged Turkish plot to invade Syria. Although in the atmosphere of East-West detente following the Cuban missile crisis of October 1962 some Turks called for closer relations with the Soviet Union, Khrushchev's policy toward the Cyprus crisis, which involved support for the Greek position and military aid for the Cypriot regime of Archbishop Makarios, was a major stumbling block in the way of a rapprochement between the two countries.[30]

All in all, the Soviet Union's position in the Middle East at the time of Khrushchev's fall in October 1964 was considerably better than when Khrushchev came to power. Of perhaps greatest significance, the Baghdad Pact had been all but destroyed by the withdrawal of its one Arab member, Iraq. In addition, the Russians had succeeded in establishing diplomatic relations with almost all the states in the Middle East and had given many of them military and economic aid. The Middle East was clearly no longer the Western sphere of influence it had been at the time of Stalin's death, and the Russians could justifiably consider themselves to be an important factor in Middle Eastern affairs.

The Soviet position, however, was far from a dominant one in 1964. In the countries in which the USSR could be said to have had the most influence—and in which it had spent the most money (Egypt, Syria, Iraq, and Algeria)—the

Communist parties remained illegal and many Communists languished in jail. Voices were already being raised in Moscow that too much had been spent with too little return. Although Arab leaders often joined the Russians in denouncing "imperialism," all had fairly good relations with the Western powers, and Russia was unable to control any of them. It was beginning to appear that, far from being exploited by the Russians as many in the West had feared when the USSR had made its dramatic entrance into the Middle East in 1955, the Arab nations were actually exploiting the Russians. They had gained large amounts of military and economic aid, while sacrificing none of their sovereignty. A Soviet commentator stated several years later:

> The existence of the world socialist system may be used to the advantage not only of Revolutionary Democrats or other representatives of the workers; certain judicious bourgeois circles in a number of countries are very successfully using this circunstance to strengthen the political sovereignty and economic development of their countries.[31]

Soviet gains were also limited in the realm of ideology. To be sure, the state sector had been enlarged and the private, or capitalist, sector reduced in many of the states of the region, particularly Egypt and Algeria. In addition, some foreign investments had been nationalized, and there had been a considerable amount of land reform. Nonetheless, these social reforms had been undertaken by nationalist regimes, operating independently of the Communist parties of their countries. Khrushchev hailed these reforms as demonstrating that a number of Middle Eastern nations had taken the noncapitalist way, and in his usual optimistic way went on to equate the noncapitalist way with the road to socialism on which the Communist nations of the world themselves had embarked. Khrushchev's successors, however, clearly differentiated between these two concepts. One Soviet commentator, in assessing the overthrow of such pro-Russian regimes as Nkrumah's in Ghana and Sukarno's in Indonesia, noted ruefully that the noncapitalist road was by no means irreversible.[32]

In sum, when Khrushchev fell in October 1964, the Soviet position in the Middle East was far better than it had been at the time of Stalin's death (it could hardly have been worse), yet it was far from a position of dominance or even preponderance of power. The nations of the Northern Tier, Iran and Turkey, remained firm allies of the United States, although both had improved relations—to a point—with the Soviet Union. Soviet influence had risen fastest among the Arab states, particularly Egypt, Algeria, Syria, and Iraq, but even in these states it was clearly limited. Each of these countries had maintained its independence of action both domestically and in foreign policy and, as argued above, tended to extract far more from the Soviet Union in the form of economic and military support than it paid in political obedience. To be fair to Khrushchev, it should be pointed out that the Middle East was not the primary area of Soviet concern during the period in which he ruled. Khrushchev's main concerns were the problems of Eastern and Western Europe and the rapidly escalating Sino-Soviet conflict. With the rise of the Brezhnev-Kosygin leadership to power, however, Soviet interest began to focus more closely on the Middle East.

THE BREZHNEV-KOSYGIN ERA,
1964-70

When the impulsive and energetic Khrushchev was replaced by the conservative and rather phlegmatic duo of Brezhnev and Kosygin, Western observers called the changeover in leadership "the triumph of the bureaucrats."[33] Like bureaucrats everywhere, they were tired of the constant administrative reorganizations of the Khrushchev era, along with his impulsive actions in foreign policy.[34] Unlike Khrushchev, who tried to spread Soviet influence everywhere in the world at a rapid pace, the new leaders appear to have decided to concentrate Soviet energies and resources on becoming the dominant power in the Middle East, while adopting a much more gradualist policy toward the growth of Soviet power in other parts of the non-Communist world. The Soviet drive for power and influence in the Middle East became increasingly evident in 1965 and 1966, both in the Northern Tier nations, which became the recipients of large amounts of Soviet economic aid, and in the Arab states of Egypt, Syria, Iraq, and Algeria. By early 1967 the new Soviet policy was in high gear, and at least part of the responsibility for the June 1967 Arab-Israeli war can be attributed to the USSR, which was exploiting the Arab-Israeli conflict to increase its influence among the Arab states.

While the Israeli victory in the Six-Day War was a temporary setback for the Russians, one consequence of the Arab defeat was a marked decline of American influence in the radical Arab states of the region.[35] As a result the Russians redoubled their efforts to oust Western influence from the Arab states, while cementing their newly improved relations with Iran and Turkey. Yet, by becoming more involved in the Middle East, the Soviet leaders encountered a number of serious problems, and although by the death of Nasser in September 1970 Soviet influence in the Middle East had reached its highest point since World War II, the Russians were still far from controlling the region. They instead found themselves paying a far higher price than ever before in terms of economic and military aid for their "influence," while running an increasingly serious risk of war with the United States—just at a time when the Sino-Soviet struggle was heating up.

In assessing the Brezhnev-Kosygin approach to the Middle East, it is first necessary to analyze the international situation that the new Soviet leadership faced when it took power in October 1964. Next, an examination will be made of the innovations and changes the new leadership made in Soviet policy toward the region. Finally, an assessment will be made of the Soviet position in the Middle East at the time of Nasser's death.

THE NEW INTERNATIONAL SITUATION

In surveying the Soviet position in the world after they took power in 1964, Brezhnev and Kosygin seem to have reached the conclusion that the further expansion of Soviet influence in Western Europe and Latin America was out of the question, at least for the time being, since these areas were of vital importance to the United States, which had demonstrated its clear military superiority over the Soviet Union during the Cuban missile crisis. Similarly, the active hostility of the Chinese Communists had confronted the Russians with a clear danger as well as an obstacle to the spread of their influence in South and Southeast Asia. While the USSR still had several important footholds in Africa, the Soviet leaders evidently decided that, because of the serious problems facing the Soviet economy, they should begin to concentrate their military and economic assistance in the Middle East, an area contiguous to the USSR and one holding greater possibilities for Soviet gains.[36]

The growing influence of the Russian military, with its call for an expanded navy, probably was a contributing factor to this decision. The key naval communication routes that run through the Middle East, and the Russian need to cope with American missile-carrying Polaris submarines already cruising in the Mediterranean at the time of Khrushchev's fall, made the region a particularly important one for the Soviet military. In 1964 a special Mediterranean unit was formed as part of the Soviet Black Sea fleet.[37]

A second contributing factor to the Soviet decision was the increasing instability in the region itself. Nasser's prestige had begun to wane, as his regime was beset with increasing economic and political difficulties, not the least of which was the failure of Egyptian intervention in the Yemeni civil war. Egypt's relations with the United States also began to deteriorate badly in the 1965-66 period.[38] In addition, the endemic Arab-Israeli conflict had begun to worsen, the frequently changing Syrian and Iraqi regimes were unable to cope with internal difficulties, and the British were hard-pressed to maintain their position in riot-torn Aden. All these developments must have tempted the Russians into greater involvement.

The Soviet leaders' attempt to gain increased influence in the Middle East was also aided by a number of events occurring elsewhere in the world in the 1965-66 period. Perhaps the most important was the large American troop commitment to Vietnam in 1965. This was a major bonus to the Russians for a number of reasons. Not only did the Vietnam War cause increasing internal turmoil in the United States itself, but it also served another major Soviet goal—the containment of Communist China. For with a half-million American troops to its south, a hostile India (supported by both the United States and the Soviet Union) to its southwest, and thirty Russian divisions along its northern border, China was indeed "contained"—from the Russian point of view, that is. Another important consequence of United States policy in Vietnam was that it tended to divert American energy and attention from other parts of the world, including the Middle East, thus enabling the Russians to operate more freely there.

A second major bonus for the Soviet Union was China's so-called cultural revolution, which occurred in 1966. This effectively removed China from competition with Russia in the Third World and greatly reduced Chinese influence in the international Communist movement. Not having to compete economically with China for influence throughout the Third World allowed the Russians to concentrate their resources in the Middle East.[39] It should be added that the cultural revolution, much like the United States involvement in Vietnam, tended to divert Chinese attention from the Middle East.[40]

Yet another bonus for the Russians came with the British decision to pull out of Aden (now the People's Democratic Republic of Yemen) in February 1966. This, together with increasing discussion in England about the necessity for pulling out of the Persian Gulf as well, must have given the Russians the impression that a major power vacuum was opening up along the southern and eastern periphery of the Arabian peninsula—a power vacuum that the Russians could fill. The fact that Western unity also seemed to be breaking down, as evidenced by de Gaulle's 1966 decision to take French military forces out of NATO, also must have been encouraging to the Russians. This French move, coupled with the British decision to pull out of Aden, made it appear very unlikely that the Western powers would develop a joint policy to confront the Russians in the Middle East.

Soviet failures elsewhere in the Third World also must have sharpened the Russian drive into the Middle East. The fall of Sukarno's regime in Indonesia in October 1965, a regime in which the Russians had invested nearly $2 billion in military and economic aid, was a blow to the Russians. Four months later, in February 1966, came the fall of Nkrumah's regime in Ghana, and the Russians lost their investment of nearly $500 million in military and economic aid. Both pro-Russian regimes were replaced by pro-Western ones.[41]

These events must have made the Russians prize even more highly the good relations they still had with a number of Middle Eastern nations, particularly the regimes of the "radical" Arab states, in which they had similarly invested extensive economic and military assistance. This was particularly true of the Syrian regime, which took power after a coup d'etat in February 1966 and announced its intention to undertake a major "socialist transformation" in Syria as well as work for improved relations with the Soviet Union. The fact that this regime took power so soon after the overthrow of Nkrumah must have been heartening for the Russians; even more heartening was the new regime's decision to permit the Syrian Communist leader, Khalid Bakdash, to return from his eight-year exile in Europe.[42] Yet the Russians were to find that their initial enthusiasm for the new Syrian regime was to become a very costly one, for it was this regime, with its encouragement of the Palestinian guerrillas, that was to help precipitate the June 1967 Arab-Israeli war.

NEW POLICY INITIATIVES

The decision of Brezhnev and Kosygin to make the Middle East a primary area of Soviet interest meant that the new Russian leaders would have to come to grips with some of the dilemmas left unsolved from the Khrushchev era. Most important of these was the role the Communist parties of the Middle East were to play in the political and economic life of the countries in which they operated. While Khrushchev had been generally ambivalent about this, the Brezhnev-Kosygin leadership adopted a clearer position. They no longer entertained much hope that any of the Communist parties of the region would seize power; indeed, confronted by a hostile Communist China, the Russian leaders must have wondered if it was to their benefit if any more countries were taken over by independent Communist parties. In any case the new Russian leaders began to emphasize the importance of good state relations with the nationalist leaders of the Middle East, and generally let the Communist parties of the region fend for themselves. In the case of the Northern Tier states, the Russians virtually disregarded the Communist parties; in the case of the Revolutionary Democratic Arab states, the parties were urged to disband and their members urged to join the large state parties of their countries, such as Egypt's Arab Socialist Union with which the Russians, in a policy change begun in Khrushchev's last months in power, were trying to develop party-to-party relations.

Thus, in April 1965 the Egyptian Communist Party was officially dissolved; a communique later published in *Al-Nahar* (Beirut) announced the termination

> of the existence of the Egyptian Communist Party as an independent body and the instruction of its members to submit—as individuals— their applications for membership in the Arab Socialist Union, and to struggle for the formation of a single socialist party which would comprise all the revolutionary forces in the country.[43]

Unfortunately for the Soviet leaders, the new strategy met with serious difficulties only two months later as Ben-Bella was ousted from office by Houri Boumadienne, the Algerian military chief, who had earlier complained about the growth of Communist influences in the Ben-Bella government. Boumadienne purged the Algerian government and the FLN of its Communist members and publicly stated that Communists would have no part in his new government.[44] For reasons of international politics, the Soviet leadership did not break relations with the new regime, even when Algerian Communists were imprisoned by it. The CPSU even continued party-to-party relations with the now Communist-free FLN, perhaps hoping thereby to maintain socialist influence on the Boumadienne regime from above. Nonetheless, party relations with the FLN proved to be an embarrassment for the Soviet Union because the Algerian Communist Party, although now illegal, continued to operate. At the 23d CPSU Congress in March 1966, the Algerian FLN, which was invited as a friendly (albeit non-Communist) party, walked out rather than see the Algerian Communist Party seated as an official delegation.[45]

Thus, the new Russian leaders had run into a dilemma. In seeking to develop close party ties with the non-Communist state parties of the radical Arab states, they invited the Algerian FLN to the conference; yet, because of the Sino-Soviet conflict and for reasons of domestic legitimacy, they had to invite the Algerian Communist Party as well. The Soviet goal to remain the leaders of the international Communist movement had once again come into conflict with its Middle Eastern policies. Unfortunately for the Russian leaders, this particular conflict was to occur again.[46]

Meanwhile, in Egypt the decision to dissolve the Communist Party had not led to the hoped-for increase in Communist influence in the Nasser regime, although it did remove a major irritant in Soviet-Egyptian relations. While the former members of the party were given posts in the Egyptian mass media, the Youth Bureau, the Ministry of Education, and even the Central Committee of the Arab Socialist Union, power remained in the hands of Nasser and his entourage, and there was no noticeable increase in socialist legislation as a result of the Communist presence. While the Marxists may have hoped to form "vanguard cadres" in the Arab Socialist Union, they were unable to do so; indeed, the only vanguard organization within the ASU was a quasi-secret police cadre system controlled by Ali Sabry and Shaari Gomaa, which arrested and periodically imprisoned the former Communists.[47]

Perhaps because of the apparent failure of the Egyptian experiments in Communist party dissolution, or because of the prestige of Khalid Bakdash who had strongly opposed it, the Soviet leadership did not actively pressure the Syrian Communist Party to dissolve following the coming to power of the pro-Russian left wing Ba'ath regime in Syria in February 1966. Instead, the CPSU established party-to-party relations with it, thus extending Soviet party relations to the third Arab state in the Middle East. The Soviet action was preceded by the decision by the new regime to permit Khalid Bakdash to return from exile, and the subsequent Soviet loan of $132 million to Syria for the construction of the Euphrates Dam. The timing of the loan, coming so soon after Bakdash's return, is clearly reminiscent of the $277-million loan to Egypt in 1964 following Nasser's decision to free imprisoned Egyptian Communists. It would thus appear that a demonstrative act by a nationalist Arab leadership toward its Communist party, one of little or no political cost to the leadership, might well bring a reward well out of proportion to the cost involved.[48]

In addition to deemphasizing the importance of the Middle Eastern Communist parties and attempting to develop close party ties with the nationalist parties of the radical Arab states, there was another policy change under Brezhnev and Kosygin. This involved a revised estimate of the desirability of Arab unity. While Khrushchev was ambivalent on the issue of Arab unity and occasionally opposed it because he feared that it would be a barrier to the spread of Russian and Communist influence, the new Russian leadership gave it a strong endorsement. The reason for this change in policy lay in the fact that beginning in 1965 the Russians tried to forge a quasi-alliance of the "anti-imperialist" forces of the Middle East under Soviet leadership. The fact that perhaps the only issue on which all Arabs can agree is opposition to Israel had led the Russians to brand Israel as the "imperialist wedge" in the Middle East and to link closely the Arab struggle against Israel with the "struggle against imperialism." One of the Soviet goals in this process was to limit the internecine conflict among the Arab nations, particularly Egypt, Syria, and Iraq, which was as endemic to the Middle East as the Arab-Israeli conflict.[49] In addition, the Russians hoped that, by becoming the champion of the Arab states against Israel, they could line up the Arab states against the West as well. Yet this policy, while it paid some dividends to the Russians, also proved to be a very dangerous one, since it almost got the Russians involved in the June 1967 Arab-Israeli war and into an open conflict with Israel and the United States in July 1970.

SOVIET POLICY TOWARD THE NORTHERN TIER
UNDER BREZHNEV AND KOSYGIN

When the new Russian leadership began to step up the Soviet drive in the Middle East, attention was first turned to the nations of the Northern Tier. A deliberate effort was made to improve relations with Turkey, and the Russians shifted their position on the Cyprus issue to gain Turkish support. Kosygin visited Ankara in September 1966, and a $200-million Soviet loan was worked out in which the Russians were committed to construct a steel mill and several other industrial projects. Interestingly enough, the agreement stipulated that the Russian loan could be repaid by the shipment of certain types of Turkish products—products that had a difficult time finding markets in the West.[50]

Soviet relations improved even more rapidly with Iran. In July 1965 the Shah paid an official visit to the Soviet Union, and in January 1966 the Russians gave Iran a $288.9-million loan for a series of industrial projects.[51] Of greatest diplomatic importance was the Soviet-Iranian agreement reached at the same time whereby the Russians would provide Iran with $110 million in military equipment, primarily small arms and transport equipment, in return for Iranian gas. While some Western commentators stated that the Russians were now making dangerous inroads in Iran, it appeared that the Shah was utilizing the Soviet arms for several purposes of his own. The first was to persuade the United States to sell Iran more sophisticated weapons, including anti-aircraft equipment, under the implicit threat that Iran would otherwise turn to the USSR.[52] Perhaps more important, however, was that the USSR, in supplying arms to Iran, had implicitly strengthened the Shah in his dealings with Iraq, a nation with good relations with the Soviet Union and one with which Iran was continuously in conflict; the new Soviet-Iranian detente enabled the Shah to focus his attention on the power struggle in the Persian Gulf. In any case, the Russians evidently found their rapprochement with Iran to be a most satisfactory one, because in April 1968, in another visit to Iran, Kosygin offered still another loan, this time for up to $300 million.[53]

By the summer of 1970 the Brezhnev-Kosygin leadership had agreed to provide no less than $788.9 million in economic aid to the nations of the Northern Tier, along with $110 million in military aid. Yet what had the Russians obtained in return? Relations had improved considerably with both Turkey and Iran, but both remained within the Western alliance system, and any thoughts of a drift toward neutralism seemed to have been aborted by the Soviet invasion of Czechoslovakia in August 1968. Soviet ships now visited Iran's Persian Gulf ports (along with Iraq's), but this merely made the Russian choice more difficult in case of a clash between the Persian Gulf powers. Indeed, as the politics of the Persian Gulf grew hotter with the British withdrawal from the region in 1971, the Russians were to find that Iran had exploited her newly improved relations with the USSR to achieve her own objectives in the region.[54] Similarly, although the Russians enjoyed a larger degree of freedom of maneuver through the straits as a result of their improved relations with Turkey, the Turks remained quite independent, as evidenced by their refusal, despite a great deal of Soviet pressure, to return the Lithuanians who had hijacked a Russian plane to Turkey in September 1970.

SOVIET POLICY TOWARD THE SOUTHERN TIER
UNDER BREZHNEV AND KOSYGIN

The Russian leadership's policy toward the Arab nations and Israel from 1964 until the death of Nasser was considerably more complex than their policy toward Iran and Turkey. Mention has already been made of the changed Soviet position on the desirability of Arab unity and the Soviet effort to promote close party relations between the CPSU and the radical Arab socialist parties of the region. Economic and military aid continued to play an important role in the Soviet-Arab relations, as it had done under Khrushchev, but Soviet political support for the radical Arab regimes, primarily Syria's, was perhaps even more important. The Syrian regime that had taken power in February 1966 espoused not only the need for a socialist transformation in Syria and close cooperation with the Soviet Union, but also military and financial assistance for the Palestine Fatah guerrilla organization led by Yassir Arafat, which began a series of terrorist attacks against Israel. These attacks placed the narrowly based Ba'ath regime in danger of retaliatory attacks by Israel, which might cause its fall; in order to avoid such a possibility the Soviet leadership urged the other Arab states, especially Egypt, to join together with Syria against the "imperialists" and Israel. This was the theme of a visit by Soviet Premier Kosygin to Cairo in May 1966 in which the Soviet leader called for a united front of progressive Arab states "such as the United Arab Republic, Algeria, Iraq and Syria to confront imperialism and reaction."[55] Kosygin's visit to Cairo was followed by a trip by Iraqi Premier Bazzaz to Moscow in late July in which the Soviet leadership publicly ended its rift with the Iraqi government over its persecution of the Kurds and the Iraqi Communist Party and urged the Iraqis to join in the anti-imperialist front of the Arab states.[56] In November 1966 the Arab united fron sought by the USSR began to take shape as Egypt and Syria signed a defensive alliance, and the Soviet leaders may have hoped that this would deter any major Israeli attack on Syria.[57] Nonetheless, the Syrian government seized on the alliance to step up its support for Palestinian guerrilla attacks on Israel, and by April 1967 the Syrian-Israeli and Jordanian-Israeli borders had become tinderboxes.

The Israelis had initially restricted themselves to retaliatory raids against the Jordanians, through whose territory the guerrillas had come from Syria. In early April they decided to retaliate directly against the Syrians. Following Syrian shelling of Israeli farmers from the Golan Heights, the Israeli air force took to the skies to silence the Syrian artillery and in the process shot down seven Syrian jets that had come to intercept them. This defeat was a major blow to the prestige of the Syrian government, and when coupled with anti-Ba'ath rioting led by Moslem religious leaders in early May, it appeared that the shaky Syrian Ba'athist government was about to fall. These developments led the Russians, who were concerned about the collapse of their main Arab ally in the Middle East and the center of anti-Western activity, to give false information to the Egyptians that Israel was planning a major attack on Syria. Nasser, then at the low point of his prestige in the Arab world, apparently seized this opportunity to regain his lost prestige and again appear as the champion of the Arabs by ordering the United Nations forces to leave their positions between Israel and Egypt, and by moving Egyptian troops to the borders of Israel. In addition, he blockaded the Straits of Tiran to Israeli shipping and at the end of May signed a military alliance with his erstwhile enemy, King Hussein of Jordan. Following the military encirclement of Israel, it appeared that war was but a few days away, and on the morning of June 5, 1967, the Israelis decided to strike first before they were attacked. In the course of six days the Israelis succeeded in defeating the armies of Egypt, Syria, and

Jordan and capturing the Sinai Peninsula, the Jordanian section of the West Bank of the Jordan river, and the Golan Heights in Syria.[58]

While Arab leaders may have hoped that the Soviet position of support for the Syrian regime, Soviet efforts to tie it to Egypt through a defense agreement, and Soviet efforts to rally an "anti-imperialist," anti-Israeli alliance among the Arab states would mean Soviet military support to the Arabs during the war with Israel, Soviet military aid was not forthcoming. The only substantive action the Russians took was to break diplomatic relations with Israel, an action also taken by the other Soviet bloc states in Eastern Europe (with the exception of Rumania) and Yugoslavia.

As might be imagined, the lack of Soviet support during the war and the Soviet efforts to achieve a cease-fire with Israeli troops still occupying Arab territory were bitter pills for the Arabs to swallow, and Soviet prestige dipped in the Arab world as a result. In an effort to compensate for their limited support of the Arabs during the war, the Soviet leaders moved immediately to rebuild the armies of Syria and Egypt and offered Soviet weapons to Jordan in an effort to attract King Hussein to the Soviet side. In addition, the Soviet leaders attempted to capitalize on the heightened military weakness of the Arab states and their diplomatic isolation (much of it self-imposed) to increase Soviet influence throughout the Arab world. Having broken diplomatic relations with the United States and Britain during the war, Egypt, Syria, Iraq, and the Sudan had nowhere else to turn for sophisticated military equipment, although French President Charles de Gaulle, in condemning Israel for attacking the Arabs, sought to spread French influence in the Arab states and at the same time to obtain new markets for France's battle-proven Mirage jet fighter-bombers. China was also not idle during this period. Immediately after the war, the Chinese diverted to Egypt four ship-loads of Australian wheat destined for China and gave Egypt a $10-million loan.[59] The Chinese proved unwilling, however, to give the Egyptians what they really wanted—an atom bomb. As Mohammed Heikal relates in *The Cairo Documents*, the Chinese leaders refused the Egyptian request and told the Egyptian delegation that if they wanted atomic weaponry they would have to develop it themselves, just as China had done.[60]

One consequence of the June war that the Soviet leaders welcomed was the oil embargo that the Arab states imposed on the United States, Britain, and West Germany. An article in the August 1967 issues of *International Affairs* stated:

> The oil weapon is a powerful weapon in the hands of the Arab countries. This is the first time in the history of the Middle East that the Western World has been made to feel who is the real owner of Arab oil. Let us add that the Western powers depend heavily on Arab oil.[61]

Despite Soviet urging, however, Arab solidarity on the oil embargo could not be maintained, particularly since the conservative Arab states—Saudi Arabia, Kuwait, and Libya—were demanding its termination.[62] In addition, both the United States (then possessing an oil surplus available for export) and Iran stepped up production to compensate for the Arab oil cutoff, and Western Europe was in no danger of running out of oil. Consequently, at the Arab summit conference in Khartoum in August 1967 the Arab states agreed to terminate the oil embargo. The rich oil states—Saudi Arabia, Kuwait, and Libya—agreed to provide Egypt and Jordan with an annual subsidy to compensate them for war losses. (Syria, which boycotted the conference, was not included in the subsidy arrangement.) In return, Nasser agreed to pull Egyptian troops out of Yemen, thus ending the threat to Saudi Arabia's southern border.

While not too pleased with the end of the Arab oil embargo and the end of "anti-imperialist" Arab unity created by the war, the Soviet leaders may have been relieved that the rich oil states were sharing with the USSR the expensive burden of supporting the chronically poor Egyptian economy. Writing in *New Times* after the conclusion of the Khartoum conference, Igor Belyaev and Yevgeny Primakov, two of the senior Soviet commentators on Middle Eastern affairs, seemed to agree with the Khartoum decision:

> It was a matter of sober calculation. Refusal to pump oil for the United States, Britain and the Federal Republic of Germany caused no actual shortage of oil and oil products in Western Europe.[63]

Nasser's agreement at the Khartoum conference to withdraw Egyptian troops from Yemen appeared to most observers at the time to mean that the Saudi-backed Royalist forces would emerge victorious from the long and bloody Yemeni civil war. To prevent this from happening, the USSR engaged in a massive airlift of military equipment to the Republican forces in late 1967 and this helped prevent a Royalist victory. Unfortunately for the Russians, however, squabbling among the Republican forces was eventually to result in a coalition government of Royalists and Republicans and a Westward turn in Yemeni foreign policy.

To the south in Aden, the Soviet leaders quickly recognized the nationalist regime, which came to power after the British withdrawal at the end of 1967, and which proclaimed Aden to be the People's Democratic Republic of South Yemen. Within two months the USSR had begun to send military equipment to the strategically located state at the entrance to the Red Sea, and it was not long before the Southern Yemeni Defense Minister journeyed to Moscow to ask for more aid. South Yemen, however, was plagued by a festering civil war between two radical nationalist groups who had fought each other as well as the British during the independence struggle. It was also beset by continuing tribal strife and an ill-defined border with North Yemen, which soon was the scene of military conflict. In this situation the Soviet Union tried to maintain as neutral a position as possible toward all groups while at the same time acquiring storage facilities and naval landing rights in the port city Aden.[64]

While the Soviet Union became active in southern Arabian affairs following the June war because of the exigencies of the political situation (North Yemen) and perceived opportunities (South Yemen), the main focus of Soviet activity in the 1967-70 period lay in its relations with the war-weakened regime of Egyptian President Gamal Nasser. Soviet-Egyptian cooperation manifested itself primarily in the diplomatic and military spheres, but the USSR also continued to lend money to Egypt for industrialization. In November 1967 the United States and the Soviet Union, together with Britain, worked out a vague formula, UN Resolution #242, which called for Israeli withdrawal "from occupied territories" (without stating how far the withdrawal should go) in return for Israel's right to live in peace within "secure and recognized boundaries" (without stating where these boundaries should be or defining the word "secure"). Resolution #242 also created a UN mediator, Gunnar Jarring, who soon began a long, tedious, and ultimately unsuccessful series of meetings with Israel, Egypt, and Jordan, all of whom had accepted the resolution while interpreting it quite differently.[65]

The failure of Jarring's diplomatic efforts, as well as various Soviet-sponsored four-power and two-power conferences to obtain an Israeli withdrawal from the Sinai Peninsula, prompted Nasser to begin a war of attrition with the newly rebuilt army against Israel in April 1969. Hoping to use Egypt's superiority in artillery to cause unacceptable casualties to Israeli forces dug in along the canal, Egyptian guns began a steady pounding of the Israeli positions. The Israelis, with only a twelfth the population of Egypt, and inferior in artillery pieces, decided to use the one weapon in which they had almost absolute superiority, their air force, to silence the Egyptian artillery. Having accomplished this with minimum losses in aircraft, the Israelis then embarked on a series of deep penetration raids into the heartland of Egypt in an effort to persuade Nasser to give up his war of attrition, and by January 1970 Israeli planes were flying at will through eastern Egypt.

This situation was humiliating to Nasser. Having lost the 1967 war and the Sinai Peninsula, he now seemed unable even to defend Egypt's heartland. Consequently, in an effort to remedy this politically intolerable situation, Nasser flew to Moscow and asked the Soviet leaders to establish an air-defense system manned by Soviet pilots and antiaircraft forces and protected by Soviet troops. The cost to Egypt, however, was a high one. To obtain Soviet aid, Nasser had to grant to the Soviet Union exclusive control over a number of Egyptian airfields as well as operational control over a large portion of the Egyptian army.

In deciding to help the Egyptians, the Soviet leadership was faced with a difficult decision. On the one hand, failure to help Nasser might mean the Egyptian president's ouster by elements in the Egyptian leadership less friendly toward the USSR at a time when the United States was trying to rebuild its position in the Arab world. In addition, the airbases that the USSR would control could be used by Russian pilots not only to intercept the Israelis, but also to fly covering missions for the Soviet Mediterranean fleet. This would be of great tactical benefit to Soviet commanders because the USSR possessed no genuine aircraft carriers of its own at the time. A final argument in favor of the Soviet commitment to Egypt was that it would be a demonstration to the Arab world that the USSR was an ally to be counted on.

Despite these clear advantages, there was one major disadvantage—the negative effect on the United States of the Soviet intervention. Up to this time, other than supplying limited numbers of military advisors, both superpowers had refrained from a major commitment of combat troops to any nation in the Middle East. Now, with between 10,000 and 15,000 Soviet troops to be stationed in Egypt and with Soviet pilots flying combat missions, there was the serious possibility of a superpower confrontation. Given American troop commitments in Vietnam and the harsh clamor in the United States not to commit any more Americans to combat duty, the Soviet leaders were probably safe in assuming that no American ground troops or pilots would be stationed in Israel. (In any case, the Israelis stated that they only wanted American materiel, not American troops.) Nonetheless, there was still the possibility that in the event of a confrontation between the Soviet Union and Israel, the United States would be drawn in on the side of the Israelis.

Finally, perhaps reasoning that their investment in Egypt, still the most powerful and most influential of all the Arab states, was too great to give up, or perhaps believing that a Vietnam-burdened Nixon administration would not act decisively in the Middle East despite its public statements to the contrary, the Soviet leaders decided to take the risk and commit pilots and combat troops to Egypt. Fortunately for the Soviet leaders, Israeli Defense Minister Moshe Dayan stated that the Israeli air force would cease its deep penetration raids of Egypt so as to avoid a confrontation with the Soviet pilots; this, initially at least, took some of the heat out of the situation. By the end of June, however, with Soviet forces engaged in establishing the air-defense system near the Suez Canal, Soviet-Israeli clashes did occur, and on one occasion the Israelis shot down five Soviet-piloted Migs. In addition, President Nixon publicly warned the Russians that the Middle East could drag the superpowers into a direct war, just as happened in 1914. Perhaps fearing such an eventuality, or perhaps wishing to consolidate their new military position in Egypt, the Soviet Union agreed to an American-sponsored 90-day cease-fire arrangement after lengthy and "frank" consultations with Nasser in Moscow.[66] The cease-fire was eventually to last for more than three years; but soon after it came into effect (August 8, 1970) and in large part because of it, Jordan was to erupt into civil war, a development to be discussed below.

While the USSR had enhanced its military position in the eastern Mediterranean through its acquisition of bases in Egypt, both Soviet and Communist influence in Nasser's regime still remained limited. Although Soviet commentator Georgi Mirsky had optimistically stated shortly after the June war in a New Times article, "It is not to be excluded that left socialist tendencies in the Arab world will gain as a result of the recent events,"[67] events were to prove otherwise. Perhaps emboldened by the results of the war, the Egyptian Marxists demanded the liquidation of the Nasser regime's right wing and the transfer of power to "revolutionary cadres."[68] These demands went unheeded. Nasser did purge some rightists, primarily to secure his own political base, although his action was widely interpreted at the time as a concession to the Russians. In an interview in Jeune Afrique on October 1, 1967, an Egyptian Communist testified to the weakness of his movement in Egypt:

> We have committed major errors, we have been "drooling" so much during the years because Nasser had permitted us to participate in national life and had given us posts in editorial offices and the university, that we have let ourselves become embourgeoises. We have lost all contact with the masses and these, abandoned to themselves, are completely disorganized. The truth is that we are tired and not at all prepared to return to prison.[69]

Despite the aid he was receiving from the USSR, Nasser also tried to maintain some ties with the West. He continued to rely on American oil companies to search for oil in Egypt. He also advised the new Libyan leader Mu'ammar Kaddafi, who came to power in September 1969 after overthrowing King Idris, to turn to France and not to the USSR for arms.[70]

While Soviet influence had increased quite sharply in Egypt, it remained quite limited in Syria and Iraq, the other two major recipients of Soviet attention in the region. For example, the Soviet leaders were unable to persuade either the Syrians or the Iraqis to accept the Soviet-backed UN Resolution #242 or to cooperate with Egypt in seeking a political settlement to the Middle East crisis. Syria and Iraq also rejected the cease-fire agreement of August 1970, much to the chagrin of the Soviet Union. In Syria, Soviet efforts were hampered by the Syrian Communist Party, which actively campaigned against Defense Minister Hafiz Assad in his struggle for power with Salah Jedid, the ex-army officer who was head of the Ba'ath party. The Syrian Communists not only harmed their own fortunes in Syria (limited as they were) but Soviet-Syrian relations as well, as the Soviet Ambassador, Nuradin Mukhdinov, was drawn into the power struggle pitting the Communists and Jedid on one side and the ultimately victorious Assad on the other.[71]

In May 1969 Assad, who was angered both by Soviet meddling in Syrian politics and by the failure of the USSR to provide what he thought were sufficient weapons, dispatched his close friend, Syrian Chief of Staff Lt. Gen. Mustafa Tlass, on an arms procurement trip to China. There, perhaps acting on Assad's instructions, Tlass allowed himself to be photographed waving the famous little Red Book of Chairman Mao's sayings. Coming only two months after the bloody Sino-Soviet clashes along the Ussuri river, Tlass's action must have been particularly galling to the Russians after all the Soviet economic, military, and diplomatic support for Syria. According to the Jerusalem *Post*, Assad reportedly had said prior to Tlass's journey:

> Why should we not boycott the Soviet Union and its supporters inside the country? If we do so, we can force them to review their stand. Either they give us what we want and what is necessary or they will lose our friendship.[72]

The Soviet leaders may have taken Assad's warning seriously, or they may have concluded that it was counterproductive to get too closely involved in internal Soviet politics. In any case by the end of 1969 they had dissociated themselves from the power struggle in Syria, which Assad seemed certain to win. The Soviet leaders may have taken some consolation from the fact that Assad was more willing to cooperate with the other Arab states than Jedid was, although the Communist Party of Syria, which had opposed him, continued to be persecuted. The persecution was severe enough for the Soviet press to take public notice; on July 18, 1970, the Soviet newpaper *Trud*, in an article signed "observer," protested against the arrest and murder of a number of Syrian Communists.[73]

The Soviet Union's relations with Iraq during the 1967-70 period were a bit warmer than with Syria although the two states continued to disagree on such Middle Eastern political issues as Resolution #242, the Iraqi government's treatment of its Kurdish minority, and its persecution of the Iraqi Communists. Iraq had long been isolated both in the Middle East as a whole and in the Arab world, and successive Iraqi governments looked to their tie to the USSR as a means of balancing off Iraq's strained relations with its pro-Western neighbors, Iran, Saudi Arabia, Jordan, Turkey, and Kuwait. From the Soviet point of view, the weak Aref regime in Iraq was not only yet another base for Soviet influence in the region; it was also a potential source of oil. By 1967 Soviet planners had begun to change their earlier optimistic predictions that the USSR would have sufficient oil and natural gas to meet all its internal needs as well as increasing amounts available for export to the Soviet bloc states of East Europe and to hard-currency customers in Western Europe and Japan. While the USSR had large reserves of oil and natural gas, most of these were located in the frozen wastes of eastern and western Siberia and would have required large infrastructure investments before they could be developed. Consequently, in December 1967 the USSR signed an agreement with Iraq to provide credits and equipment for the northern Rumelia oil field, with the USSR to be partially repaid in crude oil. In the same year the Soviet Union had also signed long-term agreements with Afghanistan to import natural gas and with Iran to import both oil and natural gas. Soviet thinking at the time seemed to revolve around the idea that the USSR could import oil and natural gas from the Middle East to serve industries in the southern part of the Soviet Union while selling Soviet oil and natural gas to Eastern and Western Europe. Such a plan would also enable the Soviet leaders to postpone, at least for a while, the huge infrastructure investments needed to develop Siberian oil and natural gas.[74]

The coming to power of the Al-Bakr regime in July 1968 had little effect on Soviet-Iraqi relations at the state level, which continued to be very good, despite the fact that Iraqi Communists continued to be persecuted. According to a reliable source, Al-Bakr even negotiated with the Communists to obtain their participation in his government; but by demanding too much (that is, the Defense Ministry) the Iraqi Communist Party wound up with nothing.[75] Nonetheless, the Soviet leadership evidently found its relations with the Al-Bakr regime to be more than satisfactory, since in July 1969 another long-term oil agreement was signed between the two countries for the development of the oil fields of northern Rumelia. In this one the USSR was to be repaid for its credits and equipment exclusively in Iraqi crude oil.[76] A *Pravda* article by Yevgeny Primakov on September 21 had warm praise for the Al-Bakr regime, although it chided the regime for failing to agree with Resolution #242 and for failing to reach an agreement with the Kurds.[77]

While the USSR and Iraq were able to agree on oil development, and the Soviet government warmly hailed the agreement reached on March 11, 1970, between the Iraqi government and the Kurds, the two nations remained divided on policy toward the Arab-Israeli conflict. Iraq opposed the ceasefire agreement of August 1970, and a *Pravda* article of August 1, 1970, called the Iraqi opposition to the ceasefire "incomprehensible" and then went on to note:

> the stand taken by the leadership of the Iraq's Ba'ath party is surprising. . . . *Without warning*, Baghdad began saying that "attempts are being made to dispose of the Palestine question" and so forth . . . the negative attitude of Iraq's Ba'ath Party leadership toward President Nasser's initiative and toward the position of the UAR government does not contribute to the actual struggle against the aggressor and the forces of Imperialism and Zionism that support aggression.[78] [emphasis added]

The fact that the Russian leadership used the phrase "without warning" probably indicates that they were not even consulted by the Iraqi regime on this important policy statement. It is interesting to note that even after an Iraqi delegation went to Moscow for talks in early August there was no change in Baghad's position. Despite Iraqi opposition to this relatively important initiative backed by the USSR, the Russians not only did not exert any pressure on the Iraqi leadership (such as cutting off or even curtailing military or economic aid); they went ahead and signed a protocol on trade and economic cooperation with the Iraqis on August 13, 1970, which called for an increase in trade and Soviet assistance. The Russians then granted the Iraqis a $34-million loan on August 30.[79] These events indicate not only a limited degree of Soviet influence in Iraq, but also a clear desire by the Russians to maintain good relations with the oil-rich and strategically located nation that had become Egypt's chief rival in the Arab world.

As the Soviet Union stepped up its efforts to oust Western influence from the Middle East following the June war, developments in the Arab states of North Africa appeared to fall nicely into place for them. In Libya, the pro-Western regime of King Idris was overthrown in September 1969 by a military junta headed by Mu'ammar Kaddafi, whose first major foreign policy demand was for the United States and Britain to leave their military bases in Libya—a demand both Western nations speedily complied with. In Algeria, Boumadienne's decision to nationalize the French-owned oil industry led to a withdrawal of French technicians, and the Soviet Union immediately sent its own technicians to replace them. It should be mentioned, however, that in the cases of both Libya and Algeria, the steps taken by the nationalist regimes to lessen Western influence in their countries did not mean they had opened the door to Soviet control. Both Boumadienne and Kaddafi pursued independent foreign and domestic policies, as their frequent clashes with both the USSR and the United States clearly indicated.

One country where the Soviet Union appeared to make deep inroads was the Sudan. Following a military coup d'etat in May 1969 Jaafar Nimeri came to power. He proclaimed the Sudan to be a democratic republic and defined the main foreign policy aims of his regime as the support of national liberation movements against imperialism, active support of the Palestinian struggle, and extension of the Sudan's ties to the Arab world and the socialist countries. Domestically, Nimeri proclaimed the formation of a single party of "workers, peasants, soldiers, national bourgeoisie and the progressive intellegen[t]sia." Communists were prominently represented in Nimeri's first cabinet, although the Communist Party, like all other existing parties, was officially dissolved.[80]

The Soviet leadership wasted little time in consolidating its relations with Nimeri's regime. The Sudanese leader was invited to Moscow in November 1969 and agreements were signed for the expansion of trade and cultural and scientific cooperation.[81] State relations continued to improve in early January 1970 as Soviet navy warships paid a visit to Port Sudan and the USSR began to supply the Sudan with military equipment.[82] As Soviet-Sudanese relations improved, the Soviet leaders apparently decided that in order to solidify ties with the strategically located nation and to avoid possible future complications, the powerful Sudanese Communist Party should dissolve (as Nimeri had demanded), its members to join Nimeri's one-party regime as individuals, much as the Egyptian Communist Party had done earlier.[83] However, the Sudanese Communist Party was split and the faction led by Secretary General Abdel Mahgoub apparently refused to comply with the Soviet requests. Nonetheless, Mahgoub was willing to support the Nimeri regime, and in an interview with the Soviet journal *Za Rubezhom*, which was broadcast over Radio Moscow in Arabic on August 11, 1969, the Sudanese Communist leader stated:

> The communists believe that the present government is a progressive one and that the May 25th movement had created the best circumstances for continuing our people's struggle for realizing the tasks of the national democratic revolution. Therefore, the Communist Party sincerely supports the new government's policy.[84]

Yet, as the situation in the Sudan developed, it became clear that Nimeri was using the Sudanese Communists to weaken his right-wing enemies, the Mahdiists. Once the Mahdiists were eliminated as a political force, Nimeri arrested and then exiled Mahgoub, who had become increasingly critical of Nimeri's policies, including the entry of the Sudan into a projected confederation with Egypt and Libya. While the anti-Mahgoub faction remained allied to Nimeri and in the government, it appeared that the Sudanese leader had learned the lesson, taught by Kassem a decade earlier, of playing off the Communists against other political forces, and that the Communist Party's future in the Sudan was limited indeed.

If the postwar atmosphere in the Arab world was conducive to weakening Western influence, it also provided fertile ground for the growth of the Palestinian resistance movement, a multitude of guerrilla organizations, which launched attacks against Israel (most of them unsuccessful), capturing the imagination of an Arab public still shocked by Israel's defeat of the regular Arab armies. As the Palestinian guerrilla organizations increased in power, they began actively competing with each other for recruits, funds, and prestige while at the same time increasingly becoming a challenge to the established governments in the Arab world, particularly those in Jordan and Lebanon, where large numbers of Palestinian refugees were located.[85] While the Soviet leadership initially played down the significance of the guerrilla organizations because it preferred to work through the established Arab states, the Russians could not long overlook either the growing power of the Palestinian guerrilla movement as a factor in Middle Eastern politics or the growing involvement of the Chinese Communists in the movement. By providing military equipment and ideological training to a number of the guerrilla organizations, the Chinese were seeking to increase their influence in the Middle East via the guerrilla movement.[86] By mid-1969 the Soviet leadership evidently decided that it was time to get involved with the guerrillas. It did so in a cautious manner, however, and it was not until after the death of Nasser and the severe beating taken by the Palestinians in the Jordanian civil war that the Soviet Union began to court the guerrillas in a serious manner.

At the Seventh World Trade Union Congress in Budapest in October 1969, Politburo member Aleksander Shelepin came out with the first public sign of Soviet support for the guerrillas:

> We consider the struggle of the Palestine patriots for the liquidation of
> the consequences of Israeli aggression a just anti-imperialist struggle of
> a national liberation and we support it.[87]

By stressing the term "liquidation of the consequences of Israeli aggression,"
however, Shelepin was manipulating the meaning of the guerrilla organizations'
fight to coincide with the Soviet-backed UN Resolution #242. Indeed, in 1969 the
guerrilla organizations were virtually unanimous in proclaiming their intention
to liquidate Israel itself, rather than to aid the Arab states in recovering the land
lost to Israel in 1967. By the end of 1969, however, after observing how clashes
with the guerrillas had shaken both the Lebanese and Jordanian governments,
Soviet leadership may have begun to envision the Palestinian movement as a
useful tool for weakening or even overthrowing the two pro-Western regimes and
replacing them with governments more friendly to the USSR.[88]

In February 1970, Yasir Arafat, who had replaced Ahmed Shukeiry as head
of the Palestine Liberation Organization (PLO), the loose federation of the
guerrilla organizations, after the 1967 war, was invited to Moscow, but the visit
was kept in low key as the invitation came from the Soviet Afro-Asian Solidarity
Organization rather than from a higher-ranking organ of the Soviet government.
The very next month, however, Arafat was given a high-level reception in Peking
and the Palestinian guerrilla leader warmly praised the Chinese for their
assistance. As Sino-Soviet competition for the allegiance of the guerrillas grew,
the Soviet leadership decided that its position would be improved if the
Communist parties of the Middle East formed their own guerrilla organization,
which would be able to participate in, and hopefully influence, the PLO from the
inside. Consequently, the Communist parties of Lebanon, Syria, Jordan, and
Iraq formed the Ansar guerrilla organization in March 1970, but as a Jordanian
Communist Party member was to complain two years later, Ansar had very little
influence in the guerrilla movement.[89]

One of the main problems plaguing the PLO was the very sharp competition
among its constituent organizations for power. Some guerrilla groups were
avowedly Marxist, such as the Popular Front for the Liberation of Palestine
(PFLP) and the Popular Democratic Front for the Liberation of Palestine
(PDFLP). Others were the instruments of Arab governments, such as Asiqa
(Syria) and the Arab Liberation Front (Iraq). Still others, such as Fatah, the
largest, proclaimed themselves ideologically neutral and were willing to accept
aid from all sides. By June 1970 the intra-Palestinian struggle for power had
reached a peak, with the PFLP openly challenging Fatah's leadership and seeking
to bring down the regime of King Hussein in Jordan as well. By this time the
guerrillas had established a virtual state-within-a-state in Jordan, and the
compromise agreement worked out in June between Hussein and the guerrillas
testified to their growing power. The acceptance by King Hussein of the
American-sponsored cease-fire agreement (Egypt and Israel also agreed) in
August set the stage for the final showdown. Fearing that the Palestinian cause
would be overlooked in a direct settlement between Israel and Jordan and Egypt,
and feeling that the time had come to topple the Hussein regime, the PFLP
embarked on a skyjacking spree that resulted in the flying of three skyjacked
passenger planes to a guerrilla-controlled airstrip in northern Jordan and their

demolition, while the troops of King Hussein, which had surrounded the guerrilla airstrip, looked helplessly on.[90]

Hussein seized this opportunity to end the guerrilla threat to his regime and began military attacks on the guerrillas. While his army was attacking the guerrilla positions, the Syrian government, then headed by Salah Jedid, dispatched an armored brigade to help the guerrillas. At this juncture the United States moved the Sixth Fleet toward the battle area and, acting jointly with Israel, threatened to intervene if the Syrian forces were not withdrawn, as both Kissinger and Nixon clearly indicated that they would not permit the pro-Western regime of Hussein to be ousted by the invasion of a client state of the Soviet Union.[91] The Soviet leadership, during this period, was conspicuous by its inaction. For this reason, or because of the strong American-Israeli stand, or, most probably, because he saw a chance to embarrass Jedid, General Assad, who controlled the Syrian air force, refused to dispatch Syrian jets to fly covering missions for the Syrian tanks. The result of Assad's decision was that the Jordanian air force and tank units badly mauled the invading Syrian army, which was forced to retreat in disarray to Syria. The emboldened Hussein then turned to finish off the guerrillas and had almost completed the job when an Arab league cease-fire arranged by Nasser came into effect.[92] It was to be the Egyptian president's last act as an Arab leader, however, because on the very next day he died of a heart attack, an event that was to lead to a transformation of the Soviet position in the Middle East. Before this transformation is discussed, however, it is necessary to evaluate the Soviet Middle Eastern position at the time of Nasser's death.

THE SOVIET POSITION IN THE MIDDLE EAST
AT THE TIME OF NASSER'S DEATH:
A BALANCE SHEET

In assessing the Soviet position in the Middle East at the time of Nasser's death, it is clear that the primary Soviet gain since Khrushchev's ouster had been an improvement in the Soviet military position in the region, although this was not an unmixed blessing for the Soviet leaders. The USSR had acquired air and naval bases in Egypt, and port rights in Syria, the Sudan, Yemen, South Yemen, and Iraq. The bases in Egypt gave air cover to the Soviet fleet sailing in the eastern Mediterranean and thus were substitutes for aircraft carriers, which the Soviet navy did not then possess. Yet the large military presence of the Soviet Union in the Middle East also contained a major risk for the Soviet leadership. There were a number of Arabs who wanted to involve the USSR in a war against Israel, regardless of the international consequences of such an action. One of the reasons that the Soviet Union accepted the American cease-fire initiative in the summer of 1970 appears to have been a desire to cool down its rapidly escalating conflict with Israel, which might soon have involved the United States as well. Thus, while the Soviet military position in the Middle East had improved by the time of Nasser's death, so too had the chances of a military confrontation between the United States and the Soviet Union—a development the Soviet leaders probably wished to avoid at almost any cost given the increasingly hostile relations between the USSR and China.

Other than improving their military position in the Middle East, there were few other concrete gains the Russians could point to from their expensive involvement in the region at the time of Nasser's death. The Russians seemed to have assumed the role of military supplier and financier of the economically weak radical Arab regimes of the area, and they appeared to be attempting to buy influence in the Northern Tier nations as well. Nonetheless, as Aaron Klieman pointed out in his 1970 study of the Soviet involvement in the Middle East, "In return for enabling the Soviets to claim influence, the Arabs expect Moscow to supply loans, weapons, technical advice, diplomatic support, and favorable terms of trade."[93] The obvious question is, Who was exploiting whom in this relationship? In addition, Soviet "influence" was far from reaching a position of control over the policies of any of the regimes in the region. The continued opposition of Syria and Iraq to such Soviet-supported peace initiatives as UN Resolution #242 and the 1970 cease-fire agreement presented serious difficulties to Soviet policy-makers, who sought to create a unified Arab stand on a Middle Eastern settlement that would be favorable to both the USSR and its Arab allies.

An even more serious problem for the Soviet Union at the time of Nasser's death was the reemergence of the United States as an active factor in Middle Eastern politics. While the U.S. position in the Arab world reached a low point following the Six-Day War, it appeared to have made a substantial recovery by September 1970. The Rogers Plan, announced on December 9, 1969, was a factor in preventing the Arab summit conference that convened at Rabat, Morocco, a few days later from issuing an anti-American statement as had been rumored in early December.[94] The cease-fire between Israel, Egypt, and Jordan that began in August 1970 was an American initiative, and although it was violated by Egypt (Israel received compensation for this by increased delivery of American weapons), it nonetheless seemed to set the climate for substantive peace negotiations. The strong American support for King Hussein's regime when Syrian tanks invaded Jordan in September 1970, during Hussein's crackdown on the guerrillas, helped restore a great deal of American influence in Jordan and in Lebanon as well. The Soviet Union's disinclination to get involved in support of one of its erstwhile clients, Syria, against a client of the United States, Jordan, was also not lost on the Arab world.

Perhaps even more important, however, was the impression spread in the Arab world by American declarations of an evenhanded policy in the Middle East, that the United States might be willing to assist the Arab states in regaining at least part, if not all, of the land lost to Israel in 1967—something the Soviet Union had been unable to do by diplomacy and was still unwilling to do by force.

Thus, the specter of rising American influence in the Arab world and the disunity among the Soviet Union's Arab clients were the major problems confronting the Soviet leadership when Gamal Nasser, the man who had been the linchpin of Soviet strategy in the Middle East, departed from the scene.[95]

NOTES

1. For an analysis of Soviet policy toward the Middle East between 1917 and 1945, see Ivan Spector, *The Soviet Union and the Muslim World* (Seattle:

University of Washington Press, 1956). This book also contains a useful survey of Czarist foreign policy toward the Middle East from 1552 to 1914. For an analysis of Soviet policy toward the Communist parties and radical movements of the Middle East in the interwar period, see Walter Laqueur, *The Soviet Union and the Middle East* (New York: Praeger, 1959), pp. 1-134. For an excellent treatment of Western involvement in the Middle East, see William R. Polk, *The United States and the Arab World*, rev. ed. (Cambridge, Mass.: Harvard University Press, 1969).

2. For a detailed examination of Soviet pressure against Iran and Turkey, see Howard M. Sachar, *Europe Leaves the Middle East 1936-1954* (New York: Alfred A. Knopf, 1972), chapter 9.

3. According to Khrushchev's memoirs, Stalin considered the Near East part of Britain's sphere of influence and felt that Russia did not have the power to challenge Britain there directly. See Strobe Talbott, ed., *Khrushchev Remembers* (Boston: Little, Brown, 1970), p. 431. Soviet support for the ouster of British and French troops from Lebanon and Syria in 1946 seems to have been motivated by the same considerations as its early support for Israel. A collection of Soviet documents pertaining to its relations with the Arab world from 1917 to 1960 is found in *SSSR i arabskie strany* (The USSR and the Arab States) (Moscow: Government Printing Office of Political Literature, 1960). The documents pertaining to Soviet support of Lebanon and Syria are found on pages 87-96 of that volume.

4. For a detailed analysis of the USSR's relations with Israel, see Avigdor Dagan, *Moscow and Jerusalem* (New York: Abelard-Schuman, 1970). For an analysis of Soviet behavior during the Israeli struggle for independence, see Robert O. Freedman, "The Partition of Palestine: Conflicting Nationalism and Power Politics," in *Partition: Peril to World Peace*, ed. Thomas Hachey (New York: Rand McNally, 1972).

5. In the 1955-56 period, while there were already some strains in Sino-Soviet relations, Russia was still the unquestioned leader of the socialist bloc. In addition, the rapprochement between Yugoslavia and the USSR that took place at the time seemed to many observers to bring Yugoslavia back into the Soviet sphere of influence. (Yugoslavia had been ousted from the socialist bloc by Stalin in 1948 and had subsequently turned to the West for aid.) Thus, Khrushchev apparently considered that any state that became Communist would automatically come under Soviet leadership. This situation was to change radically with the onset of the Sino-Soviet conflict several years later. For an excellent survey of Soviet policy towards the Middle East under Khrushchev, see Oles M. Smolansky, *The Soviet Union and the Arab East Under Khrushchev* (Lewisburg, Pa.: Bucknell University Press, 1974).

6. Two useful analyses of the background to the arms deal are Uri Ra'anan, *The USSR Arms the Third World* (Cambridge, Mass.: M.I.T. Press, 1969); and Amos Perlmutter, "Big Power Games, Small Power Wars," *Transaction* 7, nos. 9-10 (July-August 1970); 79-83.

7. For an analysis of the Middle East arms race as a cause of the Arab-Israeli wars, see Nadav Safran, *From War to War* (New York: Pegasus, 1969).

8. For a description of Soviet efforts to avoid participation in the 1956 conflict, see J. M. Mackintosh, *Strategy and Tactics of Soviet Foreign Policy*

(London: Oxford University Press, 1963), pp. 185-187. The Soviet threats against Britain, France, and Israel were not issued until after the crisis had abated, and seemed primarily directed toward a propaganda advantage with respect to the United States, which had also opposed the attack on Egypt. In 1967 Nasser's claim that American and British planes were involved in the attack on Egypt seemed to be a ploy to get the Russians to intervene on his behalf.

9. *Al Jarida* (Beirut), August 16, 1955, cited in Laqueur, *The Soviet Union and the Middle East*, pp. 219-220.

10. Press Release 50/59 (March 20, 1959), UAR Information Department, Cairo. Document found in Walter Laqueur, *The Struggle for the Middle East*, (New York: Macmillan, 1969), p. 235.

11. Data is available only on the economic aid, which consisted of an $87.5-million loan for a dam and power plant on the Euphrates River, and other projects. Kurt Mueller, *The Foreign Aid Programs of the Soviet Bloc and Communist China* (New York: Walker, 1967), p. 225.

12. For a detailed discussion of the events leading up to the union, see Patrick Seale, *The Struggle for Syria* (London: Oxford University Press, 1965); and Malcolm Kerr, *The Arab Cold War* (New York, Oxford University Press, 1970).

13. *New Times*, the Soviet foreign affairs weekly, stated on February 21, 1958: "The Soviet people rejoice in the progress achieved by the friendly Arab nations. *The USSR has never interfered in the internal affairs of any country, Arab or otherwise.*" [emphasis added]. *New Times*, no. 7 (1958): 6.

14. On March 16, 1959, the Soviet Union gave Iraq a $137.5-million loan for 35 industrial and agricultural facilities, and on August 18, 1960, a $45-million loan for construction and equipment for the Baghdad-Basra railroad. Data from Mueller, op. cit., p. 223.

15. Nasser was incensed at Soviet support for Kassem, whom he considered a dangerous rival. The Egyptian leader was even more angry at the Russians for opposing the efforts of the Nasserites in Iraq who wished to have their country join the UAR. The Russians apparently felt that their influence would grow faster in an independent Iraq. In a reception for a visiting Iraqi delegation in March 1959, Khrushchev pointedly remarked in a general attack on Nasser: "Untimely unification ultimately undermines the unity of the people, rather than strengthens it. . . . What ensues is not greater unity but a division of forces. Who profits from this . . . only the Imperialists." *Pravda*, March 17, 1959, translated in Current Digest of the Soviet Press 11, no. 11 (April 15, 1959): 8.

16. Cited in Aryeh Yodfat, *Arab Politics in the Soviet Mirror* (Jerusalem: Israel Universities Press, 1973), p. 211.

17. For an Egyptian perspective on these events, see Mohammed Heikal, *The Cairo Documents* (New York: Doubleday, 1973), pp. 152-153.

18. For an examination of Kassem's activities, see Majid Khadduri, *Republican Iraq* (New York: Oxford University Press, 1969); and Uriel Dann, *Iraq under Kassem* (New York: Praeger, 1969). Chapter 11 in M. S. Agwani, *Communism in the Arab East* (Bombay: Asia Publishing House, 1969), is also worthy of examination as it deals in detail with Kassem's manipulation of the Iraqi Communist Party.

19. The Russians got a late start in developing relations with the FLN because Khrushchev did not wish to antagonize French President Charles de Gaulle, whom he hoped to wean away from NATO. The loans that the USSR promised Algeria ($100 million in 1963 and $128 million in 1964—Mueller, op. cit., p. 226) seem also to have been aimed at gaining the USSR admission to the second Bandung Conference of Afro-Asian states, which was scheduled to be held in Algeria in 1965. For an overall discussion of Soviet-Algerian relations, see David and Marina Ottaway, *Algeria: The Politics of a Socialist Revolution* (Berkeley: University of California Press, 1970).

20. In the first installment of his memoirs, Nikita Khrushchev referred to those members of the Soviet leadership who opposed his policy toward Egypt as "those skunks, those narrow-minded skunks who raised such a stink and tried to poison the waters of our relationship with Egypt." See Strobe Talbott, ed., *Khrushchev Remembers* (Boston: Little, Brown, 1970), p. 450.

21. For analyses of the Soviet ideological convolutions, see Richard Lowenthal, "Russia, the One-Party System and the Third World," *Survey*, no. 58 (January 1966): 43-58; Aryeh Yodfat, *Arab Politics in the Soviet Mirror* (Jerusalem: Israel Universities Press, 1973), chapter 1; and Philip Mosely, "The Kremlin and the Third World," *Foreign Affairs* 46, no. 1 (October 1967): 64-77. See also Jaan Pennar *The USSR and the Arabs: The Ideological Dimension* (New York: Crane Russak, 1973).

22. "Socio-Economic Changes in the Arab Countries and 'Arab Socialism' Concepts," *World Marxist Review* 7, no. 9 (1964): 60.

23. Ibid, p. 63.

24. Ibid, p. 62.

25. Heikal, op. cit., pp. 155-157.

26. This sizable loan, like similar loans to Algeria, may have been related to Soviet efforts to gain entry into the second Bandung Conference of Afro-Asian states. The Chinese Communists strongly opposed the admission of the USSR to the conference and offered loans of their own in an effort to prevent it. A very useful chart comparing Chinese and Soviet loans to Afro-Asian countries in the 1963-65 period is found in Marshall Goldman, *Soviet Foreign Aid* (New York: Praeger, 1967), p. 190. The loan may also have been related to Nasser's decision to free a large number of imprisoned Egyptian Communists (an action taken before Khrushchev's visit) and may have served as an incentive for the Egyptian leader to allow some of them to serve in his regime.

27. The Russians justified their assistance to the feudal regime of the Iman of Yemen on the basis of his "anti-imperialist" policy toward British-controlled Aden. Following the death of the Iman in 1962, a civil war broke out in which the Egyptians intervened with large numbers of troops. The USSR supported the Egyptian intervention, although it maintained a number of military advisors there as well.

28. The loan was for a number of projects, the most important of which was a dam. Data from Mueller op cit., p. 224.

29. For a more detailed description of the Shah's problems, see Laqueur, *The Struggle for the Middle East*, pp. 30-35.

30. Ibid., p. 17.

31. Nodari Alexandrovich Simoniya, "On the Character of the National Liberation Revolution," *Narodi Azii i Afriki*, no. 6, 1966, translated in *Mizan* 9, no. 2 (March-April 1967): 48.

32. Ibid., p. 45. A Soviet evaluation of the role of the national bourgeois in the "noncapitalist way" that appeared soon after Nasser's death is found in R. Ulianovskii, "Nekotorie voprosy nikapitalisticheskogo razvitiia" (Some Problems of Noncapitalist Development), *Kommunist*, no. 4 (1971): 103-112.

33. For a detailed description of the new Soviet leadership and its policies, see Sydney Ploss, "Politics in the Kremlin," *Problems of Communism* 19, no. 3 (May-June 1970); 1-14.

34. For an excellent analysis of the factors, both domestic and foreign, that led to Khrushchev's fall, see Carl Linden, *Khrushchev and the Soviet Leadership 1957-1964* (Baltimore: Johns Hopkins Press, 1966).

35. For a description of the United States position in the Middle East at this time, see William Polk, *The United States and the Arab World*, rev. ed. (Cambridge, Mass.: Harvard University Press, 1969), chapter 19. Another useful source for examining the post-1967 situation is John Badeau, *An American Approach to the Arab World* (New York: Harper and Row, 1968).

36. An examination of Soviet policy toward sub-Saharan Africa during the early years of the Brezhnev-Kosygin leadership is found in Robert Levgold, "The Soviet Union's Changing View of sub-Saharan Africa," in *Soviet Policy in Developing Countries*, ed. W. Raymond Duncan, (Waltham, Mass.: Ginn-Blaisdell, 1970), pp. 62-82.

37. For an analysis of Soviet military strategy during the 1965-69 period, see Thomas W. Wolfe, *Soviet Power and Europe* (Baltimore: Johns Hopkins Press, 1970). For an examination of Soviet Policy in the Mediterranean, see Kurt Gasteyger, "Moscow and the Mediterranean," *Foreign Affairs* 46, no. 4 (July 1968): 676-687.

38. Badeau, op. cit., p. 158.

39. The competition was becoming very expensive, as indicated by a large number of Soviet loans to Afro-Asian countries in the 1963-65 period. These loans appear to have been motivated, at least in part, by the Soviet effort to gain admission to the second Bandung Conference of Afro-Asian states, which was scheduled to be held in Algeria in 1965.

There is some indication that Nasser was able to secure a Soviet promise to accelerate the construction of the Aswan Dam in return for supporting Soviet admission to the conference. On this point, see Sevinc Carlson, "China, The Soviet Union and the Middle East," *New Middle East*, no. 27 (December 1970): 34. In addition, as mentioned above, the Soviet decision to give $250 million in loans to Algeria during the 1963-64 period may have been motivated by the same considerations.

40. Interestingly enough, the only Chinese ambassador not to be called home during the cultural revolution was Huang Hua, China's ambassador to Egypt.

For a useful survey of Communist China's policies toward the Middle East until 1964, see Malcolm Kerr, "The Middle East and China," *Policies Toward China: Views From Six Continents*, ed. A. M. Halpern (New York: McGraw-

Hill, 1965), pp. 437-456. For a more recent analysis, see Carlson, op. cit., pp. 32-40.

41. A detailed analysis of Soviet policy toward Sukarno's regime is found in Ra'anan, op cit., part 2. For a case study of the Soviet experience with Nkrumah, see W. Scott Thompson, "Parameters on Soviet Policy in Africa: Personal Diplomacy and Economic Interests in Ghana," in Duncan, op. cit., pp. 83-106.

42. It appears that this decision was a ploy to get Soviet support for the narrowly based regime. Whatever the reason, the Russians pledged in April 1966 to help build a large Euphrates Dam and extend the Syrian railroad network. (Laqueur, *The Struggle for the Middle East*, pp. 89-90.) For an excellent study of the rise of the Ba'ath to power in Syria, see Itamar Rabinowich, *Syria Under the Ba'ath 1963-1966* (Jerusalem: Israel Universities Press, 1972).

43. Cited in Shimon Shamir, "The Marxists in Egypt: The 'Licensed Infiltration' doctrine in Practice," in *The USSR and the Middle East*, ed. Michael Confino and Shimon Shamir (Jerusalem: Israel Universities Press, 1973), p. 295.

44. For a description of these events, see Ottaway, op. cit., chapter 9.

45. For a description of the effect of this incident on Soviet-Algerian relations, see Ottaway, op. cit., p. 234; and the report by John Cooley in the *Christian Science Monitor,* April 2, 1966.

46. It was the Syrian Communist Party's turn to embarrass the Russians in 1968. During the Budapest Consultative Conference of Communist Parties, the Syrian delegate, Khalid Bakdash, attacked Rumania's position on the Arab-Israeli conflict, calling the Rumanians "tools of the Zionists," and even went so far as to claim that the Rumanians were "putting themselves outside the Communist movement." It is doubtful that the Russians, who had convened the conference in an effort to garner support for the expulsion of the Chinese Communists from the international Communist movement, wished to provoke the Rumanians to such an extent, and Bakdash was compelled to retract his remarks. The Rumanians walked out anyway. A detailed description of the conference is found in *World Communism 1967-1969: Soviet Efforts to Re-establish Control* (Washington, D.C.: U.S. Government Printing Office, 1970), pp. 63-91. For an excellent study of the effect of the Arab-Israeli conflict on Soviet relations with Eastern Europe, see Andrew Gyorgy, "Eastern European Viewpoints on the Middle East Conflict" (paper delivered to the National Meeting of the American Association for the Advancement of Slavic Studies, Denver, Colorado, March 25, 1971).

47. Shamir, op. cit., pp. 298-310.

48. For a different view of these events, see George Lenczowski, *Soviet Advances in the Middle East* (Washington, D.C.: American Enterprise Institute, 1971), pp. 113-114.

49. For an excellent study of relations between the Arab states at this time, see Malcolm Kerr, *The Arab Cold War* (New York: Oxford University Press, 1970), chapters 5 and 6.

50. Laquer, *The Struggle for the Middle East,* p. 36. For the importance of this type of agreement for a developing country, see Robert O. Freedman, *Economic Warfare in the Communist Bloc* (New York: Praeger, 1970), pp. 5-6.

51. Mueller, op. cit., p. 224.

52. For a description of Western speculation on this point, see Laquer, *The Struggle for the Middle East*, p. 40. There is also evidence that both Morocco and Jordan used the same ploy to acquire more military equipment from the United States.

53. Aaron S. Klieman, *Soviet Russia and the Middle East* (Baltimore: Johns Hopkins Press, 1970), p. 51.

54. See below pp. 65-66.

55. See the report by Hedrick Smith in the New York Times, May 18, 1966.

56. For a useful description of the triangular relations between the USSR, the Kurds, and the Iraqi government at this time, see R. S. Rauch, "Moscow, the Kurds and the Iraqi Communist Party," Radio Free Europe Research Report, September 1, 1966.

57. *Pravda*, November 22, 1966, had the following comment about the treaty: "The defense treaty signed by the UAR and Syria is called upon to play an especially important role in rebuffing the intrigues in Imperialism and Arab reaction. . . ."

58. Perhaps the best study of the events leading up to the war is found in Walter Laquer, *The Road to Jerusalem* (New York: Macmillan, 1968). See also Charles Yost, "The Arab-Israeli War: How It Began," *Foreign Affairs*, 46, no. 2 (January 1968): 304-320. For a collection of Arab viewpoints on the June war, which tends to minimize the role of the USSR in the outbreak of the conflict, see Ibrahim Abu-Lughod, ed., *The Arab Israeli Confrontation of June 1967: An Arab Perspective* (Evanston, Ill.: Northwestern University Press, 1970). For a description of the military preparations and tactics of the opposing armies, see David Kimche and Dan Bawly, *The Six-Day War: Prologue and Aftermath* (New York: Stein and Day, 1971).

59. See the report by Paul Wohl in the *Christian Science Monitor*, August 1, 1967, for a description of Chinese activity in the Middle East at this time.

60. Heikal, op. cit., p. 313.

61. L. Sedin, "The Arab Peoples' Just Cause," *International Affairs,* 13, no. 8 (August 1967): 28, cited in Lincoln Landis, *Politics and Oil: Moscow in the Middle East* (New York: Dunellen, 1973), p. 64.

62. For an analysis of Soviet policy toward the Arab oil "weapon" during the 1967 war and its aftermath, see Landis, op. cit.; Abraham S. Becker, "Oil and the Persian Gulf," in Confino and Shamir, op. cit., pp. 191-194.

63. Igor Belyayev and Yevgeny Primakov, "The Situation in the Arab World," *New Times* (September 27, 1967): 10, cited in Landis, op. cit., p. 64.

64. For an analysis of the highly complicated situation in Aden (South Yemen) at the time of the British withdrawal, see Humphrey Trevelyan, *The Middle East in Revolution* (Boston: Gambit, 1970), part 3. Trevelyan was in charge of the British withdrawal from Aden.

65. For an account of the diplomatic attempts to fashion a peace settlement after the 1967 war, see Yair Evron, *The Middle East* (New York: Praeger, 1973), chapter 3.

66. Evron, op. cit., gives a useful account both of the "war of attrition" and the negotiations leading up to a cease-fire.

67. Georgi Mirsky, "Israeli Aggression and Arab Unity," *New Times*, no. 28 (1967): 6.

68. Shamir, op. cit., p. 302.

69. Cited in Jaan Pennar, "The Arabs, Marxism and Moscow: A Historical Survey," *Middle East Journal*, 22, no. 3 (September 1968): 446.

70. For sympathetic treatments of Nasser's attempts to keep some freedom of maneuver during the post-1967 period, see Anthony Nutting, *Nasser*, (New York: Dutton, 1972), chapter 21; and Robert Stephens, *Nasser, A Political Biography* (New York: Simon and Schuster, 1971), chapter 19.

71. For an excellent study of these events, see Avigdor Levy, "The Syrian Communists and the Ba'ath Power Struggle 1966-1970," in Confino and Shamir, op. cit., pp. 395-417.

72. Jerusalem *Post*, April 11, 1969, cited in Lawrence J. Whetten, "Changing Soviet Attitudes Toward Arab Radical Movements," *New Middle East*, no. 18, (March 1970): 25.

73. *Trud*, 18 July 1970.

74. For studies of the Soviet need for Middle Eastern Oil and natural gas, see Landis, op. cit.; Becker, op. cit., and Robert W. Campbell, "Some Issues in Soviet Energy Policy for the Seventies," *Middle East Information Series* 26-27 (Spring-Summer 1974): 92-100.

75. On this point, see Uriel Dann, "The Communist Movement in Iraq Since 1963," in Confino and Shamir, op. cit., pp. 377-391.

76. For a general examination of Soviet-Iraqi relations during this period, see Y. A. Yodfat, "Unpredictable Iraq poses a Russian Problem," *New Middle East*, no. 13 (October 1969), pp. 17-20. A detailed listing of the oil agreement between Iraq and the USSR is found in the *Radio Liberty Report*, "The Broad Soviet Interest in Iraqi Oil" (Munich, April 17, 1972), p. 2.

77. *Pravda*, September 21, 1969. The agreement between the Kurds and the Iraqi government in 1966 never materialized.

78. Translated in *Current Digest of the Soviet Press* 22, no. 31: 10.

79. For an analysis of these aid agreements, see Y. A. Yodfat, "Russia's other Middle East Pasture—Iraq," *New Middle East*, no. 38 (November 1971): 26-29.

80. For studies of the highly complex situation in the Sudan, see Haim Shaked, Esther Souery, and Gabriel Warburg, "The Communist Party in the Sudan 1946-1971," in Confino and Shamir, op. cit., pp. 335-374; and Anthony Sylvester, "Mohammed vs. Lenin in the Revolutionary Sudan," *New Middle East*, no. 34 (July 1971): 26-28.

81. *Sudan News*, January 13, 1970, cited in *Record of the Arab World*, 1970, p. 419.

82. *TASS*, January 2, 1970, cited in *Record of the Arab World*, 1970, p. 418.

83. According to Aryeh Yodfat, "The USSR and the Arab Communist Parties," *New Middle East*, no. 32 (May 1971): 33, the USSR advised the Sudanese Communist Party to dissolve as early as May 1969. Shaked et al. argue that the party was urged to dissolve in 1970 after Nimeri had shown the first signs of turning against it.

84. Cited in Shaked et al., op. cit., p. 354.

85. For an excellent study of the activities and problems of the Palestinian guerrilla organizations, see William B. Quandt, Fuad Jabbar, and Ann Lesch, *The Politics of Palestinian Nationalism* (Los Angeles: University of California Press, 1973), especially parts 2 and 3.

86. For an analysis of the relations between China and the Palestinian

guerrillas, see Carlson, op. cit.; and the Radio Free Europe Research Report, "Peking and the Palestinian Guerrilla Movement," September 1, 1970. Another useful source is R. Medzini, "China and the Palestinians," *New Middle East*, no. 32 (May 1971): 34-30.

87. Cited in Paul Wohl, "New Soviet Revolutionary Stance in the Middle East," *Radio Liberty Dispatch*, May 25, 1970, p. 2.

88. For analyses of the Soviet dilemmas in dealing with the Palestinian guerrillas, see Y. A. Yodfat, "Moscow Reconsiders Fatah," *New Middle East*, no. 13 (October 1969), pp. 15-18; and John Cooley, "Moscow Faces a Palestinian Dilemma," *Mid East* 11, no. 3 (June 1970): 32-35.

89. Naim Ashhab, "To Overcome the Crisis of the Palestinian Resistance," *World Marxist Review* 15, no. 5 (May 1972): 75.

90. For a description of these events, see Kerr, op. cit., chapter 7, especially pp. 144-148.

91. For an analysis of American policy during the Jordanian civil war, see Evron, op. cit.; and Robert J. Pranger, *American Policy for Peace in the Middle East, 1969-1971* (Washington: American Enterprise Institute, 1971), pp. 39-48.

92. For a description of the atmosphere during the cease-fire talks, see Heikal, op. cit., p. 4.

93. Klieman, op. cit., p. 78.

94. An official description of the Rogers Plan, which basically calls for the withdrawal of Israeli forces from all but "insubstantial" portions of the territory captured in 1967 in return for a binding peace settlement, is found in United States Department of State, *United States Foreign Policy 1969-1970: A report of the Secretary of State*, (Washington, D.C.: U.S. Government Printing Office, 1971). For an analysis of American attempts to implement the Rogers Plan, see Pranger, op. cit.

95. For an analysis of Nasser's role as a "broker" of Soviet interests in the Arab world, see Malcolm Kerr, *Regional Arab Politics and the Conflict with Israel* (Santa Monica, Calif.: Rand Publication RM-5966-FF, 1969).

3

FROM NASSER'S DEATH
TO THE SOVIET EXODUS
FROM EGYPT

SOVIET POLICY UP TO THE 24TH CONGRESS
OF THE COMMUNIST PARTY OF THE SOVIET UNION

From the Soviet point of view, the most serious aspect of Nasser's death was that it removed the one man in Egypt so obsessed by his humiliation at the hands of the Israelis that he was willing to give up a considerable amount of Egyptian sovereignty in an effort to get revenge for his humiliation. The Russians were clearly concerned that Nasser's successor, who would not be bridled with his mistakes, might prove to be a considerably more independent person, one who even might turn to the United States for assistance. Consequently, Premier Kosygin led a large Soviet delegation to Nasser's funeral and remained in Cairo for several days of meetings with Egypt's new leadership, which was headed by acting President Anwar Sadat. The communique released at the end of the visit pledged continued Soviet-Egyptian cooperation and appealed for the "unity of action of all Arab states on an anti-imperialist basis" as the way for the Arabs to achieve success in their "just struggle for national independence, progress and a rapid solution of the Middle East conflict."[1]

Nonetheless, the presence at Nasser's funeral of a senior American official, Elliott Richardson, was a matter of concern for the Soviet leadership as it seemed to be a signal from the Nixon administration of the desire for improved Egyptian-American relations, *Pravda* correspondent Yuri Glukhov wrote on October 17:

The period following the death of Nasser has witnessed the development of bitter psychological warfare by Western propaganda which hopes to revitalize the forces of domestic reaction, smash the United Front in the UAR, foment internal crisis and *drive a wedge between the UAR and its friends. Once again the alleged inconsistency of the UAR's policy of non-alignment with the particular nature of its friendship with the Soviet Union has been raised.* Rumors have been spread about Nasser's

"behests" and his "last words" concerning the choice of a successor—
words spoken literally on his deathbed. As might be expected, the
persons named as successors are those in whom the West has a material
stake.[2] [emphasis added]

Writing a week later in *New Times*, after Sadat's succession to the Presidency
had been legitimized by a nationwide referendum, Viktor Kudryavtsev stated:

The political consolidation in the UAR has smashed the hopes of those
who thought that after Nasser's death Cairo would not be able to play
the active and important role in the Middle East as it has played so
far. . . .
   The results of the referendum are therefore a big success not only for
the Egyptian people, but for all the Arab peoples who see in the UAR a
state making an important contribution to their common struggle
against imperialist aggression.[3]

Unfortunately for the Russians, however, Sadat was later to prove far more
difficult to deal with than Nasser had been.
   In addition to the succession crisis in Egypt, the Russians were also
confronted with government shakeups in Iraq and Syria following Nasser's
death. In Iraq, Hardan Al-Takriti, one of the vice presidents, was ousted,
apparently for his role in the failure of the Iraqi troops stationed in Jordan to
come to the aid of the Palestinian guerrillas during their war with Hussein's
troops.[4] A far more serious shakeup occurred in Syria, where the pro-Russian
group of Ba'athist leaders led by Salah Jedid was finally ousted by the Syrian
defense minister Hafiz Assad—the man who had clashed with the Russians in the
past.[5] Writing in *Pravda* on November 28, 1970, two weeks after Assad took
power, Aleksei Vasilyev commented:

Imperialist propaganda and certain press organs in Arab countries
connected with Western interests have gone out of their way to raise a
fuss over the events in Syria and have tried to picture the situation as if
the Syrian Arab Republic had almost repudiated its former anti-
Imperialist policy. . . . Imperialist propaganda has been speculating on
the discrepencies [within the Syrian leadership] and has been striving in
every way possible to exaggerate their significance and scale, provoke
crisis and skepticism in Syria, and activate the forces of reaction in
Syria, and splinter the A.S.R.P. [Ba'ath Party] and other progressive
patriotic forces, including the communist party.[6]

While Vasilyev praised the new Syrian regime for "maintenance and
exten[s]ion" of the reforms of its predecessor, and its plan to develop relations
with the USSR and to join the proposed Arab federation of Egypt, Libya, and the
Sudan, he nevertheless warned the Syrian leadership:

Imperialist circles and reactionary elements in Syria have not forsaken
their plans. Stability in Syria and the success of the program of action
outlined can be assured only if the new leadership will count on the

cooperation of all patriotic and progressive forces within the country and a lasting union with the progressive regimes, and on friendship and fruitful cooperation with the socialist countries.[7]

Faced by these important domestic changes within its major Arab clients, the Soviet leaders adopted a policy of "watchful waiting" in the Middle East in the five months following Nasser's death. Unwilling to see a resumption of the Arab-Israeli conflict while the Arab world was in such a disarray, and with new regimes in office in Syria and Egypt, the Soviet Union continued to support the principle of an Arab-Israeli settlement along the lines of UN Resolution #242. The USSR also supported the mission of Gunnar Jarring, which had been reactivated in December, although the Swedish diplomat's trips to Cairo and Jerusalem were to be no more successful in 1971 than they were in 1968. Soviet policy during this period appeared to focus on consolidating relations with the new regimes rather than embarking on any new policy initiatives. There were frequent trips between Moscow and Cairo, highlighted by Egyptian Vice President Ali Sabry's long visit to the USSR in December 1970, Soviet President Nikolai Podgorny's visit to Egypt the following month to celebrate the opening of the Aswan Dam, and Sadat's flight to Moscow at the beginning of March following a breakdown in the Jarring talks. The new Syrian leader, Hafiz Assad, was also a guest of the Russians as he made a state visit to Moscow at the beginning of February. The Soviet leaders seem to have gone out of their way to establish a good working relationship with their erstwhile opponent, who also seemed to realize the advantages of maintaining Syria's economic and military ties to the USSR, although the visit was not without its strains. Thus, although Kosygin in his welcoming address to Assad mentioned Resolution #242, Assad did not; the final communique, which described the talks as taking place in an atmosphere of "frankness and friendship," also failed to mention the UN Resolution.[8] During this period visits between Soviet and Iraqi delegations were also exchanged as the Russians worked to further improve relations with the Al-Bakr regime. In addition, a Soviet delegation visited Khartoum in an attempt (which proved unsuccessful) to settle the rift between Nimeri and the Sudanese Communist Party. During this period the Russians also began to publish their monthly military journal, the *Soviet Military Review*, in Arabic, in an effort to instruct Arab officers and noncommissioned officers in Soviet tactics and ideology. Finally, at the request of the once strongly pro-Western Lebanese government, the USSR entered into negotiations for the sale of Soviet arms.

As stability returned to the Arab world, the Soviet Union once again began to urge that the Arab nations unify to combat the "imperialists." A new drive for Arab unity was already underway in the proposed federation of Egypt, Libya, and the Sudan, which was launched in December 1969 and which Syria joined on November 27, 1970.[9] The Russians moved quickly to throw their support behind the federation as an "anti-imperialist force in the Arab world" when it began to take definite shape in November 1970. An article in *Pravda* on November 11 described a meeting in which the leaders of Libya, the Sudan, and Egypt were working out the plans for the federation, commenting:

This event is concrete evidence of the Arab people's will toward unity, so that they can oppose *imperialist* plans to divide, fragment and weaken the national liberation movement in the Near and Middle East.

What serves as the true foundation for rapprochement . . . is the similar progressive social and economic measures within each of the three countries, these countries' *anti-imperialist course in foreign policy, and their policy of strengthening cooperation with the Soviet Union and the other socialist countries.*

This conference of leaders from the UAR, Libya, and the Sudan has dealt a blow to the calculations of the *aggressive* circles in Israel and that country's protectors to weaken the will of the Arabs in the *struggle against imperialism.*[40] [emphasis added]

The following day *Izvestia* correspondent L. Koryavin emphasized that this was only the first step in a broader Arab unity:

The creation of a federation of these three Arab states is also important because it builds a firm foundation for the subsequent strengthening of inter-Arab unity. The leaders of the UAR, Libya and the Sudan have repeatedly emphasized that cooperation among these three countries is not some isolated occurrence; on the contrary, these leaders intend to strengthen ties with other Arab countries in the future as well, and they are confident that the present federation will serve as the nucleus of broader Arab unity in the time to come.[11]

Syria's decision to join the federation was heartily approved by the Russians since conflict between Syria and Egypt in the past had been one of the main obstacles to the "anti-imperialist" Arab unity that the Russians so strongly supported. Indeed, the federation received its highest degree of official Soviet support during Assad's trip to Moscow when Soviet Premier Kosygin stated:

We believe that the Arab countries will unite their efforts more closely in the anti-Imperialist struggle, in the struggle for the elimination of the consequences of the Israeli aggression. During all these years, at all stages of the Near East crisis, Imperialism has placed its stakes on the lack of unity in the Arab world. Counting on this disunity, it unleashed aggression and again counting significantly on this, it is trying at present to prolong the elimination of the consequences of aggression. The Soviet Union hails the efforts of the United Arab Republic, the Syrian Arab Republic, the Democratic Republic of the Sudan, and the Libyan Arab Republic aimed at strengthening the unity of their actions in the anti-imperialist struggle and it *has no doubt that all the other countries of the Arab East will also make a contribution to the strengthening of this unity.*[12] [emphasis added]

While Egypt, Syria, Libya and the Sudan moved toward a Soviet-approved federation, the Soviet leaders were careful to maintain good relations with Egypt's main Arab opponent, Iraq, which was highly critical of the proposed federation, characterizing Sadat's meetings with Gunnar Jarring as "discussions of solutions of surrender."[13] Thus, while the Russians agreed on March 16, 1971, to give Egypt a $415-million loan to be used for rural electrification, desert reclamation, and a number of industrial projects, on April 8, 1971, the Iraqis were the recipients of a $224-million loan for the construction of an oil refinery and two oil pipelines. This Iraqi loan, just like the one in 1969, was to be repaid by oil—a commodity that the Russians were beginning to find more and more expensive to produce at home. The Soviet loan also served to strengthen the hand of the Iraqi leaders in their bargaining with the Western oil companies, which had become very heated. Interestingly enough, the large Soviet loan was offered despite the Ba'ath regime's severe persecution of the Iraqi Communist Party, persecution serious enough to draw public criticism from *Trud* on February 11, 1971, in an article protesting the murder of two Iraqi Communists in a Baghdad prison. The article asked pointedly:

> How much longer will the criminal reactionary elements in Iraq enjoy the freedom to carry out their black deeds and thus besmirch the name of their country in the eyes of progressive and democratic people?[14]

All in all, by the beginning of April it appeared as if the USSR had succeeded in rebuilding its position in the Arab world. Despite major governmental changes in Syria and Egypt, both Arab states were closely cooperating with the Soviet Union, and the Russians seemed to have established good working relationships with the new leaderships. As an added bonus for the Russians, the Syrians and Egyptians were cooperating closely for the first time since 1961 and, together with Libya and the Sudan, they were beginning to implement the Arab Federation that appeared to be closely aligned with the Soviet Union. Russian ties with Iraq remained strong (despite the persecution of the Iraqi Communist Party), and the Soviet leaders may even have begun to hope that it might not be too long before Iraq too joined the Arab federation. Thus, at the time of the 24th CPSU Congress, it appeared as if the USSR had not merely successfully weathered the changes in the Arab regimes, but had actually improved state-to-state relations with them. Consequently, the Soviet leadership saw little need to alter its policies towards the nationalist regimes—and the Arab Communist parties—despite the continued persecution of the Arab Communists, which in the case of Iraq and the Sudan had become increasingly severe. Speaking at the Congress, Brezhnev described developments in the Third World in a very optimistic light, although he was far more realistic than his predecessor, Khrushchev, in estimating the time span involved in the transition of the ex-colonial nations of the Third World to socialism:

> Today, there are already quite a few countries in Asia and Africa which have taken the *non-capitalist way of development, that is the path of building a socialist society in the long-term.* Many states have now taken this path. Deep-going social changes, which are in the interests of the masses of people and which lead to a strengthening of national independence are being implemented in these countries, and the number of these changes has been growing as time goes on. . . .
>
>   In the countries oriented towards socialism, the property of the imperialist monopolies is being nationalized. This makes it possible to strengthen and develop the state sector, which is essential as an

economic basis for a revolutionary-democratic policy. In a country like the United Arab Republic, the state sector now accounts for 85 per cent of national production. . . . New serious steps in nationalizing imperialist property have been taken in Algeria. Many foreign enterprises, banks and trading companies have been handed over to the state in Guinea, the Sudan, Somali and Tanzania. . . . Important agra[r]ian transformations have been carried out in the UAR and Syria and have been started in the Sudan and Somali. . . .

Comrades, in the struggle against imperialism an ever greater role is being played by the revolutionary-democratic parties, many of which have been proclaimed socialism as their program goal. The CPSU has been actively developing its ties with them. We are sure that cooperation between such parties and the Communist Parties, including those in their own countries, fully meets the interests of the anti-imperialist movement, the strengthening of national independence and the cause of social progress.[15] [emphasis added]

In a feature article discussing the 24th CPSU Congress in the June 1971 issue of the *World Marxist Review*, Boris Ponamarev, head of the CPSU Central Committee Department for International Communist Affairs, further emphasized the Soviet leadership's commitment to improving relations with the so-called revolutionary democracies:

The CPSU will continue to extend and deepen friendly ties with revolutionary-democratic regimes, *our comrades-in-arms* against imperialism.

The participation of national-democratic parties in the work of the 24th Congress reflects the growth of our mutual ties. In recent years this has been one of the specific directions in the alliance between the CPSU and the national-liberation forces. Ties of this kind, established these days by many fraternal parties, *actually represent a fundamentally new form of solidarity between the world communist movement and the forces of national liberation.* [emphasis added]

As a sop to the Third World's Communist parties, however, Ponamarev added:

The participation of revolutionary democracies in the CPSU Congresses, our Party hopes, will not only stimulate their greater cooperation with our Party and the world communist movement, but will also facilitate allied relations between them and the communists in their own countries.[16]

Despite the reduced importance given to the Arab Communists at the 24th CPSU Congress, however, an Arab Communist Party managed to be an irritant in Soviet relations with a "revolutionary democracy" just as happened at the 23d CPSU Congress when the FLN delegation walked out rather than see the Algerian Communist Party seated as an official delegation. In this case the Iraqi Communist Party leader, Aziz Mohammed, used his opportunity to speak (an Iraqi Ba'ath delegation had also been invited) to denounce the Ba'athist government for its persection of the Iraqi Communists and for arrogating all power in Iraq to itself.[17]

This was to be only a minor problem for the Soviet leadership, however, when compared to the events that took place soon after the 24th CPSU Congress—events that were to shake severely the Middle Eastern position of the Soviet Union and lead to the decimation of one of the most important Communist parties of the region.

THE COUP D'ETAT IN THE SUDAN

As the Soviet-supported Arab Federation reached its final stages with a Cairo meeting of the heads of state of the member nations on April 12, 1971, difficulties arose that were to cause serious problems for the Soviet Union. In the Sudan, Mahgoub's faction of the Sudanese Communist Party came out strongly against the federation. Sudanese Premier Jaafar Nimeri was forced to leave the unity talks in Cairo to fly to Moscow in an effort to get Soviet support in pressuring the Sudanese Communists, whose members occupied important posts in the government and trade unions, into giving up their opposition to the Sudan's participation in the federation. The Russians, however, were either unwilling or unable to bring effective pressure to bear on the Sudanese Communists, and the report of Nimeri's visit in *New Times* (April 28, 1971) said nothing about the Sudanese Communists or the proposed federation. The end result was that the Sudan pulled out of the talks in Cairo and was not a signatory to the preliminary agreement, which was signed in the Egyptian capital on April 17, 1971.[18]

Despite the opposition of the Sudanese Communists to the federation, the Soviet leadership greeted the signing of the preliminary agreement with enthusiasm and *Pravda* hailed it as

"a new step towards the unity of the Arab states, and a further strengthening of the battle front against the forces of zionism and neo-colonialism in the Middle East." . . . The main feature of the Federation is its progressive, anti-imperialist character. The consolidation of unity between the progressive Arab regimes leads to the strengthening of their common anti-imperialist front, the consolidation of the position of each of the three states and their inevitable victory over the forces of aggression, Zionism and neo-colonialism.[19]

On April 25 *Pravda* made it even more clear that the Soviet leadership hoped to use the federation as a device to weaken Western influence. *Pravda* stated: "The creation of the Federation has been received with alarm in Washington and Tel-Aviv because it strengthened the anti-imperialist front in the Middle East."[20] Less than four months later, however, the Russians were to take a very different position on the federation, which suddenly demonstrated anti-Communist and anti-Soviet instead of anti-Western tendencies.

While the Sudanese Communists opposed the federation, there was also strong opposition in Egypt. Seizing on Egypt's participation in the federation as an issue to challenge Sadat, Ali Sabry, in an apparent bid for power, moved to oust the Egyptian president. Sadat proved too skillful a politician, however, and succeeded in removing Sabry from his post as vice president.[21] What made this more than another Arab power struggle was that Sabry was fired on May 2, 1971—three days before the arrival of U.S. Secretary of State William Rogers in Cairo in the first official visit of an American Secretary of State to the Egyptian capital since 1953. Consequently, the removal of Sabry, perhaps the man closest to the Soviet Union of all the top Egyptian leaders, was interpreted in the West— and not only in the West—as a gesture to Rogers and a signal that the Egyptians might be willing to move closer to the United States and away from the USSR—if the United States were to bring the necessary pressure on Israel. Indeed, *New Times* commented in early May:

> The American government clearly wants to use it [Rogers' tour] to reaffirm its support for the forces in the Arab countries that are opposed to cooperation with the Soviet Union and to progressive social reforms, and at the same time to strengthen the position of the conservative elements whom Washington regards as its potential mainstay in that quarter. . . . American diplomatic efforts to set Arab countries against one another and *to drive a wedge between them and the Soviet Union* can only aggravate the situation in the Middle East and hamper the political settlement of the Arab-Israeli conflict.[22] [emphasis added]

Reinforcing such speculation were a series of events several months earlier. Mohammed Heikal, editor of *Al-Ahram* and often (but not always) a spokesman for the Egyptian government, had come out in his weekly column for an improvement of relations with the United States in order to limit U.S. support for Israel. Sadat himself had warmly greeted the chairman of New York's Chase Manhattan Bank, David Rockefeller, during the American banker's visit to Cairo.[23]

Whether the speculations on an Egyptian gesture to the United States were true or not, they were believed to be true. When Sadat followed up the removal of Sabry by a wholesale purge of all his major opponents on May 14, 1971, including Shaari Gomaa, who as head of the Egyptian secret police was another individual widely rumored to be close to the USSR, and Diaddin Daoud, who had publicly criticized Heikal for looking to the United States and for attempting to "vilify and discredit the very substance of our relations with the USSR," the speculations grew in intensity.[24]

In addition to possibly signaling to the United States for an improvement of relations, the purges enabled Sadat to strengthen his own position with respect to the Soviet Union by making it far more difficult than before for the Soviet leaders to factionalize against him in the Egyptian leadership. It is clear that the Russians were more than a little unhappy about the governmental changes in Egypt, although they proved powerless to do anything about them. Their true feelings may be understood by a *New Times* editorial citing the Beirut daily *Al-Anwar*:

> As the Beirut paper *Al-Anwar* wrote on May 14, 1971, the recent developments in Egypt "had disturbed the Arab nation and had aroused

anxiety among the masses at a time when the decisive clash with the enemy requires the mobilization of the forces and the unity of the revolutionary leadership in the face of the American-Israeli plot."[25]

The Russians themselves were disturbed and anxious. One week after the second purge, Podgorny made a trip to Egypt that resulted in the signing of the Soviet-Egyptian treaty, a document that had been under discussion for several years. There was a great deal of speculation about this treaty at the time. Some commentators alleged that the Russians had spread the mantle of the "Brezhnev Doctrine" over Egypt and had thus irreparably limited Egypt's freedom of action in the international arena. The impact of the treaty was, however, far less significant. At least from the published articles (there have been as yet no "leaks" of any secret articles), the impression obtained is that the treaty was merely a codification of the existing Soviet-Egyptian relationship. The Egyptians did not commit themselves beyond agreeing to consult regularly with the Russians, something they were doing already, and agreeing not to join any alliance hostile to the Soviet Union, something they were unlikely to do in any case. For their part, the Russians were also very careful to limit their military involvement by article eight of the treaty, which stated that military cooperation would be limited to "assistance in the training of UAR military personnel and in mastering the armaments and equipment supplied to the United Arab Republic with a view of strengthening its capacity to eliminate the consequences of aggression."[26]

Perhaps the greatest importance of the treaty to the Russians was as a demonstration that the United States had failed in its attempts to "drive a wedge between Egypt and the USSR." In a dinner speech in Cairo following conclusion of the treaty, Podgorny stated:

> The treaty between the Soviet Union and the United Arab Republic signifies a new blow to the plans of international imperialism which is trying in every possible way to *drive a wedge* into the relations between our countries, to undermine our friendship, and to divide the progressive forces.[27] [emphasis added]

Sadat's speech in reply had a very different content and tone:

> The most important thing is that you have displayed true understanding in *all* conditions. We appreciate this above all. We feel that it is true understanding that must be the criterion in evaluating anyone's position. . . . *When each of us understands the meaning and tasks of the other's struggle, when each of us understands the nature and principles, values and rights defended by the other . . . when each of us understands this, the rest will come by itself.*[28] [emphasis added]

What Sadat seemed to be saying was that he very much appreciated the fact that the Russians did not interfere during his ouster of Sabry, and that they acknowledged his freedom of action. Indeed, the signing of the treaty was itself an implicit endorsement of the Sadat regime.

The Soviet leadership, however, was not yet satisfied with the progress of events of Egypt or the reliability of Sadat. While a front-page editorial in *Pravda* on June 2 stated that the Soviet-Egyptian treaty "signifies a new blow at the plans of international imperialism which is trying in every way to drive a wedge in the relations between the two countries,"[29] three days later *Pravda* published an article by Yevgeny Primakov strongly criticizing Arab politicians who advocated improving relations with the United States as a way of increasing pressure on Washington to cease its support of Israel. Significantly, Primakov stated that the purpose of Rogers' trip was to revitalize pro-American sentiment which was still "rather rife in a number of Arab countries," and that "American maneuvers" in the Middle East were aimed at driving a wedge between the USSR and Egypt.[30]

One week later came the trip to Israel of Victor Louis, the famous Soviet correspondent long rumored in the West to have ties to the Soviet secret police. Mr. Louis's previous major international trip was to Taiwan in October 1968 at the height of the Sino-Soviet conflict. That trip had aroused a great deal of speculation in the West that the USSR was about to establish diplomatic relations with the Chinese Nationalist regime of Chiang Kai-shek, the bitter enemy of the Chinese Communists. This clearly had been a move to bring pressure on the Chinese Communists; and the same tactic, sending an "unofficial envoy" to Egypt's enemy and arousing speculation that the USSR was about to reestablish diplomatic relations with Israel, can be seen as a similar attempt to bring pressure on Sadat.

Sadat, however, did not appear to be moved by these pressures. To be sure, he appointed a former Egyptian Communist, Ismail Sabri Abdullah, as Minister of Planning. In addition, another former Egyptian Communist, Lufti Al-Kholi, now free of persecution by Sabry and Gomaa, could state that "for the first time since 1952 there exists in Egypt a national front in which Marxists participated as such and were recognized as a Marxist trend and not only as individuals."[31] However, these gestures were only sops to the Soviet Union, and the Egyptian president took a far more important step in the latter part of June when he invited Saudi Arabia's King Faisal to Egypt for consultations. The visit, which lasted a week, signaled both the end of a long period of Egyptian-Saudi hostility and a new entente between the two Arab powers that was to reach its highest point several years later in their cooperation in the October 1973 Arab-Israeli war. In June 1971, however, Sadat's rapprochement with the pro-Western king must have appeared to the Soviet leaders as yet another step by Sadat toward the United States.

The Soviet Union was to receive an even sharper blow to its Middle Eastern position in July following the abortive coup d'etat in the Sudan. As mentioned above, the Mahgoub faction of the Sudanese Communist Party had resisted Nimeri's demands to dissolve the party and had opposed the Sudanese leaders' plans to join the Arab Federation. Faced by these challenges to his power, on May 25, 1971, Nimeri cracked down hard on the Communists. He arrested seventy Communist leaders, including nearly all the central committee, and dissolved the unions that served as the Communists' bases of power.[32] While Nimeri was careful during this process to pledge that such actions would not harm Soviet-Sudanese friendship, it is clear that the Russians were not at all unhappy when Nimeri was ousted less than two months later on July 19 by a group of army officers opposed to many of his policies. Soviet correspondent Dmitry Volsky, in reporting the goals of the new regime, which, while not Communist, was supported by Maghoub's wing of the party and which pledged close cooperation with the Soviet Union, took the opportunity to comment negatively on Nimeri. In a *New Times* article, Volsky complained that some of the factories that had been nationalized in 1970 had been turned back to private ownership by Nimeri and that the ousted Sudanese leader had begun to include businessmen in his government as well.[33]

The Russians thus received a severe shock only three days later when, with the aid of Libya and Egypt, Nimeri was able to return to power. One of the Sudanese leader's first actions was to order the execution of the leading Communists in the Sudan, including the general secretary of the party, Abdel Mahgoub, and Lenin Prize winner Ahmed el-Sheikh, who were blamed for instigating the abortive coup d'etat. Here again the Soviet leadership was faced with an old dilemma: Should it sacrifice hitherto good relations with a Middle Eastern government for the sake of a Communist party?

The Russians at first adopted a relatively moderate stance to the events in the Sudan, condemning the crackdown on the Communists and the announced plans to execute the two key Communist leaders, but still holding out the hope for an improvement in Soviet-Sudanese relations. A TASS statement of July 28, 1971, commented:

> All Soviet people, profoundly sympathizing with the friendly Sudanese people, are anxiously following the development of events in the Sudan. Together with the world's progressive public, they express the hope that the Sudanese leadership will realize the danger of the path onto which it is pushing the country and the danger the present situation poses for the very destiny of the Sudanese national democratic revolution, and will find the strength to return to the path of strengthening the unity of all the national patriotic forces, thereby ensuring success in the struggle against imperialism and reaction, for the consolidation of their national independence and for the social progress of the Democratic Republic of the Sudan.[34]

When the TASS statement failed to elicit any change in Nimeri's anti-Communist campaign (Mahgoub was executed despite Soviet protest on July 28), the Soviet tone became harsher. A *Pravda* comment by "observer" on July 30 stated:

> The wire services are bringing more and more new reports about the unbridled arbitrary rule and the mass arrests and executions of patriots in the Sudan. To all intents and purposes an atmosphere of the cruelest terror against the country's progressive forces, first of all against the communists, has been established in the country.
>
> All this gives ground for drawing the conclusion that the Sudan is taking a course aimed at the complete liquidation of the Sudanese communist party and the physical extermination of its leaders, activists and rank and file communists. . . .
>
> The Soviet Union, and this is well known to all the Arab peoples, strictly adheres to a policy of non-interference in the internal affairs of

other states. . . . However, the Soviet people are not indifferent to the fate of fighters against imperialism, and for democracy and social progress. No one should have illusions on this score. For this reason, the words of certain Sudanese leaders to the effect that the repression against the communists will not effect the close relations between the Sudan and the Soviet Union sound strange, to say the least.[35]

The Russians also complained about "unfriendly actions" against Soviet representatives in the Sudan, damage to Soviet property, and threats and "acts of violence" against Russian personnel in Khartoum.

Nimeri, meanwhile, bitterly rebuked the Soviet leaders for their support of the Communists, and in a radio broadcast of August 5 stated:

The ordeal has shown us the type of friends we used to hail and call supporters of helpless peoples and who, as now has been confirmed, want to enter the Sudan and Africa with another face of colonialism. We shall not accept the Soviet Union or any other state as our colonizer.[36]

The following day Nimeri again attacked the Soviet leaders as colonizers:

The Soviets used to think Sudan is a nation which follows them but we will teach them a lesson and show them Sudanese originality. We will not accept colonization from the Soviet Union or any other country.[37]

Despite the polemical attacks between the USSR and the Sudan, diplomatic relations between the two states were not broken although Nimeri recalled his ambassador from Moscow and expelled the counselor to the Soviet Embassy along with the Bulgarian ambassador. For their part the Russians appear to have held up economic and military aid to the Sudan while also arranging demonstrations of Arab students outside the Sudanese embassy. Interestingly enough, however, the demonstrating students not only carried anti-Nimeri placards, but they also criticized Egyptian President Anwar Sadat.[38] The Egyptian leader, who had been instrumental in assisting Nimeri to regain power, not only did not condemn Nimeri's execution of the Communists, but in a major speech on July 30 after the executions, he publicly praised Nimeri and denounced the Sudanese Communists.[39] For Sadat to so defy the Russians on a matter of such importance to them (they had mounted a huge propaganda campaign to save the lives of Mahgoub and el-Sheikh) was a clear indication that treaty or no treaty, Soviet influence with the Sadat regime was quite limited.

To make matters worse, Heikal published a long article in his weekly column on July 30 in *Al-Ahram* in which he severely criticized the Sudanese Communists and, by implication, the USSR. In the article, broadcast the same day on Radio Cairo, Heikal asserted that the Communists should limit themselves to small groups of intellectuals so that the Communist ideology might become "one of the elements of fertility in the national experiment," but that they must understand that they could not be "the seed or the tree itself."[40] In addition, in a clear statement showing the limits of the Arab "revolutionary democrats' " willingness to cooperate with local Communists and the USSR, Heikal stated:

The national-liberation movement by its progressive nature, isolates the reactionary right, but this does not automatically make the Marxist left the alternative.[41]

All in all, Soviet disappointment with Sadat must have been great indeed, for the most that the Egyptian leader would do for them, once Nimeri had completed his repression of the Sudanese Communists, was to issue a joint communique with Soviet leader Boris Ponamarev, who was visiting Egypt on the nineteenth anniversary of the Egyptian Revolution, which stated that hostility to Communist causes only "harmed the people's aspirations, served the interests of the imperialists, and caused dissension within the Arab revolutionary struggle."[42] That this was only lip service, however, became evident on August 21, 1971, when Sadat flew to Khartoum and delivered a speech on Sudanese radio in which he strongly praised Nimeri and hailed the "victory of the people's will" that had brought Nimeri back to power.[43] In addition to dissatisfaction over Sadat's foreign policy, the Russians could not have been very pleased with a number of the Egyptian leader's domestic actions at the time, which included the jailing of a number of Communist sympathizers, a major speech on August 8 to Egyptian trade union leaders emphasizing national unity over class struggle,[44] and his increasing encouragement of foreign and domestic capital.

Meanwhile, as the events in the Sudan unfolded, the Soviet leaders received another major shock when Henry Kissinger arrived in Peking and announced the visit of United States President Richard Nixon to Communist China in early 1972. These developments meant that the long feared Sino-American rapprochement had become a reality and it became imperative for the Soviet leaders to adjust their policies accordingly.[45]

All in all, the spring and early summer of 1971 had not proven to be very successful seasons for Soviet policy in the Middle East, and it was not long before a reevaluation of a number of Soviet policies was underway.

REAPPRAISAL OF SOVIET POLICY

The events of May-July 1971 seem to have led to an "agonizing reappraisal" of Soviet policy toward the Middle East. The ousting of a number of pro-Russian figures in Egypt; the abortive Communist-supported coup d'etat in the Sudan, which resulted in the destruction of the strongest Communist party in the Middle East and a sharp deterioration in Soviet-Sudanese relations; Egyptian President Sadat's decision to back Nimeri's policies in the Sudan instead of those of the Soviet Union; the surprisingly rapid rapproachement between the United States and Communist China, which must have seriously complicated Soviet security planning—all seem to have prompted a major reevaluation of Soviet policy throughout the Middle East.

The first indication of a new Soviet position came in a revised evaluation of the Arab Federation, which was to take effect on September 1, 1971, following ratification votes in Egypt, Libya, and Syria. Instead of the effusive comments about the growth of "anti-imperialist" unity in the Arab world so prominent in early descriptions of the federation, the new Soviet evaluation was considerably cooler in tone—and for good reason. It must have been galling for the Russians to listen to the tribute given to the federation on August 2, 1971, by Nimeri after he had been restored to power with the help of the leaders of two of the federation's member nations:

> The attitude of the Tripoli Charter states. . . . The attitude of the sisterly UAR, of beloved Libya, kind Syria and the attitude of the other Arab sisters which cabled congratulations on the people's restoration of their revolution shows that our people's destiny and fate is one, *and has primarily proves the efficiency of the Tripoli Charter*.[46] [emphasis added]

The federation appeared to be moving in an anti-Communist and anti-Soviet direction as a result of the summer's events, a direction that could only be reinforced if the now militantly anti-Communist Sudanese regime of Nimeri should join. Consequently, the Russians began to argue that for the federation to be successful there had to be room in it for Communists and other "progressive forces." In a detailed analysis of the obstacles in the path of Arab unity—an analysis that continued to reflect Soviet fears of increased American influence in the Arab world—the Soviet commentator R. Petrov stated in an article in *New Times*:

> Another view [of Arab unity], often voiced in some nations *even at top levels* is that the movement for unity is the "supreme national cause" of all Arabs, irrespective of their social affiliation and political views, regardless of the socio-political systems of the various states. The proponents of this approach maintain that to resolve this national task it is essential to make use of any kind of support from without, whether it comes from the socialist countries or the capitalist. *It has been said for instance, that it is enough merely to neutralize or limit the role of the United States which, since it backs Israel, allegedly holds the "key" to the settlement of the Middle East conflict.*
>
>   Lately, reactionary and right wing nationalist forces in Arab countries, egged on by the imperialists, have sought to raise the sinister flag of anti-communism. *They are trying to persuade the ordinary people that it is possible to draw on the support of the socialist countries in combating imperialism and the Israeli aggression and at the same time wipe out the local Arab communists and ban the communist parties.*
>
>   The fallacy of this position is obvious. Experience, the Arabs['] included, has shown that imperialism can be successfully combated only if all the national progressive forces stand united. *Any attempt to exclude the communists and their parties from the common struggle can only weaken the united front* and play into the hands of the imperialist forces and their agents.
>
>   All true friends of the Arab people . . . are confident that in spite of the efforts of imperialism, international Zionism and the Arab reactionaries to tie up the Arab unity movement *in the straitjacket of*

nationalism and traditional conservative views, the Arab peoples will overcome the obstacles raised by ill-wishers to bar their way to freedom.[47] [emphasis added]

In making this appeal not only for Arab Communists but also for the Arab Communist *Parties,* the Russians seemed to have decided that their original scheme—the dissolution of the Arab Communist Parties and the participation of Communists in national fronts as *individuals,* had not proved efficacious, and that Soviet interests would be better served if the Communist parties retained their independent existence. This was to be a theme increasingly emphasized during subsequent months, as the Russians urged Syria and Iraq to establish national fronts where the Communists could participate as parties, albeit subordinate ones.

The events in the Sudan and Sadat's "anti-revolutionary" acts in Egypt provided an opportunity for the Arab Communists, long unhappy with the Soviet Union's preference for the one-party regimes of the revolutionary-democracies, to air openly their criticisms. Writing in the *World Marxist Review* in September 1971, Nicholas Shaoui, Secretary General of the Lebanese Communist Party, stated, after commenting on the events in the Sudan and the Arab liberation movement:

> The *Working Class,* the most revolutionary and united class and the one most interested in extending and deepening the liberation movement, *must be the center around which all the progressive and patriotic forces are brought together.*[48] [emphasis added]

The Soviet Union's reply to this demand came from Rotislav Ulianovsky, Ponamarev's deputy on the international committee of the CPSU Central Committee, who cautioned the Arab Communists against any premature thrust for power (the Sudanese case was implied although not specifically mentioned). While Petrov had appealed to the Revolutionary Democrats to allow the Arab Communists to participate in national fronts, Ulianovsky was telling the Arab Communists that their participation would be a subordinate one for a long time to come:

> Petty-bourgeois ideology, which usually has a nationalist and anti-imperialist spearhead and religious overtones, dominates the masses in one form or another *and will evidently do so for a long time to come....* The working class movement in most Afro-Asian countries is too weak, too poorly organized and too closely connected with its petty-bourgeois environment, while the positions of scientific socialism are not strong enough to warrant counting on them alone.[49] [emphasis added]

Ulianovsky went on to maintain that the Soviet policy of supporting the national democratic parties was to be continued:

> A realistic revolutionary approach to the matter reveals that socialism must very often be built not out of the ideal matter that an advanced

working class alon[e] can be, but of poor material that objective reality puts at the revolutionary's disposal. . . .

The masses . . . can be gradually led to an understanding of scientific socialism. Marxists bring out and foster the tender shoots of genuine ‘ socialism in petty-bourgeois concepts that will probably persist in Afro-Asian countries for years. We believe that this is the right line to follow. It proceeds from the idea that the national democratic parties, above all their left-wing groups, can, after starting from non-Marxist national socialism advance toward scientific socialism and, in the course of struggle and contradictions, finally adopt it. . . .

In terms of present and future interests, the important thing is not so much the fact that national democracy is still a non-Marxist trend as its actual fight against imperialism, against capitalism as a social system and the revolutionary democrats constructive efforts to build a new society. This is what determines the Marxist attitude to revolutionary democratic programs and parties.[50]

While in effect telling the Arab Communists that they had to be satisfied with the "anti-imperialist" policies of the revolutionary democrats (which, of course, were in line with the foreign policy interests of the USSR, if not the domestic interests of the local Communist parties), Ulianovsky then told the Communists that they had to endure stoically the persecution they received from the nationalist leaders:

Anti-communist measures carried out in a number of countries unquestionably make it difficult to achieve mutual understanding between Marxist-Leninists and national democrats, between progressive forces generally. Even when they are temporary, these measures affect both the substance of national democracy and the course of the national liberation movement. *However, proletarian parties do not yield to emotion, but proceed from objective class analysis.*[51] [emphasis added]

Ulianovsky went on to tell the Arab Communists that they were not yet ready to take leadership of the national liberation movement, although they should play an active role in it:

In a number of countries, national democratic parties are ruling parties playing the leading role in the national-liberation movement and in noncapitalist development. *The problem of leadership is not solved— and this applies to communist and national democratic parties alike— by declarations about who plays or should play the leading role, but by the actual position of the parties concerned.*[52] [emphasis added]

Ulianovsky concluded by telling the Communists that their alliance with the National Democrats was to be a long range one, and he justified the task he had assigned to the Communists in Marxist terms:

This alliance is not a passing development, but a long-range and lasting perspective. It came into being at the general democratic stage of the national liberation revolution. To continue and consolidate it at the socialist stage *would fully meet the objective requirements of social progress. This is, to our mind, one of the most important theoretical and practical aspects of the problem of the Marxist-Leninist approach to the Revolutionary democrats' non-Marxist socialism today.*[53] [emphasis added]

In addition to a new evaluation of the Arab Federation and a new role for the Arab Communist parties, a third major Soviet policy change took place in regard to the Soviet Union's relations with Israel—the federation's main enemy and a nation occupying territory belonging to two of the three member nations of the federation. A delegation of Israeli figures—all opposed in one way or another to Israeli Premier Golda Meir's policy in the Arab-Israeli conflict—were invited to Moscow at the beginning of September 1971 for a one-week visit. The Soviet press played up the "progressive" nature of the group, although only one was a Communist, and intimated that there were forces in Israel interested in changing its orientation in the world. *Pravda* stated on September 8, 1971:

The members of the group declared that they opposed the anti-Soviet statements of Israel's ruling circles. "The Israeli people are tired of war and the country's one-sided orientation toward the Imperialist Americans," M. Eidelbert [a member of the Soviet-Israeli friendship movements] stated.[54]

In addition to the visit of the "progressive" Israeli delegation to Moscow, there were a number of other indications of a Soviet attempt to improve relations with Israel, including the granting of visas to Israelis attending international conferences in the Soviet Union (in previous years Israelis were often barred from international conferences in the USSR) as well as particularly warm and cordial treatment for such visitors once they arrived.[55]

All of this pales, however, before the most important decision of all taken by the Soviet leadership in regard to Israel—the decision to sharply increase Jewish emigration from the USSR to Israel from an average of 300 per month to 3,000 per month. It had long been one of the most cherished dreams of Israeli leaders to obtain Soviet consent for Russian Jews to emigrate to Israel, and this had been one of the factors complicating Soviet-Israeli relations almost since the founding of the Jewish state in 1948.[56] While there may have been a number of domestic political considerations which motivated the decision of the Soviet leaders to allow increased emigration, the foreign policy implications of the decision were of great importance. In the first place, large numbers of the departing Jews were of military age, and a relatively significant proportion were professionals (doctors, engineers, scientists) who could make an important contribution to the Israeli war effort. Thus, while the Russians were supplying Egypt with advisers and modern weapons with which to fight Israel, they also were supplying Israel with both military manpower and individuals with skills vital to both the military and civilian sectors of the Israeli economy.[57]

There have been a number of hypotheses offered to explain the Soviet decision on allowing large-scale Jewish emigration. A number of scholars argue that the Jews are "infecting" other Soviet minorities with their nationalism, and for this reason the Russian authorities wish to get rid of them. Others argue that the release of the Jews is a sop to Western opinion since the plight of Soviet Jews is now a cause celebre in the Western world; that by giving way on this relatively unimportant issue (to the Soviet leadership), the USSR could improve its relations with the West (which deteriorated sharply after the invasion of Czechoslovakia), an improvement made necessary by need for foreign trade and the Sino-American rapprochement. Indeed, the Russians had long overestimated Jewish and Zionist influence in Washington, and by allowing increased numbers of Jews to emigrate to Israel, the Soviet leadership may have hoped to gain the support of the "Zionist lobby" for Soviet objectives. A third school of thought contends that the exodus of Soviet Jews to Israel is an overt sign of Soviet displeasure with the Sadat regime and is a means of bringing pressure upon it in the pattern of Victor Louis's trip in June.[58]

There is also a fourth hypothesis that bears some examination. Given the events of the summer, the Russians had clearly decided not to back Egypt in any new war against Israel; yet, without a war, it appeared impossible to secure the opening of the Suez Canal, a major goal of Soviet policy. Following the Sino-American rapproachement, it must have seemed urgent for the Russians to build up their southern flank against China, and the USSR's signing of a long-term treaty with India in August 1971 was one way of implementing this policy. An open canal, in addition to enabling the Soviet Union to supply India more rapidly in case of a war with Pakistan, an eventuality that appeared more and more inevitable as the summer wore on, would also enable the USSR to supply its northeastern flank against China more effectively than the highly vulnerable trans-Siberian railroad. Finally, with British withdrawal from the Persian Gulf scheduled for the end of 1971, an open canal would enable the Russians to move their Mediterranean fleet there speedily if the need developed. Yet the canal could not be opened without the agreement of Israel, and in the absence of Soviet willingness to exert military force against the Jewish state, it may well be that the Soviet decision to increase Russian Jewish emigration, when coupled with other moves to improve Soviet-Israeli relations, might have been, in part at least, a signal to the Israeli government that they might expect further benefits should they be willing to open the canal on the proper terms.[59]

A fourth significant Soviet policy change that followed the reversals in the Sudan and Egypt was a major effort to broaden the base of Soviet ties in the Middle East. Having concentrated their attention over the past few years in the core area of the Arab world (Egypt, Syria, Iraq), the Russians now moved to improve their position in a number of other states as well. There was a flurry of diplomatic activity between the Soviet Union and the Middle East beginning with a visit by the premier of the People's Democratic Republic of Yemen (South Yemen) to Moscow on September 30. Next came Kosygin's state visits to Algeria and Morocco in the first ten days of October, Egyptian President Sadat's trip to Moscow on October 12, and a visit by Yasir Arafat of the PLO (again at the invitation of the Soviet Afro-Asian Solidarity Organization) on October 20. Indeed, the virtual squeezing of Sadat's visit between Kosygin's trip to North

Africa and Arafat's visit to Moscow may well have been an indication to the Egyptian leader that the Soviet Union was not dependent on its position in Egypt for influence in the Arab world, but that it was ready and able to court a number of other Arab leaders as well—including some of Sadat's chief Arab opponents.

The Soviet Union did not restrict itself to established Arab states in its efforts to rebuild its position in the Arab world, but turned to the two main Arab guerrilla organizations as well. At the beginning of September 1971, the Soviet Afro-Asian Solidarity Organization invited a delegation from the Popular Front for the Liberation of the Occupied Arab Gulf (PFLOAG) to Moscow for the first time, following a major Soviet press buildup of their successes against the pro-Western ruler of Oman. This was followed a month later with an invitation to Arafat by the same organization. Of particular interest in the Arafat visit was *Pravda's* description of the talks:

> The Palestinian and Soviet sides noted the importance of the unity of all progressive forces of the Arab world and the necessity for the further strengthening of their alliance with the true friends of the Arab people—the countries of the Socialist commonwealth. In this connection, emphasis was laid on the *danger of attempts to undermine Arab-Soviet friendship, to split the ranks of the Arab anti-imperialist movement, and to tear it from the common anti-imperialist front.* These attempts inflict damage on the Arab People's liberation aspirations and national interests and serve only the interests of international imperialist and Zionist circles.[60] [emphasis added]

While the Russians were now trying to enlist Arafat and his organization in their renewed drive for influence in the Arab world, the Palestinian guerrillas also stood to gain from the visit. Following his return from Moscow, Arafat stated that the talks with the Soviet leaders had been "very successful" and that he had found the Moscow climate "warmer" than on his previous visit in February 1970.[61] The situation had changed markedly for both sides since that time. Badly mauled by the Jordanian army in September 1970 and July 1971, Arafat's forces were greatly weakened and the Palestinian guerrillas were no longer the independent force in Arab politics they once were. Since the guerrillas were in far greater need of Soviet support than at the time of Arafat's February 1970 visit, the Russians may have assumed that the PLO would be more open to Soviet influence. Consequently, although the Chinese Communists continue to back the PLO (a delegation from Fatah, the largest guerrilla group in the PLO, went to Peking two weeks before Arafat's visit to Moscow and got a pledge of continued Chinese assistance from Chou En-lai[62]), the Russians, by reportedly pledging training, medical care, and equipment to the Palestinians, seemed for the first time to be attempting to bring them under the Soviet wing. Interestingly enough, the Soviet invitation to the PFLOAG guerrillas had also come at a time when the guerrilla organization had been weakened because of the efforts of the new Sultan of Oman, who had been trained at Sandhurst, and his British officers.

While the Russians were moving to improve relations with the PFLOAG and the PLO, they did not neglect their relations with the governments with which the two guerrilla organizations were at odds. The Russian government signed a number of agreements with Hussein's regime in Jordan, including one that provided Soviet experts to assist the Jordanians in exploration for minerals; it concluded an $8-million arms deal with Lebanon in early November;[63] and it invited the head of the Yemeni Arab Republic (North Yemen), an opponent both of the regime in South Yemen and the PFLOAG, for a state visit to Moscow on December 7, 1971. The Soviet Union even welcomed good relations with the conservative governments of the New Persian Gulf States, Bahrein, Oatar, and the Union of Arab Emirates—regimes that the PFLOAG had sworn to overthrow.[64]

The explanation for these apparently contradictory Soviet moves seems to lie in the Russian leaders' attempt to broaden as much as possible the Soviet base of operations in the Middle East. Given the rapid changes, coups d'etat and counter coups d'etat so endemic to Arab politics, the Russians seem to have decided to strive for as much influence as possible with all the actors within the Arab world so as to be on reasonably good terms with whoever might emerge victorious in the numerous power struggles, while at the same time trying to be in a position to reinforce anti-Western trends in the region wherever possible.

One consequence of the broadening of the Soviet thrust into the Arab world was a corresponding limitation of the Soviet relationship with Egypt. As discussed above, the Soviet leaders were quite disenchanted with Sadat following his ouster of Ali Sabry and Shaari Gomaa and his support of Nimeri. Additional areas in which the Russians were clearly unhappy with Sadat were the greater freedom he gave to private capital and his reconciliation with a number of Egypt's leading landowners and capitalists whose property had been expropriated under Nasser. Sadat's ending the arbitrary seizures of private property that had occurred under Nasser, encouraged Egyptians again to make investments in shops and land. In addition, Sadat made a bold move to attract foreign capital by establishing a hard-currency bank for international trade and development.[65]

The Russians made public their criticisms of Sadat's regime in mid-August following the execution of the Sudanese Communists. In an article in *New Times* sharply critical of the new leadership of Egypt's Arab Socialist Union (Sabry had been one of its leaders before he was purged, and the head of the ASU delegation to the 24th CPSU Congress had met the same fate[66]), the Soviet commentator V. Lykov, after pointedly reminding the Egyptians no less than three times of the importance of Soviet aid, commented:

> There is no discounting the difficulties the Egyptians are confronted with in accomplishing what they have set out to do. The role that belongs in this to the ASU [Arab Socialist Union] would be hard to overrate. *But the ASU is still very young and its new functionaries are younger still in organizational, political experience.* Survival of a specious, purely formal approach [is] still very strong. There also persists, as a legacy of the past, fear of participation by the broad working masses in conscious working activity. And *local reactionaries do their best to cultivate the idea that people of the Marxist way of thinking must not be allowed to share in active political life, even under ASU slogans.*
>
> The success of the ASU program will be solidly assured if the masses, including the progressive intellectuals, see it as their own vital concern,

the tangible future of their country. And so, the key to its successful fulfillment to movement in the long term, toward socialist reconstruction lies above all in the active enlistment of the masses. That applies to the armed forces too. The greater their political understanding, the firmer will be the forces' stand in any and every situation, the more confidently will they defend their country, knowing what social gains they are fighting for. And then there will be true unity of rear and front, and a guarantee against any attempts to use the army against the country's reconstruction along socialist lines, such as there have been in some other countries.[67] [emphasis added]

Relations between the USSR and Egypt continued cool in September. In that month came the visit of British Foreign Secretary Sir Alec Douglas-Hume to Cairo, the first visit of a British Foreign Secretary to Egypt since the Suez war of 1956. It proved to be a successful visit in that it resulted in an agreement on compensation for British subjects whose property had been nationalized, and it paved the way for a British share in the financing of the Sumed pipeline from Suez to Alexandria. Douglas-Hume's successful visit to Cairo, which followed by only four months the visit of U.S. Secretary of State William Rogers, seemed to indicate another move to the West by Sadat's regime—a development not greeted with favor in Moscow, considering the enormous Soviet investment in Egypt.[68]

Thus, as the date of Sadat's trip to Moscow approached, Soviet-Egyptian relations seemed to have hit a new low. Writing on the first anniversary of Nasser's death (and only two weeks before Sadat's scheduled visit), *Pravda* columnist Pavel Demchenko stated:

> The imperialist states and in particular the United States are doing their best to undermine (Soviet-Egyptian) relations and isolate Egypt from the Socialist states. It is no secret that the reactionary elements in Egyptian society would like to forget the course aimed at unifying the progressive anti-imperialist elements which had been pursued by the late President.
>
> The attempts of the imperialist and their allies within Egypt to destroy Nasser's policy were thwarted by the signing of the Soviet-Egyptian treaty of friendship and cooperation in May of this year. However, the attempts to cloud Soviet-Egyptian relations, as an Egyptian journalist put it, have not ceased.[69]

It was one of the goals of Sadat's trip to Moscow to remove the "dark cloud" over Soviet-Egyptian relations, as the Egyptian leader told a group of Egyptian university professors before his departure.[70] Nevertheless, the primary issue in Soviet-Egyptian relations, at least as seen from the Egyptian side, was not easy to resolve. Sadat had already committed himself to the thesis that 1971 was to be the "year of decision" in Egypt's conflict with Israel, and it appeared to be his main goal to obtain Soviet support for military operations against the Israelis. On August 19, 1971, the editor of *Al-Ahram*, Hasanein Heikal, had pointedly stated:

> Any Arab defeat which the USSR does not help prevent will bring the Arab world and the Soviet position in it to the pre-1952 condition when

Imperialism was the absolute master and in full control of the Arab area.[71]

In an even more open example of an Egyptian attempt to exploit the Soviet Union, the Egyptian government spokesman, Tahsin Beshir, interviewed by the foreign editor of the London *Times* in an article appearing on October 7, 1971, commented that Sadat was preparing "to bring about a superpower confrontation between the U.S. and the USSR" if Israeli troops did not withdraw from the Sinai Peninsula. With what might be termed brash effrontery, Beshir went on to say that Sadat would be able to manipulate the Soviet leaders to do what he wanted because "the Middle East is the only area outside Europe where the Soviet Union could exercise power and therefore it could not afford to offend Egypt."[72]

The Russians, however, who had given Egypt huge sums in economic and military aid, and who almost had been drawn into a military confrontation with the United States in June 1967, were not then willing to let themselves be so exploited. In the official Soviet description of the Moscow talks between Sadat and the Russian leaders, there were frequent references to "a spirit of frankness" and "exchanges of opinions"—indications that there were a number of disagreements. In his speech of October 12, Sadat continued his theme that war was the only way to secure Israeli withdrawal and that he expected the Soviet Union to support Egypt in its time of need:

We have proceeded from the conviction that force and force alone is the way to exert pressure on Israel and eliminate aggression against our lands. Force and force alone is the path of opposition to any aggression that may be undertaken against our territory by Israel—this hotbed of aggression that imperialism has created in Arab soil. . . .

The peoples of the Soviet Union have always stood by us. They have been our friends in happy and difficult times. *Our people believe that the Soviet Union will stand by us at a time when we shall have to decide our destiny and the destiny of freedom on our soil and throughout the Arab world.* Such is our faith in your position, in the position of all socialist states, in the position of all freedom-loving and peace-loving peoples.[73] [emphasis added]

By contrast, Soviet President Podgorny's speech emphasized the need for a peaceful solution to the Arab-Israeli conflict, and the joint communique issued at the end of the talks was a clear reflection of Soviet, not Egyptian, priorities. The UN resolution of November 22, 1967, was repeatedly stressed, and anti-Communism and anti-Sovietism "resolutely condemned." The most the Egyptians were able to extract from the discussions was a somewhat vague statement that the two sides "agreed on measures aimed at the further strengthening of Egypt's military might."[74]

Most galling of all for the Egyptians, however, must have been the Soviet insertion into the communique of the following statement, which seemed to commit the Egyptians to a peaceful settlement:

The Soviet side noted with satisfaction that Egypt's constructive

position with respect to the achievement of a *peaceful* settlement of the
Near East crisis and its clearly expressed desire to reach—through the
mediation of Gunnar Jarring, the special representative of the U.N.
Secretary General—a just settlement on the basis of the fulfillment of all
provisions of the November 22, 1967 Security Council Resolution and
the pullback by Israel to the lines of June 4, 1967, enjoy the support of
all *peace-loving* states and peoples.[75] [emphasis added]

In an effort to maintain some positive ties to the Sadat regime following the
unsuccessful visit, the Russians gave final approval on November 1 for the
construction of a $110-million aluminum plant at Nag Hammadi, which when
completed would have an output of 100,000 tons of aluminum per year.[76]
In the period following the Soviet-Egyptian talks, the Soviet government in
its public statements on the Middle East continued to emphasize the need for a
peaceful settlement of the Middle East conflict. Despite Sadat's increasingly
bellicose speeches, the Russians clearly indicated that they would not support an
Egyptian attack on Israeli-held territory—"year of decision" or not. The Russians
were not willing to risk a confrontation with the United States, whose president
had just been invited to visit the Soviet Union in May 1972, and who was in the
process of planning his trip to China, for the sake of a rather fickle Arab ally. In
addition, the Russians had other concerns at the time, the most important of
which was the growing conflict between India and Pakistan.
Limitations of space preclude an extensive analysis of the Soviet role in the
Indo-Pakistani war of 1971. It is nonetheless necessary to discuss briefly the
effects of the conflict on the Soviet position in the Middle East. The USSR's aid to
Hindu India against Moslem Pakistan was unpopular among the Egyptian
masses (Egypt served as a transit point for Soviet equipment going to India),
although Sadat made no official comment condemning the USSR.[77] However,
Kaddafi, the Islamic fundamentalist leader of Libya, openly denounced the
Soviet role as "confirming the Soviet Union's imperialist designs in the area."[78] In
addition to putting the Russians' Arab supporters in an embarrassing position,
the war also enabled Iran to conquer more easily the three strategically placed
islands at the head of the Persian Gulf, which the Shah of Iran had long coveted.
Iraq, Iran's main opponent in the competition for control over the Persian Gulf
following the British withdrawal, appealed in vain for assistance against the
Iranian move. Egypt, which was Iraq's main opponent in the Arab world, was
neither in the position or in the mood to render support, and the semiofficial
Egyptian newspaper *Al-Jumhuriyah* had said in response to an earlier Iraqi plea
by Iraqi President Al-Bakr that the "bigger Arab powers cannot, under present
circumstances, take part in defending the Arab character of the three islands
because they are preoccupied with the Israeli aggression."[79] The Soviet Union,
which was involved in a deterring action against the United States during the war
and had no desire to worsen relations with both Iran and Pakistan, remained
silent.[80] Iraq, more isolated than ever, was thus limited to breaking diplomatic
relations with England, which was accused of "collusion," and expelling 60,000
Iranian citizens from her territory in reprisal for the Iranian seizure of the
islands.[81] Iraq's growing isolation, however, and her military inferiority with
respect to Iran were to lead the Arab nation into a treaty with the Soviet Union
several months later. A second consequence of the Iranian action that the Soviet

leaders found quite positive was Libya's decision to nationalize British Petroleum's interests in Libya because of Britain's "complicity" in the Iranian action. This was the first purely political nationalization of a Western-owned oil company in the Arab world, and the Soviet leaders evidently hoped it was the forerunner of many to come.

By the start of the new year, therefore, the Russian position in the Middle East was a mixed one. On the one hand, the Soviet leaders had considerably strengthened their strategic position in relation to China by backing India in a successful war against Pakistan. With Pakistan no longer a major threat, India could concentrate its forces against China, thus complicating China's security problems considerably—given the Russian buildup along China's northern border. On the other hand, Soviet popularity in the Arab world had dipped even further because of its aid to Hindu India against Moslem Pakistan and because of the Soviet decision to increase sharply Jewish emigration to Israel. The Jewish immigration was a particularly sore point for Arab leaders even before the decision to increase it, as the Kuwaiti newspaper *Al-Rai Al-Am* had stated on March 21, 1971:

> We knew very well that every Jew arriving in Israel becomes a soldier in its army. . . . Mindful that Moscow has always been careful to give us only defensive weapons, we can now see the difference between these weapons and the manpower it is sending to Israel to use the offensive weapons already there. The Russians, like the Americans, want us to remain at the mercy of the enemy so we will always need Moscow and remain under its control.[82]

In addition, Soviet-Sudanese relations remained poor. Since Sadat's "year of decision" had passed without a war, the Egyptian leader began openly blaming the Soviet Union for lack of support in Egypt's confrontation with Israel.[83] Consequently, as the new year began, the main Soviet tactical goal seemed to be to arrest the growing wave of anti-Sovietism in the Arab world.

THE SOVIET-IRAQI TREATY AND THE SOVIET EXODUS FROM EGYPT

The Soviet leadership's efforts to arrest the rising tide of anti-Sovietism and anti-Communism in the Arab world initially centered around an effort to utilize the Communist parties of the Middle East to counter these negative trends. The congress of the newly legalized Lebanese Communist Party in Beirut in early January 1972 provided a good opportunity for this since the party congress attracted government-party delegations from Egypt, Syria, and Iraq, as well as Communist parties from the Middle East, the Soviet Union, and Eastern Europe. One of the main functions of the congress was the denunciation of Communist China, which, having been recognized by Turkey and Iran during the summer and Lebanon in November, was becoming increasingly active in Middle East affairs. The congress resolutions also condemned rightist trends in the Arab world, and the Soviet Union received support for the convening of a congress of all the "progressive and patriotic organizations of the Arab countries" whose goal was to be the mapping out of a "general line of struggle against imperialism, Zionism, and reaction."[84] The goal of the Soviet leaders in arranging such a conference was spelled out by Lebanese Communist Party member Nadim Abd Al-Samad in an interview with *Pravda* on January 26, 1972:

> The Central Committee of the Lebanese Communist Party feels that there is an urgent need to convene a pan-Arab conference of progressive forces now. This is all the more necessary under conditions of increasing pressure on the Arab liberation movement. One of the forms this pressure takes is the attempt by certain circles to arouse anti-communist and anti-Soviet sentiments.[85]

A second facet of the Soviet leadership's use of the Arab Communist parties to curb anti-Sovietism in the Arab world was their call to the leaders of Iraq and Syria to accept the Communists as junior partners in a national front. This theme was clearly spelled out in an article by Ulianovsky in *New Times* titled "The Arab East: Problems of a United Progressive Front," in which the author claimed that both the Syrian and Iraqi Communists had made numerous concessions to the ruling Ba'ath party in order to enter the national fronts of their countries, and that the Communists clearly recognized the Ba'ath as the "leading force" in each front.[86] In calling for the participation of Communist parties as junior partners in a national front, the Soviet leaders had thus clearly given up their earlier plan of having the Communist parties dissolve. Their experiences with the effects of a dissolved Egyptian Communist Party may have convinced them of the futility of that approach. By clearly emphasizing the junior partner character of Communist participation in the national fronts, the CPSU evidently hoped to allay the fears of the Ba'athist leaders that the Communist parties would utilize their positions to seize power. The apparent Soviet hope was that by working within the framework of a national front the Communist parties could more effectively influence the foreign and domestic policies of the Ba'athist regimes than they could either as individuals within the regime or as illegal opposition parties outside them.[87]

While perhaps welcoming the Soviet abandonment of the policy of calling for the dissolution of the Arab Communist parties, Syrian and Iraqi Communists were not as enthusiastic about entering coalitions where they would be subordinate to the Ba'ath, whatever the benefits to Soviet foreign policy. The Syrian Communist Party actually split over this issue (among others), and the CPSU was very hard put to mend the breach, which pitted the majority of the Syrian Communist Party's central committee against the pro-Russian general secretary Khalid Bakdash.[88] Given Assad's March 1972 description of the proposed national front, which stated that the Ba'ath party would have the "majoritarian presence in all institutions of the Front" and that the Ba'ath were given the *exclusive* right to carry on "political recruitment, organization, and propaganda in the ranks of the armed forces and among the student masses," it is not surprising that many Syrian Communists felt that joining the national front under these conditions might well mean the effective end of the Syrian Communist Party.[89] In any case, Assad cleverly selected Communists from each of the two factions to serve in his government, thus playing them off and weakening the Syrian Communist Party still further.

While the Russians were upgrading the importance given to the Communist parties of the Middle East, their relations with Egypt remained cool. Sadat made yet another trip to the Soviet Union in February 1972, but he was in a much weaker position than on his previous visit. His bluff on war with Israel had been called, and student riots had broken out in Cairo two weeks before he left for Moscow. The Russians, with Nixon's visit to the USSR only three months away, were in no mood to pledge support for an Egyptian military venture against Israel. Once again, the joint communique following the visit stressed the UN Resolution of November 22, 1967, and the need for a peaceful settlement of the Arab-Israeli conflict. As a sop to the Egyptians, the Russians made another vague allusion to giving the Egyptians military aid by stating that "the two sides again considered giving Egypt assitance in the field of further strengthening its defense capability and outlined a number of concrete steps in this direction."[90] The absence from the talks of Egyptian Defense Minister Mohammed Sadek, however, suggested that these "concrete steps" might be a long time in coming. It is interesting to note that following his return from Moscow, Sadat declared that the Egyptians would have to "prepare themselves for an extended political and military struggle" in order to recover the Israeli-occupied territories.[91]

While the Soviet Union's relations with Egypt remained cool, they rapidly warmed with Iraq. Just as in the 1958-59 period, when Soviet displeasure with the Egyptian regime of Nasser led it into a close relationship with Nasser's Arab rival, Premier Kassem of Iraq, so too in 1971-72 when the Soviet leaders grew disenchanged with Sadat, they moved to improve relations with the regime of Sadat's arch-rival in the Arab world, Iraqi President Hassan Al-Bakr.

Mention has already been made of the large loan given to the Iraqi government on April 8, 1971, despite Soviet opposition to a number of Iraq's policies. Following the ouster of Ali Sabry and Shaari Gomaa, the two individuals in the Egyptian regime closest to the Soviet Union, the Russian attitude toward Iraq's Ba'athist regime became much more favorable. Thus, in an article on July 14, 1971, entitled "Iraq on the Path of Changes," *Pravda* columnist R. Petrov praised the Ba'athist regime for having properly reconsidered the policies of its previous period in power in 1963 when it had actively suppressed and slaughtered Iraqi Communits. Petrov was particularly pleased with the Iraqi regime's announced desire to create a national front that would unite "all progressive anti-imperialist organizations, including the communist party of Iraq." While warning that the Iraqis still faced many difficulties—not the least of which was the "remnants of anti-communism and mistrust of Iraqi communists in the Ba'ath party and in the military," Petrov concluded his analysis on a positive note:

However, in leading Iraqi circles as a whole, every year brings increased understanding of the importance of establishing an atmosphere of genuine trust and cooperation among all the progressive forces of the people.[92]

Soviet-Iraqi relations grew still warmer following the abortive coup in the

Sudan several days later. Faced by a hostile Saudi Arabia and Iran to her south and east, and with her western neighbor Syria having joined the Arab Federation led by Egypt, Iraq was isolated both in the Arab world and in the Middle East as a whole. The Iraqis had probably hoped that by supporting the military coup d'etat against Nimeri, the Sudan might be weaned away from its ties with Egypt and into a close relationship with Iraq. When the coup failed and Nimeri returned to power, the Soviet Union was the only country that exceeded Iraq in its condemnation of Nimeri's activities—albeit for different reasons.[93]

Iraq's isolation grew stronger as its Persian Gulf rival Iran seized control of the three strategically placed islands in the Persian Gulf during the Indo-Pakistani war, and all Iraqi appeals for assistance to her fellow Arab states were in vain. At the same time the truce between the Iraqi government and the Kurds had broken down, with Kurdish leader Mullah Mustafa Barzani accusing the Iraqi government of trying to assassinate him and of not fulfilling the agreement of March 11, 1970.[94] The Iraqi government then began arresting large numbers of Kurds, while other Kurds returned to Barzani's mountain fortresses to prepare for war. To make matters worse for the narrowly based Ba'athist government, Iranian Foreign Minister Abbas Khalatbari stated in early December 1971 that Iran would aid the Iraqi Kurds should civil war between the Kurds and the Iraqi government break out again.[95] Meanwhile, the Iraqi government continued to have difficulties in its negotiations with the Western oil companies. Frustrated and isolated, Iraq turned to the Soviet Union. One week after Sadat had departed from Moscow, the number-two man and heir-apparent of the Iraqi regime, Saddam Hussein, came to the Soviet Union for a one-week visit. In his welcoming speech, Kosygin continued the usual Soviet line of praise for the evolution of the Ba'athist regime:

> We see that important changes are taking place in the life of the Republic of Iraq. . . . The efforts of the Ba'ath party and other progressive parties and organizations of Iraq aimed at the creation of a National Front of all the country's progressive forces will undoubtedly facilitate the movement of the Iraqi people along the path of progressive social and economic transformation.[96]

Saddam Hussein's speech, however, was considerably more explicit and included an outright request for an alliance with the USSR:

> The conviction is growing among our people that it is necessary to unite the progressive forces in every Arab country and to strengthen the ties between our countries—Iraq and the Soviet Union. . . . While highly appreciating the fraternal assistance that your great country is giving us and other Arab states, we are at the same time looking forward to the day when there will be *qualitative progress* in the nature of relations between us.
>
> We think that the firm strategic alliance between our peoples, parties and governments is the foundation on which economic, technical, cultural and other relations are being built and will continue to be built.[97] [emphasis added]

For reasons of its own, the Soviet Union was also interested in a treaty arrangement. In the first place it would give the Russians another strong point in the Arab world and make it less dependent on its position in Egypt. Perhaps even more important, a treaty with Iraq would strengthen the Soviet Union's position in the Persian Gulf at a time when politics in the oil-rich region were in a great state of flux.[98] Nonetheless, there must have been some fears in the Kremlin that the Iraqis might use an alliance with the Soviet Union as a strategic cover for an attack on Iran—much as India had utilized the alliance it signed with the USSR in August 1971 as a diplomatic base from which to launch its attack on Pakistan. It was perhaps for this reason that the joint communique released on February 18, 1972, merely stated:

> The two sides have agreed, taking the present exchange of opinions into account, to study additional measures that could be undertaken in the near future adequately to strengthen the relations that have developed between the two states and to raise these relations to a new and higher level, formulating them into a treaty.[99]

The Russians also obtained Iraqi approval to include in the joint communique the by now ritual condemnation of "imperialist attempts to disseminate anti-communism and anti-sovietism in the Arab world."

In mid-March the Iraqis made one last attempt to end their isolation in the Arab world by proposing an alliance between Egypt, Syria, and Iraq—allegedly as a means of dealing with King Hussein's plan to establish a federation of the eastern and western banks of the Jordan River. Having once again been rebuffed by their fellow Arabs, and spurred by the announcement of President Nixon's forthcoming visit to Iran, the Iraqis turned once more to the Soviet Union. This time their wish was granted. On April 9, 1972, during Kosygin's visit to Iraq to inaugurate the northern Rumelia oil fields, which the Russians were helping to develop, a treaty was signed between the two countries.

The treaty bore a number of similarities to the Soviet-Egyptian treaty signed eleven months earlier. Lasting for fifteen years, the treaty provided that Iraq and the USSR would contact each other "in the event of the development of situations spelling a danger to the peace of either party or creating a danger to peace." In addition, the two sides agreed not to enter into any alliance aimed against the other. The Soviet commitment on military aid, however, was even more vague than in the case of the Egyptian treaty, stating merely that the two sides "will continue to develop cooperation in the strengthening of their defense capacity."[100]

Thus, in less than one year, the USSR had signed treaties with three of the major nations along its southern periphery: Egypt, India, and Iraq. This was a diplomatic undertaking in many ways reminiscent of the brief period in 1921 when the Soviet Union signed treaties with Turkey, Afghanistan, and Iran. The Soviet-Iraqi treaty, however, contained some possible dangers for Soviet policymakers. In the first place, it was more than likely that Iraq, emboldened by the treaty, would be more aggressive in its relations with Iran. Second, by signing the treaty, the Soviet leadership seemed to have written off the Kurds, whose leader, Barzani, complained to a *Le Figaro* correspondent on April 10 (the day after the treaty was signed) that the weapons that Iraq would receive under the treaty would be used against the Kurds.[101]

Despite the treaty it is apparent that serious disagreements remained between the two countries. Thus, the final communique reported that the negotiations took place in an atmosphere of "frankness" and that "exchanges of opinions" had occurred between the two sides.[102] The Russians may well have been concerned that the Iraqis would use the newly signed treaty with the USSR as support in its conflict with Iran and hence advised the Iraqis to be cautious. Any such Soviet concern was evidently justified, because on April 10, 1972—the day after the signing of the treaty—Iran reported that Iraq had precipitated five border clashes. As if to emphasize the real Iraqi purpose in signing the treaty, the semiofficial Baghdad newspaper *Al-Jumhouria* commented that "the treaty has filled the hearts of the Iranian leaders with fright."[103] Another result of the treaty with which the Russians could not have been too happy was a further deterioration in Iraqi-Libyan relations as Kaddafi branded the treaty "imperialist." (This is of particular interest, since a Libyan delegation had visited the Soviet Union from February 23 to March 4, 1972, and had signed an agreement on economic and technical cooperation with the USSR at that time.)

A more positive effect of the Soviet-Iraqi treaty for the Russian leaders was the announcement on July 1, 1972—less than two months after Kosygin's visit to Iraq—that the Iraqi government had nationalized the Iraq Petroleum Company (IPC) oil field at Kirkuk (one of the three main oil fields owned by the Western consortium). As mentioned above, the Iraqis had been involved in a long wrangle with the IPC, which had cut production in the Kirkuk field by 44 percent in March because of a drop in Mediterranean oil prices. There is little doubt that the Russians actively encouraged the Iraqi nationalization decision. Soviet spokesmen had long urged the Arab states to nationalize their oil holdings and thus strike a blow at "Western imperialism"; and by February 1972 Soviet spokesmen had begun to point out that unlike the situation at the time of the Arab oil boycott after the June 1967 war, both Western Europe and the United States were now vulnerable to Arab oil pressure.[104] On March 14, 1972, Radio Moscow reminded the Arabs that the former chairman of the U.S. Joint Chiefs of Staff, Arthur Radford, had said that the loss of Middle East oil to the West would be a catastrophe, and the broadcast went on to emphasize what it called the "growing sentiment" among the Arabs to use oil as a weapon to exert pressure on the United States because of its "anti-Arab policies."[105] In April 1972 the Soviet journal devoted to the United States, *SSha*, published an article emphasizing Western dependence on Middle East oil and noting the statement of President Nixon's adviser Peter Flanigan that if the United States loses the petroleum of the Near East, its "influence on Western Europe and Japan will be greatly weakened."[106]

Meanwhile, the Western oil companies were steadily retreating in the face of price demands from the Organization of Petroleum Exporting Nations (OPEC), and the oil-producing nations were now also demanding an increasing percentage of the companies' oil for their own use. Consequently the Soviet leaders may have seen the IPC nationalization as another major blow to the whole structure of Western oil holdings in the Middle East and a reinforcement of the trend leading eventually to the full nationalization of Arab oil and the consequent weakening of the Western alliance system headed by the United States. In the meantime the increasing Soviet involvement in the development of Iraq's oil industry, highlighted by the northern Rumelia agreement, would be a demonstration to the Arabs that if cut off by the West they could turn to the USSR as an alternate source of oil development capital. Indeed, a week *before* Iraq's nationalization, *Pravda* commentator Irina Pogodina stated:

> The recent commissioning of oil fields in North Rumelia, which were opened up with USSR assistance, has created new opportunities for the Iraqi people in their struggle against domination by foreign monopolies. . . . Iraq's fruitful cooperation with the socialist states, which is developing successfully, has created auspicious conditions for the country's achievement of *full* economic independence.[107] [emphasis added]

The Soviet government was quick to hail the Iraqi announcement of the Kirkuk nationalization and the subsequent decision by Syrian Premier Hafiz Assad to nationalize the IPC pipeline complex radiating across Syria. Writing in *New Times*, Pavel Demchenko stated:

> The decision of the Iraqi and Syrian governments to nationalize the property of the Iraq Petroleum Company (IPC) struck a telling blow at the mighty oil empire foreign capital has built up in the Middle East and North Africa in the past half-century. . . .
> The implications of this go far beyond the purely economic aspect and throw light on the potential contained in united action by Arab countries to gain control over their own natural resources which in the independence and strengthening of their anti-imperialist positions. [sic][108]

Nonetheless, despite their enthusiastic acceptance and encouragement of the nationalization decision, the Iraqi government's action was not without cost to the Soviet leaders. The day after the nationalization, Iraqi Foreign Minister M. S. A. Baki flew to Moscow in quest of economic and technical assistance to help compensate for the expected losses and difficulties resulting from nationalization. Lacking a tanker fleet of its own, and possessing only a limited refining capacity, Iraq was hard put to market its oil. To make matters worse, the regime had also lost about $780 million in hard-currency revenue as a result of the nationalization. While the Russians may have welcomed the increased dependency of the Iraqi regime, a situation that could lead to closer cooperation in exploiting the unstable situation in the Persian Gulf (assuming such cooperation could be achieved without unduly alarming Iran), the Russians would have to pay for this dependency. Thus, five days after Baki's arrival, an agreement was signed stipulating that the Soviet Union would help Iraq transport its oil, build a refinery in Mosul (near the Kirkuk field) with an annual capacity of 1.5 million tons, and help prospect for oil in southern Iraq. The Russians also agreed to give further assistance to the Baghdad-Basra oil pipeline. This agreement, like previous Soviet-Iraqi ones, stipulated that the USSR would be paid for its assistance by importing Iraqi oil.[109]

The Soviet assistance, however, was far from meeting all of Iraq's needs. The Iraqi regime faced a severe shortage of hard currency—something the Russians with their own hard-currency problems (aggravated by the need to buy large amounts of wheat abroad) could not supply. The Iraqi government sought to diversify its export outlets by gaining markets in hard-currency areas, and agreements were signed with both France and Italy covering part of the output of the Kirkuk fields. Despite these moves, however, the Iraqi government was still forced to institute an austerity program to compensate for its decreasing supply of vitally needed hard currency.[110]

While Soviet-Iraqi relations on a state-to-state level continued to improve, the Russians were not without criticism of the Iraqi government's domestic policies. *Izvestia*'s political commentator, V. Kudryavstev, writing one week after the IPC nationalization, complained that the Iraqi popular front (containing Communists and other "progressives"), which the Ba'athist government of Iraq had promised as far back as 1970, had not yet come into existence:

> *The tasks confronting Iraq under its program of social and economic transformation are so great that the Baath party alone cannot cope with them. It would be an illusion to believe that this program can be fulfilled without the cooperation between the Baath on the one hand and the Iraqi Communist Party and the Democratic Party of Kurdistan on the other. . . .* In March 1970, I had occasion to talk to Saddam Hussein, Deputy General Secretary of the Baath regional leadership and Vice-Chairman of the Revolutionary Council; at that time he was already talking about the necessity of creating a national front of all the country's progressive forces, especially since the March 11, 1970 agreement on the peaceful solution of the Kurdish problem had facilitated the implementation of this task. But now two years have gone by, and still there are only talks about the creation of this vitally necessary front.[111] [emphasis added]

By June 1972, it might have occurred to the Russians that the Iraqi call for a popular front, together with the inclusion of two Iraqi Communists in nominal positions in the Iraqi Cabinet that occurred in May 1972, could well have been a ploy to gain Soviet support—much as the Syrian Ba'athist regime's decision in 1966 to allow the return of Syrian Communist Khalid Bakhdash from exile was a ploy to get Soviet assistance for the Syrian regime. Whether or not the Russians would be able to exploit Iraq's new dependency to force the creation of a genuine "popular front" remained very much in doubt, and Iraqi actions, such as the decision to permit the United States to open an "Interest Section" in the Belgian Embassy in Baghdad in August 1972, seemed to indicate that the Iraqis were interested in limiting their dependence on the USSR. Nonetheless, despite conflict over the Ba'ath regime's internal policies, in the realm of foreign policy it appeared as if the two governments were working closely together and the immediate prospects were of even greater cooperation in the future.

While Soviet-Iraqi cooperation was increasing, the Soviet relationship with the Sadat regime in Egypt was running into further difficulties. Egyptian President Sadat, who had been able to get the desired support from the Soviet

Union in his conflict with Israel, faced serious criticism at home. The prolonged "no war-no peace" situation was causing increasing frustration, as Israel, which was receiving a continual flow of American military and economic assistance, seemed ever more firmly entrenched in the occupied Sinai Peninsula.

Two months after his unproductive visit to Moscow in February, Sadat made yet another visit to the Soviet capital—this time just before the Nixon-Brezhnev summit talks, which both Sadat and Israeli Prime Minister Golda Meir feared might lead to an imposed Soviet-American Middle East settlement injurious to their interests. As he later remarked in a speech to Egypt's Arab Socialist Union, Sadat told Brezhnev during his Moscow visit that Egypt would never agree either to a limitation of arms shipments to the Middle East or to a continuation of the "no war-no peace" situation, or to the surrender of "one inch of Arab lands" in an imposed peace by the superpowers. Perhaps even more important, however, Sadat once again expressed his desire for advanced weapons (fighter-bombers similar to the Phantom, which could reach the Israeli heartland, and ground-to-ground missiles) along with Soviet support for renewed hostilities against Israel.[112] The Russians, however, with more important global issues at stake, proved unwilling to sacrifice their relations with the United States on behalf of a small ally—and a relatively fickle one at that. Although the joint communique at the end of Sadat's visit contained the statement that Egypt had a right to use "other means" (*drugie sredstva*) to regain territories occupied by Israel should a peaceful solution prove impossible, the Russians committed themselves to nothing more than "considering measures aimed at further increasing the military potential of the Egyptian Arab Republic.[113] Far more to the point was the communique released after the Soviet-American summit conference, which reaffirmed the two superpowers' "support for a peaceful settlement in the Middle East in accordance with Security Council Resolution No. 242," and declared their willingness to play a role in bringing about a settlement in the Middle East "which would permit, in particular, consideration of further steps to bring about a military relaxation in the area."[114] In addition, each power pledged to warn the other in the event that a dangerous local conflict threatened to arise and "to do everything in their power so that conflicts or situations do not arise which would seem to increase international tensions," and also not to seek "unilateral advantage at the expense of the other."[115] *New Times* correspondent Y. Potomov strongly emphasized the Soviet Union's interest in Soviet-American cooperation and in a peaceful solution to the Arab-Israeli conflict in a commentary on the significance of the Soviet-American talks on the Middle East:

> It is in place to emphasize in this connection the great significance of the support expressed in the joint Soviet-American communique on the talks between the Soviet leaders and the U.S. President for a *peaceful* settlement in the Middle East in accordance with the Security Council resolution of November 22, 1967. . . . All who really seek *peace* in the Middle East and the world should bar the way to the reckless adventurist forces that are prepared to sacrifice the interest of *peace* and security of the peoples for the sake of their own selfish interests.[116] [emphasis added]

Having thus been rebuffed once again by the Soviet leadership in his quest for effective support against Israel, and beset by an increasing sense of frustration as well as a rising level of discontent in Egypt, Sadat began to plan a major shift in Egyptian foreign policy. It should be noted that frustration with the perceived lack of Soviet support was by no means confined to Sadat. In March, a seminar sponsored by *Al-Ahram* on Soviet policy towards the Middle East and attended by Soviet and Egyptian delegates revealed a great deal of mutual hostility; the Egyptians complained that the Russians were promoting Communist ideology in the Arab world, while the Soviet delegates complained about the prominence of the petty bourgeois and the hostility displayed toward Egyptian Communists. Particularly sharp in his criticism was Ismail Fahmy, a senior counselor at the Egyptian Foreign Ministry (and later to become Egypt's Foreign Minister), who complained that the "no war-no peace" situation in the Middle East was being used by the Soviet leaders to further their own interests.[117] Then, in early April, a number of prominent Egyptians on the right of the Egyptian political spectrum, including Abd Al-Latif Baghdadi and Kamal ad-Din Hussein, who like Sadat were among the original group of officers who overthrew King Farouk in 1952, complained in a memorandum to the Egyptian president:

It is now time to reconsider the policy of extravag[a]nt dependence on the Soviet Union. That policy, five years after the defeat, has not deterred the aggression nor has it restored the rights. . . . The relationship with the Russians must return to the natural and secure framework of relationships between a newly independent country which is anxious to protect that independence and a big state whose strategy—by virtue of ideology and interests—embodies the desire to expand its influence. . . . It is time now for Egypt to return to a secure area between the two superpowers. . . . There is no doubt that going beyond the limits of that area was one of the causes of the catastrophe. The policy of alliance with the devil is not objectionable only until it becomes favorable to the devil.[118]

Sadat made this note public in an interview with the Beirut daily *Al-Hayat* on May 18, probably as a trial balloon to gauge public opinion toward an anti-Russian shift in Egyptian foreign policy. The *Al-Hayat* interview was followed the next day by the publication of the discussions of the *Al-Ahram* seminar, and in June and early July by a series of editorials by the editor of the Egyptian daily *Al-Ahram*, Hassanein Heikal, who not only continued the theme that Egypt should seek a more neutral position in world affairs, but went one step further by asserting, as had Ismail Fahmy, that the Soviet Union, just like Israel and the United States, was actually profiting from the continuation of the "no war-no peace" situation.[119]

In addition to Egyptian dissatisfaction with the lack of Soviet support, there were a number of other serious irritants in Soviet-Egyptian relations. Friction was increasing between the Soviet military advisers and Egyptian officers, and Egyptian Defense Minister Mohammed Sadek frequently complained to Sadat about alleged slurs made by the Russian advisers as to the capability of the officers and troops under his command. In addition, the Soviet bases in Egypt had been declared off limits to Egyptians, even, on occasion, to Sadat himself, and this revived unpleasant memories of the situation that had occurred when the British controlled Egypt only twenty years before.[120]

The Russians, however, also had some grievances. Sadat's increasingly close alignment with Libya's Kaddafi, the most vocal anti-Soviet leader in the Arab world, was not well received in the Kremlin, and the Soviet efforts to bring Iraq into a closer tie with Egypt may be considered an attempt to counter this trend. Perhaps even more serious was the growing Soviet displeasure at what appeared to be a partial restoration of capitalism in Egypt. Georgi Mirsky, one of the Soviet Union's top experts on Egypt, made the following rather caustic comments about domestic developments in Egypt on the eve of the twentieth anniversary of the Egyptian revolution:

> In many villages, richer peasants, who profited from the agrarian reforms and who hold the village elders and other local chiefs in the hollow of their hands, call the tune. In urban areas, even though the state controls 85 percent of the industrial production, there is a strong private sector which incorporates not only shopkeepers and artisans, but also growing numbers of middlemen, profiteers, building contractors and other such bourgeois elements. The higher paid bureaucrats display a tendency to link up with the private sector. All these elements, as progressive Egyptian and foreign newsmen note, today represent the main danger at home to Egypt's socialist orientation; for the Revolution, as they emphasize, has a long way to go before every goal is accomplished.[121]

If there remained any Egyptian hope for possible Soviet support in a war against Israel, it was dispelled in late June with the publication of the report of a team of Soviet Communists who were sent to Syria in an attempt to make peace between the two contending factions of the Syrian Communist Party, one of which was pro-Moscow and the other independent. This report, which was leaked to the Beirut daily *Al-Rayah* by the independent faction of the Syrian Communist Party, contained a number of specific criticisms of Arab and Arab Communist policy. In the first place, the Russians voiced a great deal of skepticism about the possibility of genuine Arab unity because of the lack of a "joint economy." Second, the Russians rejected the slogan of "Arab nationalism" for Arab Communists, stating that "to run after popularity through nationalism will only have a bad result." Most important of all, the Russians came out for a political rather than a military solution to the Arab-Israeli conflict: "The reason is not only that we do not want war, but because war will result in disasters for the progressive Arab regimes"—a clear indication that the Russians showed little confidence in the fighting ability of the "progressive Arab regimes," including Egypt.[122]

Another factor that must have caused considerable concern to Sadat during the prolonged period of "no war-no peace" was that Egypt's position of leadership in the Arab world, which had once been paramount under Nasser, seemed to be slipping away. Thus, despite Sadat's bitter denunciations of the United States in May and June 1972 because of its support for Israel, the regime in North Yemen, once closely aligned with Egypt, announced the restoration of diplomatic relations with the United States on July 2, 1972. At the same time, Sudanese Premier Jaafar Nimeri, whom Sadat had helped to restore to power following the coup d'etat against him less than a year before, spoke very warmly of United States aid to the war-ravaged southern section of his country and stated that the Sudan was "seriously considering" the reestablishment of diplomatic relations with the United States, an action that took place less than three weeks later.[123]

Thus, Sadat, beset by internal frustration and rising domestic discontent, and whose leadership was under increasing challenge in the Arab world, decided on a dramatic action before the twentieth anniversary celebration of the Egyptian Revolution to electrify his country and end the malaise that had been deepening in Egypt because of the apparently interminable continuation of the "no war-no peace" situation. Following the failure of a final arms-seeking trip by Egyptian Premier Aziz Sidky to Moskow on July 14, and complaining that "while our enemy has a friend in the world (the United States) which acts rashly and escalates, we have a friend (the USSR) which calculates and is cautious," Sadat announced on July 18, 1972, the "termination of the mission of the Soviet military advisers and experts, the placing of all military bases in Egypt under Egyptian control, and the call for a Soviet-Egyptian meeting to work out a new relationship" between the two countries.[124]

There is little doubt that these moves were popular both among the Egyptian masses and among the officer corps that is the backbone of the Sadat regime. To foreign observers the whole country appeared invigorated during the celebration of the twentieth anniversary of the revolution just two days later. [125] Yet a greater degree of domestic popularity was clearly not the only motive for Sadat's action. The Egyptian leader was seeking to regain a freedom of action in foreign affairs and break out of the cul-de-sac that the Egyptian relationship with the USSR had gotten Egypt into. Apparently acting on the recommendation of the note addressed to him on April 4, 1972, Sadat was endeavoring to place Egypt "on the more secure ground between the two superpowers." His reasoning seemed to be that since the Soviet Union had been unable to get Israel to withdraw from the occupied territories by diplomatic means, and was unwilling to expel her by force, Egypt would turn to the United States and Western Europe for assistance.

Despite the close American tie to Israel, the Egyptians had not forgotten that it was primarily American pressure that had forced the Israelis to withdraw from the Sinai in 1957. Indeed, Heikal had editorialized on August 21 in *Al-Ahram* that "no one can convince Egypt that the United States is incapable of bringing pressure on Israel."[126] High-ranking American officials such as Henry Kissinger and President Nixon had made no secret of their desire to get the Russians out of Egypt and thereby weaken the entire Soviet position in the eastern Mediterranean. Deprived of their air bases in Egypt and lacking aircraft carriers to provide air cover for their fleet, the Russians were clearly put at a tactical disadvantage with respect to the American fleet in the Mediterranean, and Sadat must have assumed that the United States would be grateful for his expulsion of the Russians. The weakening of the Soviet presence in the Mediterranean was also of benefit to Western Europe, and Sadat may have hoped that the Europeans might reciprocate by bringing pressure on Israel by withholding Common

Market tariff concessions then under negotiation as well as by selling Egypt advanced weaponry.

Egypt's move toward a more nonaligned position was officially expressed by Egyptian Minister of Information, Dr. Mohammed el-Zayyat (the man who was to become Foreign Minister one month later), in a news conference for foreign journalists on July 22:

> We joined Nehru and Tito in non-alignment and we urged other emerging nations to do the same. We have *never deviated from this road.* This is the foundation of our behavior and it is important for the understanding of everything.[127] [emphasis added]

On the same day, the government-controlled Cairo newspapers prominently displayed a declaration by Ismail Sabri Abdullah, Minister of State for Planning, advocating an "open-door" policy for foreign investments. The statement cited the existence of a new law, made public in September 1971, giving guarantees for foreign investments. This open appeal for Western investment in Egypt was a marked policy change from the days when Nasser was nationalizing Western factories.[128]

In addition to courting support in the West, a second facet of Sadat's new policy was a move toward further union with oil-rich Libya. Indeed, on July 23, only six days after the expulsion of the Russians, Libyan leader Kaddafi saw fit to publicize his offer to Sadat of a union of Egypt and Libya—something that had been under consideration since Sadat's unsuccessful trip to Moscow in February 1972. Considering the major benefits that would flow to Egypt as a result of such a union, particularly access to Libya's immense oil revenues, and the strongly anti-Communist and anti-Soviet position held by Kaddafi at that time, it is quite conceivable that the expulsion of the Russians might have been the condition demanded by Kaddafi before the Egyptians could gain access to Libya's hard-currency reserves, then estimated by some Western sources at $3 billion.[129]

On July 31 Kaddafi and Sadat met at Tobruk, and two days later an agreement was reached to establish a "unified political leadership" to work out plans for the unification of the two countries in finance, education, and political and constitutional organization by September 1973.[130] There were numerous advantages that would accrue to Egypt as a result of such a union. In the first place, as mentioned above, Egypt would gain access to Libya's approximately $3 billion in hard-currency reserves as well as an estimated $2.5 billion in yearly oil revenues. With some of this money, Sadat could not only pursue an independent path of economic development at home—should the Russians renege on their promised capital loans to Egypt—but Egypt now could also buy advanced weapons on Western markets. It was rumored that the Egyptians had already begun to shop in England for Rapier antiaircraft missiles and Chieftain tanks. Second, the defense potential of Egypt would clearly be improved by Sadat's ability to position Egyptian aircraft and tanks in Libya out of the range of Israeli aircraft until he was ready to use them, and by the fact that Libya was receiving tanks and armored personnel carriers from Italy and Mirage jet fighters from France. Interestingly enough, the French government, which had placed an embargo on exports of weapons to "combatants," stated that the Mirages would continue to flow to Libya until the Libyan-Egyptian union took "more concrete shape" (that is, until September 1973). This assured Libya of at least eighteen more Mirages, and many observers doubted that the French government, which had sought to increase its influence in the Arab world under both de Gaulle and Pompidou, would cease to supply the first-class jet fighter-bombers even after that date.[131] Finally, the fact that the United States had major oil holdings in Libya would give Sadat a means of pressure against the United States to weaken its support of Israel.

The Soviet Union, of course, lost heavily by Sadat's decision to expel the Russian military forces from Egypt. Although it was now far less likely to get dragged into a war with the United States in the Middle East—and this fact must have sweetened the exodus somewhat—its strategic position in the Mediterranean was clearly weakened. Without the airfields in northern Egypt it was unable to give air cover to the Soviet Mediterranean fleet, and without its airfield in southern Egypt near Aswan it lost control over a major strategic foothold in northeast Africa. While the Russians retained the right to visit Egyptian ports, even this was contingent upon a modicum of Egyptian goodwill, and the Egyptians could use this as a bargaining chip to assure the continued flow of Soviet economic aid or, at the minimum, the completion of aid projects already under way.

What made matters worse for the Russians was that while their position in the Middle East worsened, the positions of their two main rivals for influence in the area, the United States and China, were strengthened. Mention has already been made of the resumption of diplomatic relations between Northern Yemen and the United States on July 2, 1972, and between the Sudan and the United States on July 19, 1972. United States relations also improved with Algeria as the American Federal Power Commission approved plans for the El Paso Gas Company to import $1 billion in natural gas from Algeria (although neither the company nor Algeria was very happy about the price), and the Algerian government promptly returned both the aircraft and the million dollars in ransom that a group of Black Panthers had hijacked to Algeria. Even the militant Iraqi government perceived the need to allow an American government presence in Baghdad and, as mentioned above, an agreement was reached in late August for two American foreign service officers to open an American Interest Section in the Belgian Embassy in the Iraqi capital.

The increased American presence in the area was also highlighted by the trip of Secretary of State William Rogers to Kuwait, Northern Yemen, and Bahrein (where the United States had a small base) in July, and the opening of a "home port" for the United States Sixth Fleet in Piraeus, Greece, in early September. The home-port arrangement enabled the Sixth Fleet to increase its service in the Mediterranean by sharply reducing the separation period between the sailors and their families, many of whom took the opportunity to move to Greece.[132]

The Chinese Communists, jubilant over the Egyptian decision to expel the Russians, were also moving to improve their position. Taking advantage of Soviet mistakes in the Sudan the previous summer, the Chinese supplied the Nimeri government with $80 million in loans following the abortive coup, along with military equipment. Ethiopia, the Sudan's strategically placed southern neighbor, was the recipient of an $87.5-million loan in October 1971, and the

Chinese further improved their position in northeast Africa by signing two civil air agreements with the Ethiopian government in May and July 1972.[133] During the summer of 1972, the Chinese also hosted representatives of the Northern Yemeni and Southern Yemeni governments in Peking, and in September the wife of the Shah of Iran was an honored guest in the Chinese capital as the Chinese Communists sought to capitalize on the strain in Soviet-Iranian relations following the Soviet-Iraqi treaty.

After a long period of coolness, Sino-Egyptian relations also began to improve, a process hastened by the Soviet departure from Egypt, which received considerable attention in the Chinese press. Following his unsuccessful visit to Moscow in February 1972—an event that increasingly appeared as a turning point in Soviet-Egyptian relations—Sadat approved a sharp increase in Egyptian trade with Communist China from $12.5 million to $85 million per year. Sadat may have also hoped that his expulsion of the Russians would induce the Chinese to allow Egypt to make use of the unused portion of the $90-million loan that the Chinese had promised in 1965, and the Egyptian leader dispatched an economic delegation to China, possibly for this purpose, in early August.[134]

A rapprochement between the two countries (after a period of strained relations in which the Chinese Communists had been accused of stirring up the student riots in Cairo in February 1968), when coupled with China's moves in the Sudan, Ethiopia, and North and South Yemen, and the recent improvement in Sino-Iranian relations—all presaged an increase in influence for China in the Middle East, a prospect that probably made the Russians little happier than did the resurgence of American influence in a region that the Russians had endeavored to make their private sphere of influence.

With its expulsion from Egypt, the Soviet Union had thus suffered another major blow to its influence in the Middle East, while the Middle Eastern positions of its two main rivals, China and the United States, had sharply improved in the "zero-sum game" competition for influence in the region. The Middle East, however, remained a highly volatile region. Fortunately for the Soviet leadership, events within the region were soon to give the USSR an opportunity to recoup some of its lost prestige.

NOTES

1. *Pravda*, October 4, 1970.

2. Translated in *Current Digest of the Soviet Press* (hereafter *CDSP*) 22, no. 42: 15.

3. Victor Kudryavtsev, "The Political Consolidation in the UAR," *New Times*, no. 43 (1970): 7.

4. New York *Times*, October 16, 1970. See also Michael Field, "Iraq-Growing Realism among the Revolutionaries," *New Middle East*, no. 29 (February 1971): 27.

5. For an analysis of the events in Syria, see J. Gaspard, "Damascus After the Coup," *New Middle East*, no. 28 (January 1971): 9-11.

6. *CDSP* 22, no. 48: 25.

7. Ibid., 26.

8. For a translation of the speeches and the final communique, see *CDSP* 23, no. 5: 1-6.

9. For an analysis of the origins and development of the federation, see Peter K. Bechtold, "New Attempts at Arab Cooperation: The Federation of Arab Republics 1971—?" in *Middle East Journal* 27, no. 2 (Spring 1973): 152-172.

10. *CDSP* 22, no. 45: 17-18.

11. *CDSP* 22, no. 45: 18.

12. *Pravda*, February 2, 1971. Translated in *CDSP* 23, no. 5: 3.

13. In opposition both to the Jarring talks and to the proposed federation, the Iraqi regime tried to organize a "Progressive Arab Front" in cooperation with the Popular Democratic Front for the Liberation of Palestine (PDFLP). See *Middle East Monitor* (hereafter *MEM*) 1, no. 6 (April 15, 1971): 1.

14. Cited in "Review of the Soviet Press," *New Middle East*, no. 31 (April 1971): 9.

15. *Documents of the 24th Congress of the Communist Party of the Soviet Union* (Moscow: Novosti Press Agency Publishing House, 1971), pp. 23-24, 28.

16. Boris Ponamarev, "Under the Banner of Marxism-Leninism and Proletarian Internationalism: The 24th Congress of the CPSU," *World Marxist Review* (hereafter *WMR*) 14, no. 6 (June 1971): 13.

17. Aziz Mohammed's speech was printed in *Pravda*, April 9, 1971.

18. For the text of the federation, see *MEM* 1, no. 7 (May 1, 1971): 3-5. The joint declaration at the time the federation was announced stated: "The three presidents affirm that the Democratic Republic of the Sudan and its struggling Arab people, who have contributed—under the leadership of Chairman Ja'afar Muhammed an-Nimeri and his brother members of the Revolutionary Command Council—earnestly and effectively to the Progress of action within the framework of the Tripoli charter, will remain active in the unionist struggle and in close contact with the Federation of Arab Republics until it is able to join."

19. Cited in "Review of the Soviet Press," *New Middle East*, no. 33 (June 1971): 45-46.

20. Ibid., p. 46.

21. Perhaps the best analysis of these events is P. J. Vatikiotis, "Egypt's Politics of Conspiracy," *Survey* 18, no. 2 (Spring 1972): 83-99. See also Peter Mansfield, "After the Purge," *New Middle East*, no. 33 (June 1971): 12-15.

22. *New Times*, no. 19 (1971): 16.

23. See Raymond Anderson, "Egypt is Seeking to Win U.S. Favor," New York *Times*, March 12, 1971.

24. Another of the men purged by Sadat was Abdel-Mahsen Abdel Nur, Secretary General of the Arab Socialist Union, who had headed the ASU delegation to the 24th CPSU Congress the previous month. For a discussion of the men purged, see Jaan Pennar, *The USSR and the Arabs: The Ideological Dimension* (New York: Crane Russak, 1973), pp. 84-88.

25. *New Times*, no. 21 (1971): 16.

26. The text of the treaty is found in *New Times*, no. 23 (1971): 8-9. For a reasoned analysis of the treaty, see Nadav Safran, "The Soviet-Egyptian Treaty," *New Middle East*, no. 34 (July 1971): 10-13.

27. *Pravda*, May 29, 1971. Translated in *CDSP* 23, no. 22: 5.

28. Ibid.

29. *Pravda*, June 2, 1971.

30. *Pravda*, June 5, 1971.

31. Shimon Shamir, "The Marxists in Egypt: The 'Licensed Infiltration' Doctrine in Practice," in *The USSR and the Middle East*, ed. Michael Confino and Shimon Shamir (Jerusalem: Israel Universities Press, 1973), p. 313.

32. For a discussion of these events, see Anthony Sylvester, "Mohammed vs. Lenin in Revolutionary Sudan," *New Middle East*, no. 34 (July 1971): 26-28.

33. Dmitry Volsky, "Changes in the Sudan," *New Times*, no. 30 (1971): 11. This issue of *New Times* appeared in the brief interval between the time Nimeri was overthrown and the time he returned to power.

34. *CDSP* 23, no. 29: 3-4.

35. Ibid., p. 5.

36. Radio Sudan (Obdurman), August 5, 1971.

37. *Agence France Press*, August 6, 1971. Cited in R. Waring Herrick, "Sudan in Sino-Soviet Relations Since the July Countercoup," *Radio Liberty Report*, February 7, 1972.

38. Cited in report by Bernard Gwertzman, New York *Times*, July 30, 1971.

39. *OFNS* report from Cairo by Colin Legum, cited in Jerusalem *Post*, August 9, 1971.

40. Pennar, op. cit., p. 50.

41. Ibid.

42. For the text of this communique, see Nicholas Choui, "The Middle East Crisis and the Arab Liberation Movement," *WMR* 14, no. 9 (September 1971): 31.

43. Radio Sudan (Obdurman), August 21, 1971.

44. *International Herald Tribune*, August 9, 1971.

45. For an analysis of the effect of the Sino-American rapprochement on Soviet policy, see George Ginsburgs, "Moscow's Reaction to Nixon's Jaunt to Peking," in *Sino-American Detente and its Policy Implications*, ed. Gene T. Hsiao (New York: Praeger, 1974), pp. 137-159.

46. Radio Sudan (Obdurman), August 2, 1971.

47. R. Petrov, "Steps Toward Arab Unity," *New Times*, no. 35 (1971): 22.

48. Shaoui, op. cit., p. 34.

49. Rostislav Ulianovsky, "Marxist and Non-Marxist Socialism," *WMR* 14, no. 9 (September 1971): 121-122.

50. Ibid., pp. 122, 125.

51. Ibid., pp. 125-126.

52. Ibid., pp. 126.

53. Ibid., p. 127.

54. Translation in *CDSP* 23, no. 36: 21.

55. Jewish Telegraph Agency (JTA) report in *Jewish Exponent* (Philadelphia), September 10, 1971. The warm treatment of Israelis by the Soviet government during this period was to stand out in sharp contrast to the official hostility during Israeli participation in the World University Games in the summer of 1973. See below, p. 117.

56. On this point, see the study of Soviet-Israeli relations from 1948 to 1970 by Avigdor Dagan, *Moscow and Jerusalem* (New York: Abelard-Schuman, 1970).

57. For a recent Soviet attempt to play down the significance of Jewish emigration to Israel, see "Zionist Fabrications and the Reality," *New Times*, no. 16 (1972): 12-13. Interestingly enough, the author of the article, Soviet Deputy Minister of Internal Affairs, Boris Shumilin, pointedly remarked that "from the Arab countries alone some 800,000 Jews have gone to Israel."

58. A similar Soviet motive may be seen in Rumania's permission to 100,000 Rumanian Jews to emigrate to Israel in the 1959-60 period when Soviet-Egyptian relations were at a low point. In 1959 Rumania was still a docile satellite of the USSR (it was not to take an independent position until 1962) and it is unlikely that the Rumanian government could have taken such a step without Soviet permission, if not actual prodding. There is some evidence, however, that the Rumanian government gained financially from its decision to let its Jews go, and the money it received from the Jewish exodus helped finance its ambitious industrialization plans. (Interview with David Ben Gurion, the late Prime Minister of Israel, Sde-Boker, Israel, August 1, 1971).

59. *Der Spiegel* reported that Victor Louis had offered a yearly emigration quota for Soviet Jews and a pledge not to transfer Soviet troops east of the Suez Canal if Israeli troops withdrew from it. Cited in *New Middle East*, no. 36 (September 1971): 43.

60. *Pravda*, October 30, 1971. Translated in *CDSP* 23, no. 44: 18.

61. New York *Times*, January 1, 1972.

62. Ibid.

63. *Al Nahar* (Beirut), November 4, 1971. Cited in *Middle East Monitor* 1, no. 19 (November 15, 1971): 3. For a background to the arms deal, which was as much related to domestic political pressures as to defense needs, see E. Romane, "Soviet Arms to Lebanon?," *Radio Liberty Report*, July 28, 1971.

64. See *New Times*, no. 8 (1972): 6.

65. For a discussion of these policies, see the New York *Times*, January 31, 1972, "Economic Review of Africa," pp. 60, 67.

66. See note 24 above.

67. *New Times*, no. 34 (1971): 8.

68. For a suspicious Soviet account of the British official's visit, see *New Times*, no. 39 (1971): 17.

69. *Pravda*, September 28, 1971, translated in *New Middle East*, no. 38 (November 1971): 12.

70. New York *Times*, October 12, 1971.

71. Cited in *New Middle East*, no. 37 (October 1971): 39.

72. Cited in *New Middle East*, no. 38 (November 1971): 4.

73. *Pravda*, October 1971. Translated in *CDSP* 23, no. 41: 6-7.

74. Ibid., pp. 7-8.

75. Ibid., p. 7.

76. See the report by William Dullforce in the Los Angeles *Times*, November 3, 1971. Announcement of the agreement may have been an economic sop to Egypt to compensate for the failure of the USSR to provide the needed

military support. On the other hand, it may also be viewed as an attempt to keep up the underlying pattern of economic cooperation, despite political differences. Thus, it would be similar to the Soviet decision in late 1958 to build the Aswan Dam despite increasingly sharp differences with then President Nasser over political issues.

77. For a review of Arab opinion on the war, see *Middle East Monitor* 2, no. 1 (January 1, 1972): 3-4.

78. Cited in the Jerusalem *Post*, December 17, 1971.

79. *Al-Jumhuriyah*, July 1, 1971. Cited in *Middle East Monitor* 1, no. 12 (July 15, 1971): 5.

80. For an analysis of the triangular relations of the USSR, the United States, and China in the politics of the Indian subcontinent, see William J. Barnds, "China and America: Limited Partners in the Indian Subcontinent," in Hsiao, op cit., pp. 226-248.

81. Deportation of Iranian citizens, who lived in Iraq near the Shii holy cities of Karbala, Najaf, and Kaziman, had been used as a political tactic by the Iraqi government on earlier occasions when it had wished to demonstrate its displeasure with Iranian policies. The fact that the ruling elite of Iraq are Sunni Moslems, while the vast majority of the Iranian population, including the Shah, are Shii Moslems, has exacerbated the conflict between Iran and Iraq.

82. Cited in *Middle East Monitor* 1, no. 6 (April 15, 1971): 2.

83. For Sadat's speech explaining his decision not to go to war in 1971, see *New Middle East*, no. 41 (February 1972): 42.

84. For a description of the congress, see *New Times*, no. 5 (1972): 15.

85. *CDSP* 24, no. 4: 19.

86. *New Times*, no. 41 (1972): 18-20. A more theoretical treatment of this problem is found in Ulianovsky's article, "O edinom anti-imperialisticheskom fronte progressivnikh sil v osvobodivshikhcia stranakh" (On the unity of the anti-imperialist front of progressive forces in the newly independent states), *Mirovaia ekonomika i mezhdunarodnaia otnosheniia*, no. 9 (September 1972): 76-86.

87. The full theoretical implications of the new Soviet policy on national fronts remained to be worked out, however, and throughout 1972 and 1973, the pages of *Mirovaia ekonomika i mezhdunarodnaia otnosheniia; Kommunist; Narodii Azii i Afriki; International Affairs*; and *World Marxist Review* were filled with articles analyzing the different ramifications of the new policy.

88. For an excellent treatment of the rift in the Syrian Communist Party, see the Radio Free Europe Research Reports by Kevin Devlin April 13, 1972, June 7, 1972, and August 23, 1972.

89. Kevin Devlin, Radio Free Europe Research Report, April 13, 1972, p. 5. Thanks to the split in the Syrian Communist Party, the outside world got a close view of Soviet attitudes both towards the Arab Communists and to Arab nationalism. The report of the Soviet commission seeking to heal the rift was "leaked" by the dissident Communist faction and broadcast in Arabic from Beirut and then monitored and translated by the Foreign Broadcast Information Service. For a brief examination of the report, see the analysis by Paul Wohl in the *Christian Science Monitor*, August 21, 1972. The report of the Soviet commission did not differ very greatly in its analyses of Arab society from both Soviet and Arab Communist analyses appearing in the *World Marxist Review*.

90. *Pravda*, February 5, 1972. Translated in *CDSP* 24, no. 5: 10.

91. Cited in *New Middle East*, nos. 42-43 (March-April 1972): 66.

92. *CDSP* 23, no. 28: 17.

93. In his July 30, 1971, critique of the USSR and Arab Communism following the coup in the Sudan, Heikal had commented: "The Sudanese Communist Party then turned to strange alliances, including elements in contact with the Iraqi Ba'ath Party which is a suspect party all around." Haim Shaked, Esther Souery, and Gabriel Warburg, "The Communist Party in the Sudan 1946-1971," in Confino and Shamir, op. cit., p. 362.

94. *L'Orient Le Jour*, November 18, 1971. Cited in *Middle East Monitor* 1, no. 20 (December 1, 1971): 4.

95. Cited in *Middle East Monitor* 2, no. 1 (January 1, 1972): 2-3.

96. *Pravda*, February 12, 1972. Translated in *CDSP* 24, no. 7: 7.

97. Ibid., p. 8.

98. There was an unsuccessful coup d'etat in the gulf sheikdom of Sharja on January 25, 1972, while there was a successful one on February 22, 1972, in another sheikdom, Qatar.

99. Translated in *CDSP* 24, no. 7: 8.

100. The text of the treaty is found in *New Times*, no. 16 (1972): 4-5.

101. Cited in *Middle East Monitor* 2, no. 9 (May 1, 1972): 4.

102. *Pravda*, April 10, 1972.

103. UPI report from Beirut, cited in Jerusalem *Post*, April 21, 1972; Radio Tehran, April 15 and 16, 1972.

104. See I. Bronin, "Arabskaia neft—SSha—zapadnaia Evropa" (Arab Oil—the USA—Western Europe), *Mirovaia ekonomika i mezhdunarodnaia otnosheniia*, no. 2 (February 1972): 31-42.

105. Cited in Foy D. Kohler, Leon Goure, and Mose L. Harvey, *The Soviet Union and the October 1973 War* (Miami: Center for Advanced International Studies, University of Miami, 1974), p. 80.

106. A. K. Kislov, "The United States in the Mediterranean: New Realities," *USA*, no. 4 (1972): 23. Cited in Kohler et al., op. cit., p. 27.

107. *Pravda*, May 24, 1972. Translated in *CDSP* 24, no. 21: 14.

108. Pavel Demchenko, "Arab Oil for the Arabs," *New Times*, no. 25 (1972): 10.

109. *Isvestia*, July 22, 1972. Translated in *CDSP* 24, no. 29: 18-19.

110. For a discussion of Iraq's efforts to overcome these difficulties, see the report by John Cooley in the *Christian Science Monitor*, June 21, 1972.

111. *Izvestia*, June 8, 1972. Translated in *CDSP* 24, no. 24: 13-14.

112. The full text of Sadat's speech, which gave the Egyptian leader's view of the development of Soviet-Egyptian relations, was in the Radio Cairo domestic service broadcast, July 24, 1972.

113. Text of the communique in *Pravda*, April 30, 1972.

114. The text of the joint Soviet-American communique, which gave very little space to the Middle East situation, can be found in *New Times*, no. 23 (1972): 36-38.

115. Ibid.

116. V. Potomov, "A Just Peace for the Middle East," *New Times*, no. 24 (1972): 16.

117. Cited in *Middle East Monitor* 2, no. 12 (June 15, 1972): 4.

118. Translated in *Radio Liberty Dispatch*, "Egypt and the USSR: Implication of Economic Integration," July 13, 1972, p. 6.

119. For a survey of the Egyptian press at the time of Soviet exodus, see the report by Ihsan A. Hijazi in the New York *Times*, July 19, 1972.

120. For a perceptive view of the domestic situation in Egypt at the time of the Soviet exodus, see P. J. Vatikiotis, "Two Years After Nasser: The chance of a New Beginning," *New Middle East*, no. 48 (September 1972): 7-9.

121. Georgi Mirsky, "The Path of the Egyptian Revolution." *New Times*, no. 30 (1972): 23.

122. For the text of this most interesting report, see *Al-Rayah*, June 26, 1972, pp. 12-21. Translated in special supplement to the *Foreign Broadcast Information Service Daily Report*.

123. For a discussion of the domestic and foreign background to the Yemeni and Sudanese decisions, see the report by John Cooley in the *Christian Science Monitor*, July 5, 1972; and the report by Henry Tanner in the New York *Times*, July 18, 1972.

124. Text of the statement in the New York *Times*, July 19, 1972.

125. See the report by Henry Tanner in the New York *Times*, July 24, 1972.

126. Cited in the report by John Cooley in the *Christian Science Monitor*, July 24, 1972.

127. Cited in the report by Henry Tanner in the New York *Times*, July 23, 1972.

128. Ibid.

129. For a discussion of the potential benefits to Egypt of the union, see Malcolm Kerr, "The Convenient Marriage of Egypt and Libya," *New Middle East*, no. 48 (September 1972): 4-7.

130. For the text of the agreement, see the New York *Times*, August 3, 1972.

131. Reuters (Paris), cited in Jerusalem *Post*, August 4, 1972. The observers were later proven correct, since despite clear evidence that the Libyan government had sent its Mirages to Egypt for use in the October 1973 war against Israel, the Pompidou government continued to sell Mirages to Libya.

132. This agreement was not particularly popular, however, among either sections of the Greek people who perceived it as an endorsement of the Greek military dictatorship, or among a number of U.S. Senators.

133. New York *Times*, September 4, 1972.

134. For a thorough examination of Chinese policy toward Egypt and the rest of the Arab world at this time, see W. A. C. Adie, "Peking's Revised Line," *Problems of Communism* 21, no. 5 (September-October 1972): 54-68.

CHAPTER

4

FROM THE 1972 EXODUS
TO THE OCTOBER 1973
ARAB-ISRAELI WAR

SOVIET POLICY UP TO THE MUNICH MASSACRE

Despite the major loss to the Russians' Middle East position, the initial Soviet reaction to Sadat's expulsion decision was relatively mild, although as time went on and as Soviet-Egyptian relations began to deteriorate sharply the Russian commentators became more explicit in their criticism of Egyptian policy. The communique on the Soviet Exodus, printed in *Pravda* on July 20, 1972, was terse:

> The Soviet military personnel in the Arab Republic of Egypt have now fulfilled their mission. In consideration of this fact and *after a suitable exchange of opinions* between the two sides, it has been deemed expedient to bring back to the Soviet Union those military personnel who were assigned to Egypt for a limited period of time. These personnel will return in the near future.
>
> As was noted by ARE President A. Sadat in his address to the July 18, 1972 session of the Arab Socialist Union Central Committee, the measures now being taken "in no way affect the basic principles of Egyptian-Soviet friendship."[1] [emphasis added]

More to the point was an article in the pro-Moscow Lebanese Communist daily *Al-Nida* on July 19, 1972, which accused Sadat of surrendering to "the U.S. imperialist and reactionary influence" and charged the Egyptian leader with giving the impression that the USSR was to blame for Arab suffering resulting from the continued Israeli occupation of Arab land.[2] The following day *Al-Nida* presented what it said was the background to the expulsion decision:

> It was obvious that Egypt was experiencing an acute struggle and that the Egyptian right was launching a rabid campaign aimed at striking at

the friendship and cooperation with the Soviet Union and at paving the way for acceptance of the US capitulationist solution. . . .

. . . The decision taken by Sadat was to end the struggle that had been going on in Egypt for some time. . . . The struggle reached a climax when Lt. General Sadek, who is known for his hostility to the Soviet Union, called on Sadat at the head of a military delegation. Sadat was asked to take a decision for removal of the Soviet advisers from Egypt and to reconsider the foundations of Soviet-Egyptian relations. The request was accompanied by a threat of interference by the Army command openly to impose the decision and to interfere in the political affairs [of Egypt].[3]

Pravda itself warned on July 23, 1972 (the day after Egyptian Information Minister Mohammed el-Zayyat's press conference in which Egypt's nonalignment was stressed), that in a number of countries, including Egypt, "right-wing reactionary forces" were trying to undermine Soviet-Arab friendship.[4]

Soviet-Egyptian relations worsened further following the Egyptian rejection of a note from Brezhnev to Sadat requesting a high-level meeting. On August 13, 1972, el-Zayyat stated that "there were many things to be settled before a Soviet-Egyptian summit meeting could settle future relations."[5] On August 19, 1972, Sadat told the Egyptian People's Council that he had rejected the "language, contents and type" of the message he had received from Brezhnev. The Egyptian leader further stated that the Soviet Union's refusal to supply the requested arms "aimed to drive us to desperation and the brink of surrender," but that Egypt would, God willing, obtain the needed arms elsewhere.[6] Two days later it became evident where Sadat was looking for arms. In an interview in *Le Figaro* Sadat blamed the Russians for not understanding Egyptian psychology and stated that the Western Europeans now owed Egypt a response to the "initiative" he had taken to help them.[7]

The deterioration in Soviet-Egyptian relations intensified as a war of words broke out between Soviet and Egyptian newspapers in mid-August. The editor of the Cairo daily *Akhbar-Al-Yom*, Abdul Koddous, rumored to be a close personal friend of Sadat, charged the Russians with expansionist designs in Egypt, failure to supply the needed weaponry, and dividing the Middle East into spheres of influence with the United States in a "new Yalta agreement."[8]

On August 29, *Izvestia* strongly attacked Koddous and indirectly warned Egypt of the danger of losing Soviet diplomatic support:

> The editor-in-chief of *Akhbar-Al-Yom* dares to slander the USSR, alleging that it is not fulfilling the article of the treaty referring to cooperation between the USSR and the ARE in the military field.
> . . . This "absurd allegation" may gladden the imperialists and the Israeli rulers, but is capable only of harming the Egyptian people and their just struggle to eliminate the consequences of the Israeli expansion.[9]

New Times columnist Y. Potomov joined in the attack on Koddous and clearly warned the Egyptians that their weakened position had put them at Israel's mercy:

Koddous and some of his colleagues have at times lost their bearings, forgetting on which side of the barricades are the enemies of the Egyptian and other Arab peoples. One of the cardinal features of the present propaganda campaign conducted against the Arab peoples is its patently anti-Soviet slant. . . . One of the favorite devices used by the enemies of the Arab peoples is the myth of "Soviet presence" in countries which draw on the generous aid of the Soviet Union in upholding their freedom and independence.

Particular emphasis is placed on discrediting Soviet military aid to the Arab countries. Not only imperialist propaganda but also the right-wing forces in Arab countries acting in unison with it spare no effort to smear this aid. They circulate fabrications to the effect that the USSR does not supply the Arab countries enough weapons to combat the aggressor because it allegedly seeks to perpetuate a "no war-no peace" situation in order to preserve its "military presence" in the area.

Evidently, some people in the West and also in Tel Aviv *assume that Egypt has now seriously weakened itself* and that hence the time has come to bring out the old projects for "direct" negotiations and interim agreements without any definite clear-cut commitment by Israel to withdraw its troops from the occupied countries.[10] [emphasis added]

The Egyptian press, however, refused to be cowed by Soviet attacks, with Koddous even proposing on September 2, 1972, that the Soviet press, like Brezhnev, take a holiday on the Crimea. The next day Moussa Sabry, a columnist for the Egyptian daily *Al-Akhbar*, went even further than Koddous in his attacks on the USSR by asserting that the Russians had been involved in the anti-Sadat plot led by Ali Sabry in May 1971.[11]

There is no telling how much further the deterioration in Soviet-Egyptian relations might have gone[12] when a group of Palestinian terrorists killed eleven Israeli athletes at the Olympic Games in Munich and set off a chain of events that greatly upset the pattern of Egyptian diplomacy. But before the consequences of this event are considered, it is necessary to examine Soviet policy towards other sections of the Arab world following the USSR's expulsion from Egypt.

As their relations with Egypt deteriorated rapidly, the Russians sought to shore up their positions elsewhere in the Arab world. In Syria, Premier Assad did not follow Sadat's example by expelling his Soviet military advisers, although there is some indication that he extracted a large price in Soviet aid for his "restraint." Soviet-Iraqi relations grew still warmer, and the Russians made a deliberate point of contrasting their improved relations with the Iraqi Ba'athist regime with the chill in Soviet-Egyptian relations. The Soviet leaders also moved to increase their influence within the Palestinian guerrilla movement through both endorsements in the Soviet press and by shipments of weapons. Finally, by imposing a prohibitive exit tax on educated Russian Jews seeking to emigrate to Israel, the Russians moved to counter Arab criticism that, while professing aid to the Arab cause, the Russians were in fact contributing to Israel's war potential.

Syrian leader Hafiz Assad, despite frequent protestations of Syrian-Soviet friendship, had been careful to keep the Russians at arms length. As mentioned above, his faction in Syria's Ba'ath party had ousted the more pro-Soviet Jedid faction in November 1970. Unlike either Egypt or Iraq, the other two areas of primary Soviet influence in the area, Syria had resisted Soviet requests to sign a fifteen-year treaty of friendship and cooperation. Nonetheless, Assad was more than willing to accept large amounts of Soviet economic aid, and the Russians were involved in a large number of construction projects in Syria, the most important of which was the Euphrates Dam.[13]

The Soviet Union was also the major supplier of weapons to Syria, and Russian advisers helped train the Syrian army and air force, although their numbers were far more limited than in Egypt. Like Egypt, Syria had a serious security problem with respect to Israel, and periodic clashes had erupted on the Syrian-Israeli border since the June 1967 war. Following the Lod massacre of May 29, 1972, in which a group of Japanese terrorists working for one of the Palestine guerrilla organizations killed 26 people at Lod Airport near Tel Aviv, the Israeli army made a number of strikes deep into Lebanon in an effort to destroy the guerrilla bases. In one strike, in an area only 25 miles from Damascus, the Israelis captured four high-ranking Syrian officers together with their Lebanese liaison officer.[14] These Israeli actions may have prompted Assad's visit to Moscow in early July, which resulted, according to the joint communique, in an agreement "on measures for the strengthening of the Syrian Arab Republic's military potential" and in an agreement on economic and technical cooperation.[15]

It was perhaps because of his heightened sense of vulnerability to Israel, or because the Russian "presence" in Syria was far less significant than in Egypt, or perhaps even to extract still more Soviet aid, that Assad did not follow Sadat's example by expelling the Soviet advisers from Syria. In an interview published in the Beirut newspaper *Al-Anwar* on August 10, 1972, and partially reprinted in *Pravda* the next day, Assad was quoted as saying:

> The interests of the Syrian people require the continuation of the Soviet military specialists' mission in our country. The Soviet specialists have been working in Syria for a long time, and I believe that the necessity for continuing their mission is not subject to discussion.[16]

Assad went on to say, however (in a section of the interview *Pravda* did not publish), that "we here in Syria and Egypt wish the Soviet Union would meet our request (for arms) in a better and more effective manner."[17]

While Soviet-Syrian relations remained good, if a bit distant, the USSR's relations with Iraq continued to improve rapidly, with frequent exchanges of delegations between the two countries. The Russians demonstratively publicized their improved position in Iraq as a counter to their worsened relations with Egypt. Thus, on July 21, 1972, only four days after the Soviet exodus from Egypt began, *Izvestia* made public the details of the Soviet-Iraqi aid agreement of June 7, 1972. In addition, the Russians made frequent use of statements by Iraqi leaders to justify Soviet policies in the Middle East, as the Iraqis took the leading role in combating "anti-Sovietism" in the Arab world. A *New Times* article in late August by I. Gavrilov claimed that the Iraqi people were "unanimous in their opposition to (anti-Soviet) ideological subversion by imperialism and Arab reaction," and cited the following report from the Baghdad *Observer* as "characteristic to their attitude":

The imperialists and reactionaries are currently acting in unison to undermine Arab-Soviet friendship. This is part of a sweeping design whose object is to deprive the Arab people of powerful Soviet support, disunite the progressive Arab countries in general, and isolate the regime in Iraq in particular.[18]

Another source utilized by the Russians for combating the rising tide of anti-Sovietism in the Arab world was the Palestinian guerrillas. A delegation of the Palestine Liberation Organization headed by Yasir Arafat made a prolonged visit to Moscow from July 17-27—just at the time when Sadat was expelling the Russians from Egypt. *Pravda*, on July 28, cited the PLO's statement of their appreciation of Soviet support for the Palestinian cause and their declaration that

all attempts by the imperialist and reactionary circles to disrupt the friendship between the national liberation forces in the Arab world and the Soviet Union and other socialist states are incompatible with the interests of the Arab peoples.[19]

In return for their ringing endorsement of Soviet policy toward the Arab world, Arafat's group for the first time reportedly got direct shipments of Soviet arms (hitherto they had gone to the Arab governments on whose soil PLO units were stationed),[20] as well as much greater Soviet press coverage in their struggle against Israel and the antiguerrilla elements in Lebanon. Writing an extensive feature article in *Pravda* on August 29, Pavel Demchenko described the history of the growth of the guerrilla movement and bitterly attacked Israel for its mistreatment of the Palestinians. Perhaps hoping to maintain the Soviet tie to the Hussein regime in Jordan, however, Demchenko made no direct mention of Hussein's bloody destruction of the guerrilla movement in his country in September 1970 and July 1971, which had led a number of the guerrillas to cross the Jordan River to surrender to the Israelis rather than to Hussein's troops. The Soviet journalist was, however, critical of "acts of desperation," such as hijackings of passenger planes and the blowing up of nonmilitary targets, which did "serious damage to the entire Palestinian Resistance Movement and made its support by progressive and democratic forces more difficult."[21]

Demchenko was also critical of the right-wing and anarchistic groups in the Palestinian movement, which he considered tools of the Israelis and Arab reactionaries who were "using them to set a barrier on the path to organizational and political unity." Demchenko's solution to the dilemma of the Palestinians and their relative ineffectiveness, which he candidly admitted, was the unification of the Palestinian resistance in the framework of a national front—similar to the national front policy the Soviet leaders were promoting in Syria and Iraq:

The facts indicate that the forces of imperialism and reaction have clearly stepped up their activity in the Arab East recently, setting themselves the goal of weakening the national liberation struggle of the Arab peoples and liquidating the Palestinian Resistance Movement. Naturally, this creates new difficulties for the movement and insistently confronts it with a number of cardinal problems, problems that are now being widely discussed by the progressive Arab public.

Among these problems is the determination, on the basis of the actual correlation of forces, of the place and role of the Palestinian movement in the common front of the Arab peoples. What is involved here, among other things, is cooperation with the progressive Arab governments in the struggle for the elimination of the consequences of the Israeli aggression, the settlement of the Near East crisis, and the liberation of the occupied territories. This calls for advancing slogans and setting tasks corresponding to each stage of the struggle, i.e., for the delineation of strategic and tactical tasks. Faik Warrad, a member of the Palestine National Council, has written as follows on this score:

"The experience of the Arab people of Palestine and of other peoples indicates that the policy of 'all or nothing' does not serve the people's interests. Every true revolutionary must take into account the alignment of forces and their coorelation [sic] at every separate stage and, consequently, must distinguish what is possible and realistic from what is impracticable."

This task can be fulfilled only after the unification of the ranks of the Palestinian movement *within the framework, for instance, of a national front with a political program that will take into account the diversity of the situation and of the forms of struggle* and will help to begin work among the Palestinians in occupied territory and among the refugges, [sic] especially in Jordan, since without a mass base the movement cannot develop.

The first shifts in this direction have already become evident. At a session held in Cairo several months ago, the Palestinian National Council came out for the unification of the resistance movement. Since that time, the movement's press has been unified, and a single information agency has been set up. In July the Soviet Union was visited by a PLO delegation headed by Yasir Arafat, the chairman of its executive committee. During the talks that took place, the PLO representatives reported that at present the consolidation of the ranks of the Palestinian resistance is continuing and its *unity growing stronger on a progressive anti-imperialist* basis. . . . Recent facts make it possible to draw the conclusion that attempts to isolate the Palestinian movement, to assign it a special mission in the Arab East, are receding into the past. What is gaining the upper hand is the realization that a just solution to the Palestine problem can be achieved only within the framework of a common liberation struggle of the Arab peoples and that the natural allies of the Palestinian resistance movement are the Arab and international progressive forces, the Soviet Union and other socialist countries.[22] [emphasis added]

In addition to their drive for support in Syria, Iraq, and among the Palestinian guerrillas, the Russians also sought to gain support throughout the Arab world by their decision on August 3, 1972, to charge what amounted to a prohibitive "head tax" on educated Jews seeking to emigrate to Israel. While this decision may also have been made to secure a large amount of desperately needed hard currency from Jewish communities around the world wanting to ransom their brethren in the USSR—hard currency that would pay for wheat imports from the United States—the head tax also had the effect of drastically curtailing the number of educated Jews able to emigrate to Israel.[23] This, in turn, would reduce the increasingly bitter Arab complaints that the Russian supply of skilled manpower to Israel was enhancing Israel's military capabilities.

Despite these Soviet moves to improve their position in the Arab world following the exodus from Egypt, on balance their position in the Middle East was considerably weakened. Indeed, there is no telling how much further this process would have gone when a group of Palestinian terrorists killed eleven Israeli athletes at the Olympic Games in Munich, and set off a chain of events which greatly upset the pattern of Egyptian diplomacy and gave the Russians an excellent opportunity to strengthen their position in the Middle East.

LIMITED RECONCILIATION WITH EGYPT

The immediate effect of the terrorist acts in Munich was to strike a major blow at Sadat's hopes to persuade the Western European and American leaders to bring pressure on Israel to withdraw its troops from occupied Egyptian territory. Hardest hit were Egypt's relations with West Germany, where the terrorist acts took place. Willy Brandt, whose government had painstakingly negotiated the resumption of diplomatic relations with Egypt less than three months earlier (after a seven-year break following West Germany's establishment of diplomatic relations with Israel in 1965), criticized the lack of Egyptian assistance in his efforts to negotiate a settlement with the terrorists. In response, the Egyptian leadership asserted that West Germany was trying to evade responsibility by making false charges against Egypt and other Arab nations. The German government then began to take strong action, including deportation, against Arabs residing in West Germany who were accused of conspiring with terrorist organizations, and this brought a warning from the new Egyptian Information Minister Abdel Hatem that "arbitrary measures against Egyptians were continuing and escalating in Germany, and these extraordinary measures may call for similar Egyptian action."[24] The deterioration of Egypt's relations with West Germany, her second leading trade partner (after the USSR) and a potential source of both economic and technical assistance, reached the point in mid-September that Egypt's new Foreign Minister, Mohammed el-Zayyat, canceled a scheduled visit to West Germany, which was part of a planned tour of West European capitals in search of support against Israel.

Zayyat did complete a trip to England, but here again terrorist activities hampered Egyptian diplomacy. Just as Zayyat arrived in London the Israeli agricultural attache, Dr. Ami Shachori, was killed by a letter bomb mailed to the Israeli embassy—an action that inflamed English public opinion against the Arabs.[25]

The United States, whose close alignment with Israel Sadat had hoped to sever by his expulsion of the Russians, stood even more strongly behind the

Israeli government following the Munich massacre. Indeed, the American Ambassador to the United Nations, George Bush, exercised a rare U.S. veto when a Security Council resolution condemning Israel for its reprisal raids against Palestinian guerrilla bases in Syria and Lebanon, following the Munich killings, did not also condemn the terrorist acts that provoked the reprisal raids.

The events at Munich, with their repercussions on Egypt's relations with Western nations, probably hastened the pace of the Egyptian-Libyan union as Sadat became ever more dependent on Libyan support. On September 18 Sadat and Kaddafi reached an agreement that proclaimed Cairo as the capital of the union and provided for a single government, a single political party, and a single president elected by popular vote.[26] The process of union may also have been speeded by increased Egyptian fears of an Israeli attack following the Munich massacre, fears that the Russians did everything possible to encourage.

The Israeli government was under great domestic pressure to avenge the athletes murdered at Munich and did not hesitate long. Having suffered a similar terroristic attack at Lod Airport only three months before, the Israelis apparently decided to attempt to strike a telling blow against the guerrillas by launching a series of air strikes deep into Lebanon and Syria against suspected terrorist bases. The air assault was followed a week later by an armored strike into Lebanon aimed at destroying as many guerrillas and guerrilla bases as possible. Lebanese and Syrian resistance was relatively ineffectual as the Israeli forces roamed at will in the two countries. Three Syrian bombers, counterattacking Israeli positions in the Golan Heights, were shot down.[27] The Israeli assaults, coming on the heels of similar although far more restricted ground strikes into Lebanon following the Lod massacre in June, served once again to underline Syria's vulnerability in relation to Israel, as did numerous statements by Israeli leaders, such as Deputy Premier Yigal Allon, that Israel would henceforth take "active measures" to "deny the Arab terror organizations the necessary bases, facilities and other assistance in their inhuman war."[28]

The Soviet Union seized upon the opportunity presented by the Israeli attacks to launch a special airlift of weapons to Damascus to reinforce the Syrian defenses. This airlift, which generated front-page headlines both in the Arab and Western press, underscored the Soviet argument that the Arabs could only turn to the USSR in their time of need.

Soviet propaganda had been emphasizing this theme ever since Sadat's expulsion order. A week before the Munich massacre, Dmitry Volsky, in a *New Times* article titled "A Frank Talk with Some Arab Colleagues," wrote:

Isn't it a fact that the US and NATO Mediterranean bases and the US Sixth Fleet which has now obtained a convenient new harbor in Greece, have repeatedly been used for pressure on Arab countries? From which it is clear what damage would be done in the interests of these countries by undivided US and NATO naval control in the Mediterranean? . . . If Iraq and Syria have today successfully challenged a mighty oil concern like Iraq Petroleum, which has leading powers behind it, could they have done it without enjoying the firm support of the Soviet Union and the Socialist community?[29]

Following the Israeli attacks on Lebanon and Syria, the Russians warned the Arabs that they could expect further Israeli attacks and that they could not hope for support from the West. An editorial in *New Times* pointedly stated:

> By bombing Palestinian refugee camps in Lebanon and Syria and villages in these countries and Jordan, killing and maiming hundreds of civilians, Tel Aviv has again shown the world the brigand nature of its policy. And its spokesmen let it be known that they do not mean to rest content with this. They openly threaten further aggressive action against Arab countries. None other than Israel's Chief of General Staff, General Elazar, has declared that air strikes "are not the only means" his army has used and continues to use. Another member of the Israeli command, asked by a newsman whether Egypt might come under attack, replied "I will answer with an Arab proverb—everyone in his turn."
>
> Public opinion in the Arab countries is drawing the inference from Israel's provocative actions which the imperialists are encouraging. What if not encouragement is the US veto in the Security Council on a resolution condemning Tel Aviv's barbarous acts? *All of it is helping the Arabs to realize how illusory are hopes that the imperialists are prepared to help curb the Israeli expansionists and eliminate the consequences of their aggression.* And the danger of such illusion is greater than ever now. For Tel Aviv is using them not only to hold on to the occupied territories but to make new aggressive moves against the Arab states.[30] [emphasis added]

In an effort to increase Arab fear of Israeli attacks still further—and thus make the Arabs feel constrained to turn to the USSR for assistance—the Russians subsequently even began to propagate the old myth about Israel's alleged desire to expand her borders "from the Nile to the Euphrates." Writing in *New Times* at the end of September, V. Rumyanstev claimed that the Israelis

> are seeking not only to induce the Arabs to accept the annexation of the territories seized in 1967, but to accustom them to the Zionist idea of creating a "Greater Israel from the Nile to the Euphrates."[31]

The Russians also utilized the Israeli attacks on the Palestinian guerrilla camps to dramatize their position as supporters of the Palestinians and thus to win more influence in the Palestinian resistance movement. While the Western press unanimously condemned the Munich murders, the Russian press was far more moderate in tone, referring to them only as a "tragic incident."[32] The Russians, however, denounced the Israeli attacks on Palestinian refugee camps (which often housed guerrilla bases) while most of the Western press accepted the Israeli raids as legitimate reprisals for the Munich massacres. The Russians underlined their concern for the Palestinian cause at this crucial time by airlifting medical supplies to Lebanon to help treat the victims of the Israeli attacks, and the guerrillas claimed that the USSR was now shipping them arms directly.[33]

Although receiving an increasingly sympathetic treatment in the Soviet press, the Palestinian movement also once again came in for some Soviet advice. V. Kornilov, writing a feature article in *New Times,* continued the Soviet criticism of such extremist groups as Black September, and once again emphasized the need for unity among the Palestinians, although his discussion of the possibilities of unity were a bit less optimistic than pre-Munich Soviet commentaries on the Palestinian movement:

> What the extremist groups have done and are still doing has not brought about any change for the better in the tragic lot of the Palestinians. Nor could it. On the contrary, what they have done, paradoxical as it might seem, has been grist to the mill of the Zionist ringleaders. Tel Aviv exploits the acts of terror perpetrated by the Palestinian extremists to pass off its pre-planned acts of aggression against Lebanon and Syria as "retaliation," and to step up its propaganda campaign against the Palestinians and Arabs generally, a campaign the Western bourgeois press has joined. All this damages the prestige of the Palestinian movement, and seriously. . . .
>
> In short, despite Israeli terror, despite the machinations of imperialism and Arab reaction, a trend is emerging, *albeit with difficulty,* towards the gradual consolidation of the Palestinian resistance movement. There is an increasing awareness within the PLO that for the Palestinian movement to achieve any measure of success it needs a clear cut political program which, proceeding from reality, would set explicit, feasible tasks. Most leaders of the various Palestinian organizations are coming to see more and more distinctly that both the extremism of certain groups like the Black September organization and the attempts of reactionaries in the Arab world to harness the Palestinian movement to their own interests are equally prejudicial to the cause for which many Palestinian Arabs are ready to give their lives—the liberation of Israeli-occupied territory.[34] [emphasis added]

The events at Munich and the Israeli response to them occasioned a trip to Moscow by Iraqi President Hassan Al-Bakr, and his visit of September 14-19, 1972, underlined the close cooperation now existing between the USSR and Iraq.[35] At a banquet honoring Al-Bakr, Soviet President Podgorny took the opportunity to once again attack the "slanderous assertions" aimed at undermining Arab-Soviet friendship,[36] and Podgorny also emphasized a theme that was becoming increasingly prominent in Soviet policy statements about the Arab world—the close relationship between Arab unity on an "anti-imperialist basis" and the unity of the "progressive forces" within each Arab state.[37] This theme was more fully developed in a *New Times* article by R. Ulianovsky, deputy head of the CPSU Central Committee's international department, entitled "The Arab East: Problems of a United Progressive Front," in which the author appealed to the Ba'ath leadership in both Syria and Iraq to follow through on their promises to implement their national fronts. He stated that once the fronts were established genuine Arab unity could be achieved.[38]

One of the goals of the new Soviet position on Arab unity may have been to counter the union movement between Egypt and Libya that was developing on an anti-Communist basis. It may also have been aimed at settling the smoldering dispute between the rival wings of the Ba'ath parties ruling in Damascus and Baghdad, each of which had good relations with the Soviet Union but poor relations with each other. If such a development were to occur, it would wean Syria away from its confederation with Egypt and Libya and end Iraq's isolation in the Arab world. This would also provide a bloc of relatively pro-Soviet Arab states in the eastern segment of the Arab world.

Yet there still seemed to be little possibility of unity on the Soviet terms. In both Iraq and Syria, the Communists and other "progressives" remained relatively powerless, and the inherent conflict among the various elements in the national fronts of the two nations was not overlooked by Ulianovsky:

It is not accidental that the internal and foreign enemies of the national democratic regimes are trying to set the participants of the progressive coalitions against each other. Resorting to underhand machinations, they either seek to bar the communists from the united front or insist on the dissolution of the communist and other left parties.[39]

In an effort to overcome such difficulties, throughout 1972 and early 1973, numerous Soviet conferences and articles in Soviet scholarly journals were devoted to working out the theoretical and practical aspects of Communist participation in national fronts. One conference, held under the auspices of the *World Marxist Review* at the time of Al-Bakr's visit, brought together Soviet and nonruling Communist party delegates along with representatives from Egypt's Arab Socialist Union and the Iraqi and Syrian Ba'ath parties to discuss "problems of anti-imperialist unity." The editor-in-chief of the *World Marxist Review*, K. Zarodov, began the discussion of the national front problem by stating:

The question requiring further theoretical investigation concerns the united front of progressive forces in national movements with maturing social contradictions. In some countries they grow into class antagonisms; that being so, is there a political perspective for a United Front?[40]

Zarodov went on to answer his own question, and he then gave the current Soviet interpretation of the meaning of "class struggle" in the developing countries:

Many Afro-Asian communist parties give an affirmative answer. Broad political unity of the nation's healthy progressive anti-imperialist forces is made possible by the fact that the national liberation revolution has not fully discharged its democratic mission. Hence, through [sic] contradictions between individual classes and social groups persist, there is still a considerable area of common interest in resolving crucial national issues. . . .

Political development guided by a united front does not eliminate or preclude class struggle. *In fact, unity of the nation's progressive forces is a principal form of class struggle in present-day Afro-Asian conditions.*[41] [emphasis added]

Zarodov concluded by telling the Communists in the Afro-Asian countries, much as Ulianovsky had done the year before, that they had to endure anti-Communist actions by the nationalist leaders for the sake of maintaining the anti-imperialist coalition:

In countries ruled by Revolutionary democrats, the Communists see their patriotic and class duty in facilitating progressive change. At times they point to shortcomings in the work of revolutionary democratic regimes. But this is the constructive advice of sincere friends and allies. But some Revolutionary Democratic leaders at times seem unable or reluctant to distinguish between friends and foe, ally and enemy. Unfortunately, the leaders of a number of countries, who, on the whole, take an anti-imperialist stand, regard cooperation with the communists as little short of retreat from national revolution or betrayal of national tradition. . . . We have a situation in which communists are faced by the dual task of supporting Revolutionary-democratic leaders and at the same time working for the consistant application of democratic policy [sic] principles. The struggle, therefore, is not against the Revolutionary democrats, but for alliance with them; the struggle is for the comprehensive and vigorous pursuit of socialism.[42]

A second issue raised at the conference was the need for the national democratic transition stage for Third World states. Soviet spokesmen supported the principle, but it was challenged by Lebanese Communist Party member G. Batal who questioned the "catagorical need" for a transition stage at which the general democratic tasks were given priority over the "building of socialism." Batal went on to imply that the social backwardness should not be a barrier to Communists seizing power:

Given revolutionary government capable of directing the process, a country's backwardness, the relative weakness of its working class, and inadequate social differentiation are not obstacles to socialist construction. The Democratic Republic of Vietnam is proof of that.[43]

A further challenge to the Soviet position came from Jordanian Communist Party member K. Ahmad, who complained that there was still "no general, thought-out and developed theory to disclose the essence of what we term non-capitalist development." And, in a challenge to Soviet theorists who had worked for almost a decade to work out just such a formulation, Ahmad asserted:

That theory must neither be a utopia based on a random collection of elements relating to another era, nor the result of hasty innovative generalizations or bold extrapolations that are practically useless, even as a hypothesis.[44]

While Soviet theorists and Arab Communists debated various aspects of the national front policy, Iraqi President Hassan Al-Bakr made it quite evident that he had not come to Moscow only for lectures on the desirability of national fronts. Instead, he was seeking Soviet support in Iraq's sharpening conflict with Iran over the Persian Gulf, and it appears that he succeeded in moving the Soviet leaders even closer to the Iraqi side. Thus, in a major speech, Al-Bakr condemned

> actions against the historical rights of the Arab nations in the Persian Gulf, and attempts to impose colonialism on the countries of this area.[45]

The final communique echoed the same theme, although in somewhat milder terms:

> The two sides declared their full support for the struggle that the Arab peoples of the Persian Gulf are waging to rebuff the imperialists' aggressive plans which are jeopardizing their freedom and independence. They affirmed that the peoples of the Persian Gulf must be guaranteed the right to decide their own destiny without outside interference.[46]

Of even greater importance to Iran-Iraqi relations however was the Soviet-Iraqi agreement

> on *concrete* measures for the further strengthening of the defense capability of the Republic of Iraq with a view to increasing the *combat readiness* of its armed forces.[47] [emphasis added]

Perhaps to counter the impression of the Soviet Union's "leaning to one side" in the Iran-Iraq conflict, the Russian leaders invited the Shah of Iran and his wife (who had just returned from Peking) to visit Moscow on October 10, less than a month after Al-Bakr's departure. Reports circulated both in Moscow and Beirut that Al-Bakr had requested that the Russians mediate the Iran-Iraq conflict since, given Iraq's difficulties following the nationalization of Iraqi Petroleum Company's Kirkuk fields and continued problems with the Kurds, the Iraqis were in no position to see an escalation of their conflict with Iran.[48] If this was indeed the Soviet goal (and in a dinner speech Podgorny referred to "the need for an improvement in the relations between Asian states"),[49] no mention of such an agreement was made in the final communique. Nonetheless, the Soviet Union and Iran did agree to a fifteen-year economic treaty, which, while increasing the Soviet share of Iran's trade, still left it far behind the shares of the United States and West Germany—Iran's most important economic partners.

The two nations also reached an agreement on Soviet assistance in enlarging the Isfahan metallurgical works to bring its capacity up to four million tons of steel per year, along with other projects. Nevertheless, differences of opinion clearly remained and the final communique referred to the talks as having taken place in a "frank" atmosphere and stated that the two sides had "exchanged opinions concerning the situation in Asia."[50]

The purpose behind the Shah's trip to Moscow, which so closely followed Al-Bakr's visit to the Russian capital, bore close resemblance to the reason for the visit of Soviet President Podgorny to Turkey immediately after the signing of the Soviet-Iraqi treaty in April. It appears in both cases that the Russians had hoped that the improvement in the USSR's relations with Iraq, a nation on poor terms with both Turkey and Iran, would not lead to a deterioration in either Soviet-Turkish or Soviet-Iranian relations. While in the case of Iran the economic agreements may have helped assuage some of Iran's anger, the final Soviet-Iranian communique contained many indications of strained relations, and Podgorny's visit to Turkey resulted in an even more limited communique, the "Declaration on the Principles of Good-Neighbor Relations with the Turkish Government." The Turks, clearly unhappy at the strong Soviet support for Archbishop Makarios on Cyprus and the appearance of Soviet weapons in the hands of antigovernment Turkish terrorists, were in no mood to enter into a closer relationship with the USSR. Indeed, one of the principles listed in the declaration stated that "the present Declaration in no way affects commitments earlier assumed by each of the states in regard to third countries ... and international organizations," thus tacitly emphasizing Turkey's continued close relationship to the United States and its participation in NATO.[51]

While the Soviet Union was shoring up its positions elsewhere in the Arab world and trying to maintain a balance in its relations between Iran and Iraq, Soviet relations with the Sadat regime in Egypt remained very tense. Although, despite Soviet predictions, Egypt was not hit by an Israeli retaliatory strike (possibly to avert the possibility that Egypt might be forced to call the Russians back), Sadat was clearly discomfited by the events in Munich. With his attempts to win over Western Europe and the United States for the time being, at least, having come to naught, and condemned both at home and throughout the Arab world for failing to protect Syria and Lebanon from Israeli attacks, Sadat decided to try to stabilize Egypt's relations with the USSR before they deteriorated any further.

Consequently, on September 28, 1972, the second anniversary of Nasser's death, Sadat delivered a major policy address in which he sought to regain some of the momentum in Middle Eastern events. In the first place he issued a call for the establishment of a Palestinian government in exile, which he pledged to support, stating—and here he was in close agreement with the Russians—that the divisions within the Palestinian movement hurt it more than Israel or King Hussein. Second, he officially rejected the proposal offered by U.S. Secretary of State William Rogers earlier in the month at the UN for an interim agreement and proximity talks. Using bitter language, perhaps reflecting his frustration at the failure of the United States to reward Egypt for expelling the Russians, Sadat stated: "Mr. Rogers is a man who is not living in this age. . . . There will be no partial settlement and no direct negotiations. . . ." Finally, and perhaps most important of all, Sadat changed his tone toward the Russians. The Egyptian leader declared that he had sent a letter to Brezhnev that was "friendly and cordial in spirit."[52]

Conceivably the reply Sadat was expecting was delivered by Hafiz Assad, Premier of Syria, who made a hurried trip to Cairo after returning from a secret visit to Moscow. In any case it was revealed only two days after Sadat's speech that Egyptian Premier Aziz Sidky would undertake a trip to the Soviet Union on October 16.[53] Nonetheless, the tone in the government-controlled Egyptian press remained quite cool to the USSR until the very eve of Sidky's departure. Thus, Sadat himself, in an interview published in the Lebanese weekly *Al-Hawadess* on October 5 and reprinted in Cairo newspapers two days later, stated that a peaceful settlment as desired by the Russians meant "surrender to American and Israeli terms," and complained openly that

> the Russians had become a burden to us. They would not fight and would give our enemy an excuse for seeking American support and assistance.[54]

Two days later, Sadat's confidant, *Al-Akhbar* editor Abdul Koddous (by now a bete noire of the Russians), warned that the Egyptian people must expect "tough negotiations" in Moscow and that all Assad's visit to Moscow accomplished was the invitation of Sidky.[55] In this article, of which the Chinese reprinted selected excerpts in the Peking *Review*, the Egyptian editor also belittled the value of Soviet assistance and argued that the Russians had utilized their position in Egypt to exploit the Egyptians:

> The Soviet Union benefited from military centers in Egypt so that it became an existing power in the Mediterranean. In addition, Egyptian airfields did away with the need of building aircraft carriers which would have cost the Soviet people millions of dollars. The Soviet Union employed these airfields for its international purposes and transported arms to India via these airfields during the war with Pakistan. Again, the Soviet Union benefited since Egypt was an important factor in its rapprochement with the United States, which is based on freezing the situation in the Middle East. On the other hand, Egypt did not benefit from this peaceful coexistence between the two superpowers. In fact, Egypt did not benefit from this friendship which did not prevent the immigration of Soviet Jews to Israel.[56]

This, however, was the last negative comment in the Egyptian press before Sidky's departure. Perhaps prompted by an incident in Cairo's Hussein Mosque on October 12, where an Egyptian captain tried to stir a mass protest by calling for immediate war with Israel,[57] or counseled by his advisers to set a more favorable climate for Sidky's visit, Sadat had changed his tone considerably by October 15, when, in a speech to Egypt's People's Assembly, he stated that Egypt would never have a "two-faced" foreign policy but would always value fully the friendship of the Soviet Union. In addition, the Egyptian leader called the Soviet-Egyptian friendship "strategic" and not "tactical," while warning the United States that it would have to "pay a price" for its support of Israel. Sadat also declared that he was eager to see Sidky's mission succeed.[58]

However eager Sadat may really have been, there appear to have been real limits on the accomplishments of Sidky's trip to Moscow. In the first place, unlike his earlier trip in July, the Egyptian premier did not get to see Brezhnev, but had to be satisfied with meeting Kosygin and Podgorny. Second, there was no mention of continued Soviet aid, either military or economic, in the final communique, which described the talks as having taken place "in an atmosphere of frankness and mutual understanding." About the only thing that Egyptians could point to from the talks (assuming there were no secret protocols), was a rather pro forma Russian pledge, frequently found in joint communiques, that the Russian leaders had accepted an invitation to come to Egypt, although no date was set for their visit.[59]

Upon Sidky's return to Egypt, a general debate was begun in the top ranks of the Egyptian leadership about the proper relationship with the USSR. The editor of *Al-Ahram*, Mohammed Heikal, a man often at odds with the USSR, counseled renewed friendship with the Russians in his weekly column in the October 20, 1972, issue, stating that "a sound, healthy relationship with the USSR is vital." Heikal went on to urge that Egypt continue to seek its weapons from the Russians because other suppliers were politically unreliable:

> We are able to get some weapons from sources other than the USSR under certain conditions and in certain quantities; just the same, I am worried about unknown factors in the international arms market.[60]

On October 25, 1972, Sidky delivered his report to a mixed Arab Socialist Union-government meeting, stating that the Russians had promised to resume aid to Egypt, although he did not mention precise quantities. Sadat followed with a speech in which he told the assembled delegates that "it was up to them" whether Egypt should continue to rely primarily on Soviet support or should end her cooperation with Moscow. He somewhat restricted their parameters of choice, however, by stating that there was little hope in the foreseeable future of replacing the USSR as Egypt's principal supplier of arms. Sadat went on to say that if Egypt should choose continued cooperation with the Soviet Union, its scope would never return to the pre-July 18th situation.[61]

The Egyptian leadership apparently decided on continued cooperation with the Russians, because on the very next day Defense Minister Sadek, one of the most anti-Russian of the Egyptian leaders, was either fired or else resigned from his position. This may well have been one of the prices exacted by the Russians for renewed aid; in any case, his ouster was followed by that of the Navy Commander, Rear Admiral Fahmy Abdel Rahman, another of the outspoken anti-Soviet Egyptian leaders. Sadek was replaced by Ahmed Ismail, Egypt's Military Intelligence Director, who, unlike Sadek, had neither alienated the Russians nor possessed sufficient popular appeal to pose a challenge to Sadat himself.[62]

Sadek's fall from the second most powerful position in Egypt gave rise to a great deal of speculation both in Egypt and abroad. While most commentators saw Sadek's ouster as the price demanded by the Russians for a resumption of military aid (and the arrival in Egypt of Sam-6 antiaircraft missiles together with Russian technicians soon after Sadek's "resignation" reinforced this belief[63]), Abdul Koddous, writing a front page article in *Akhbar-Al-Yom* sought to put an end to such speculation. According to Koddous, Sadek had been dismissed because of insubordination and failure to carry out Sadat's orders when the Egyptian president discovered that "some directives to General Sadek had not reached the various commands, while others had not been implemented."[64]

A related factor that could have contributed to Sadek's dismissal was the rising tide of unrest in the Egyptian army—the base on which Sadat's power rested. There had been a mutiny among Egyptian soldiers stationed at the canal in late September. This had been followed by the incident at the Hussein Mosque on October 12 and what the BBC reported as an abortive military coup on October 21.[65] Sadat may well have been displeased with Sadek's inability to control dissension in the army; this together with the Egyptian general's continuing refusal to accept the necessity for a limited rapprochement with the Soviet Union may have led to Sadek's ouster.

Whatever the actual reason for Sadek's resignation, the Russians were clearly happy to witness the departure of the most outspokenly anti-Soviet leader in the Egyptian hierarchy. While *Pravda* reported his ouster in a brief two-column story on October 28, 1972, under the title "resignation accepted," the Soviet party newspaper gave much more space to a speech by his successor, Ahmed Ismail, four days later. The new Egyptian defense minister spoke warmly of Soviet economic and military aid to Egypt, and stated that the USSR had fulfilled all the obligations it had pledged to Egypt. In addition, Ismail strongly attacked the United States for its aid to Israel and asserted that "nothing good" could be expected from the United States. Ismail also echoed the Soviet line on the goals of American policy in the Middle East:

The goal of American policy is to isolate the Arabs from the USSR and keep the Soviet Union as far as possible from the Middle East. The United States is also seeking to prevent unity in the ranks of the Arabs.[66]

Despite the warmth of his speech toward the Soviet Union, however, Egypt's new defense minister also reportedly told Western diplomats soon after taking office that "the Egyptian Army Command will never again allow Russian advisers to get key command and advisory posts in the Egyptian armed forces"— a policy goal that Ismail evidently shared with Sadat.[67]

Nonetheless, thanks to the Munich massacre and the sharp upsurge in fighting between Israel and the Arabs that followed it, the Soviet position in the Middle East had markedly improved from its low point in early September, as the Arabs felt more dependent on Soviet military supplies for their sharpening conflict with Israel. The Soviet leadership may have concluded from this that a limited degree of warfare in the region was a net bonus for the Soviet Union, as long as it did not escalate into a war between the two superpowers, since during the period of relative Middle Eastern calm (September 1970 to September 1972) the Russian position had deteriorated steadily. Indeed, the Soviet position had improved so much as a result of the post-Munich developments that on October 26, 1972, Sudanese President Jaafar Nimeri, who had clashed so bitterly with the Russians the year before over the abortive Communist-supported coup d'etat against his regime, announced that the Sudan would restore full diplomatic relations with the Soviet Union by the end of the year.[68] In addition, the Soviet leadership must have welcomed the deterioration in relations between the Arabs and the West, particularly the United States and West Germany, which occurred after the Munich terrorism. Interestingly enough, one of the comments made by the terrorists about the goals of their operation coincided with a similar objective of Soviet policy:

> The operation was aimed at exposing the close relations between the treacherous German authorities and United States imperialism on the one hand and the Zionist enemy's authorities on the other.[69]

Thus, thanks to another twist in the volatile politics of the Middle East, developments in the region began to take a turn favorable to the USSR, and the Soviet leadership now sought to reinforce this trend, although a number of serious problems still hampered their overall policy toward the region.

TO THE NIXON-BREZHNEV SUMMIT

While the Russians had clearly improved their position in the Middle East by the end of October, they still faced a number of problems in their attempts to expand their influence in the region. In the first place, North Yemen (the Yemeni Arab Republic) and South Yemen (The People's Democratic Republic of Yemen—PDRY) were on the verge of full-scale war, and the Russians must have been very concerned when the South Yemeni Premier Ali Nasser stated in an interview with the Beirut newspaper *L'Orient le Jour* on October 6 that "the Soviet Union will not stand with folded arms in the event of an invasion of South Yemen."[70] Relations were scarcely better between Iran and Iraq, and serious clashes between the Kurds and Iraqi government forces made the situation at the top of the Persian Gulf even more difficult for Soviet policy-makers. Another problem facing the Russians was their limited position in Egypt, which was still the most important Middle East state despite Sadat's problems. Finally, the Russians continued to worry about American influence in the region and the possibility that a disheartened Egypt might yet agree to a Middle East settlement on American terms.

In an effort to settle the Yemeni conflict, the USSR had long advocated union between the two Yemens since this would enable the Russians to avoid being dragged into a war between them while still enabling Moscow to maintain influence in the geographically strategic area at the Bab-el-Mandab Strait, which controlled the entrance to the Red Sea, whose importance would sharply increase if the canal were to be reopened. Talks designed to halt the fighting between the Yemens were postponed in mid-November so that South Yemeni President Salem Ali Rubaya could visit Moscow at the end of the month.[71] In evaluating the progress of the PDRY at the time of Rubaya's visit, *New Times* correspondent Yuri Gvozdev called the conflict between the two Yemens "imperialist instigated."[72] The joint communique published at the conclusion of the visit on November 26 stated that the Soviet side "greeted with satisfaction" South Yemeni measures to end military operations on the border with North Yemen, and "supported PDRY efforts for the normalization of relations between the two

Yemens."[73] The Soviet leadership was, consequently, more than satisfied when, only two days later, the two Yemens signed an agreement to unite. Nonetheless, the accord was a fragile one, and the statement by North Yemen's ambassador to France in mid-December that King Faisal of Saudi Arabia supported Yemeni unity on an "Islamic basis" might well have convinced the Russians that the Saudi monarch was continuing his efforts to overthrow the socialist regime in South Yemen.[74]

If the Soviet leaders proved able to score a moderate success in calming tensions between North and South Yemen, they faced a far more difficult task in the Iran-Iraq conflict. Soviet-Iranian tensions had sharply increased since the signing of the Soviet-Iraqi treaty in April 1972, and the Soviet decision to give Iraq more weaponry during Al-Bakr's visit to Moscow in September further angered the Iranians. Complicating Soviet-Iranian relations at this time was yet another factor—their support for opposite sides in the guerrilla war raging in the Dhofar region of Oman. While the USSR (and Iraq and the PDRY) supported the Popular Front for the Liberation of the Occupied Arab Gulf (PFLOAG) with military supplies, Iran supplied both troops and equipment to the Sultan of Oman's forces. Interestingly enough, however, perhaps in an effort to minimize this area of disagreement, the Soviet Union's official descriptions of the Sultan's forces in 1972 referred only to "British mercenaries," and not to Iranian troops.

Events in February and March 1973 were to force the Russians to quicken their diplomatic efforts to keep the Iran-Iraq conflict under control. On February 10 both Iraq and the USSR were publicly embarrassed by the disclosure that 300 Soviet-made machine guns and 60,000 rounds of ammunition had been found in the Iraqi embassy in Islamabad, Pakistan.[75] The weapons were evidently destined for the Baluchistani Liberation Front, which demanded that an independent Baluchistan be made up of Baluchistani-populated territories now controlled by both Iran and Pakistan. The Soviet leadership, whose relations with the new Bhutto regime in Pakistan were slowly improving following the Indo-Pakistani war of 1971, referred to this incident as a "regrettable circumstance,"[76] although they could not have been overjoyed by this public disclosure of their linkage, however slight, to an attempt to partition the territory of two states with which they were trying to maintain good relations.

Less than two weeks later came the announcement that Iran had concluded the largest single military sales agreement ever arranged by the U.S. Defense Department—a $2-billion order for U.S. weaponry consisting of helicopter gunships, supersonic interceptors, Phantom jet bombers, and C-130 cargo planes, along with other military equipment.[77] The arms race in the Persian Gulf was now on with a vengeance. It was perhaps in an effort to slow down this arms race—and avoid new arms requests from Iraq—that Soviet Premier Aleksei Kosygin in a visit to Iran to celebrate the opening of the Soviet-built Isfahan steel works on March 15, pointedly stated:

We are pleased that good relations have developed between our countries and we intend to do everything in our power to make Soviet-Iranian relations even firmer in the future . . . and we feel that [this] corresponds to the interests of the people of the other Asian countries as well, *particularly those bordering the Soviet Union and Iran,* insofar as their security and peaceful future to a certain extent is bound up with the foreign policy course of their neighbors, including the Soviet Union and Iran. But if we want the security of the states to be based not on an arms race—no genuine security can be built on such a foundation—but on the continuing relaxation of tensions and the strengthening of mutual trust among countries, then the efforts of each party concerned are required. Conversely, the militant policy of any one country will inevitably inflame the sitution in an entire region, and often throughout the world, forcing its neighbors to take some kind of measures to defend their national interest.[78] [emphasis added]

As soon as Kosygin returned to Moscow, however, Iraq took its turn to inflame the Persian Gulf conflict. On March 20 Iraqi troops crossed into Kuwaiti territory and seized two Kuwaiti border posts. The very next day Iraqi Vice President Saddam Hussein made a hurried visit to Moscow to confer with the Russians about the situation. The lack of Soviet enthusiasm for the Iraqi move can be seen by the *New Times* comment on this episode. Citing "Arab capitals" (a usual Soviet technique to express displeasure indirectly) the *New Times* article stated:

The dispute has caused anxiety in Arab capitals, inasmuch as Zionist and imperialist quarters have seized upon it to sow dissension in the Arab world and to weaken the Arab Front of struggle to eliminate the consequences of the Israeli aggression. The leaders of a number of Arab countries have urged the Iraqi President and the Emir of Kuwait to make every effort to resolve the conflict without delay.[79]

Thus, by invading Kuwait, the small gulf state between Iran and Iraq, the Iraqis had not only inflamed their conflict with Iran still further, but they had also apparently made even more difficult the "anti-imperialist Arab unity" the Russians were striving to create.

While the Iraqi troops eventually pulled out of Kuwait, although no final agreement was reached, the Shah made it quite clear that Iran would go to Kuwait's aid if she requested assistance. In addition, in an interview with a correspondent of the *Christian Science Monitor,* the Shah called for a NATO-like pact for the Gulf's riparian states and announced that Pakistani and Iranian army chiefs of staff had begun consultations in Tehran.[80]

While the conflicts between North and South Yemen and between Iran and Iraq were serious problems for Soviet policy-makers dealing with the Middle East, the central Soviet problem was American influence in the Middle East and the lingering possibility that the United States and Egypt might yet work out a Middle Eastern arrangement contrary to Soviet interests. To avoid such a possibility, the Soviet leaders stepped up their efforts in encouraging the Arabs to unite their efforts against Israel. The Soviet tactic seems to have been that were the Arabs to work together, the moderately pro-Russian regimes of Syria and Iraq (together with the Palestinian Liberation Organization, whose leader, Yasir Arafat, was echoing the Soviet line in return for Soviet economic and military support) would prevent any anti-Russian policy from being adopted. Fortunately for the Russians, two developments in the Middle East helped facilitate their policy. On the one hand, the Arab-Israeli conflict reached new heights of intensity following Israel's shooting down a Libyan airliner in February and the Israeli raid on the PLO headquarters in Beirut in April. Second, Egypt was also following a policy of trying to unite the Arabs for a confrontation with Israel, although Sadat's willingness to work closely first with Libyan leader Mu'ammar Kaddafi and subsequently with Saudi Arabia's King Faisal was not particularly to the liking of the Russians, because Arab unity on an Egyptian-Libyan or Egyptian-Saudi Arabian axis would fall far short of the Arab unity on the "progressive, anti-imperialist" basis that the Soviet leaders had long espoused.

In one of the first major Soviet policy-statements following their expulsion from Egypt, the Russians had been concerned about just such a development:

> The reactionary elements and certain nationalist elements seek to compromise the very ideas of Arab-Soviet friendship and to counterpose appeals for "reliance on Arab forces alone" to the slogan of strengthening the united Arab front and militant solidarity with all the forces of progress on an anti-imperialist basis. . . .
>
> A fact well worth noting is that Arab reaction's anti-Soviet sallies have been accompanied by the weaving of plots against progressive Arab regimes—plotting that is supported by Saudi Arabia, which is performing the role of promoter of imperialist policies in the Arab East. . . .
>
> The Arab peoples realize the necessity of strengthening national and pan-Arab unity; however, as the Lebanese newspaper Al Shaab points out, in present day conditions such a consolidation can be effected only on an anti-imperialist and progressive social basis and not at the expense of Arab-Soviet friendship.[81]

In an effort to promote the "anti-imperialist" Arab unity they were seeking, the Soviet leadership helped sponsor two pan-Arab congresses of "progressive forces" in November. On November 11, an international seminar with the theme "Oil as a Weapon in the Struggle against Imperialism and Israeli Aggression" was convened in Baghdad. According to the Soviet description of the seminar, which was attended by a Soviet delegation as well as delegations from Arab countries, the object of the conference was to "expose the plunder of the Arab countries by the imperialist monopolies, and the link between these monopolies and Israel."[82] At the end of November, an all-Arab "Popular Congress of the Palestine Revolution" was held in Beirut under the sponsorship of the Arab Communist parties. The congress set up the "Arab Front for Participation in the Palestinian Resistance," and a declaration approved by the meeting pledged to "liquidate the imperialist presence and its strategic and economic interests in the Arab homeland."[83] Attending the conference were the Communist parties of the Arab world, along with delegations from the Iraqi, Syrian, South Yemeni, Algerian, and Egyptian governments and representatives of the USSR and Soviet bloc states in East Europe. An editorial in the February 1973 issue of the *World Marxist Review* hailed the formation of the Arab Front as evidence of the increasing cohesion of the anti-imperialist forces in the Arab World:

The formation, at a conference in Beirut last November, of the Arab Front in support of the Palestinian Revolution, in which communists, revolutionary-democrats, and other patriotic parties and organizations of 14 Arab countries are represented, is evidence of the increasing cohesion of the anti-imperialist forces.[84]

While the Soviet leadership was working for Arab unity "on an anti-imperialist basis," Egyptian leader Anwar Sadat was convening a number of pan-Arab conferences in November and December in an effort to build a united Arab front against Israel. Having first sought Soviet and then American support against Israel, and having failed in both quests, Sadat, under great domestic and foreign pressure to go to war, decided that the only solution for Egypt was to mobilize the capabilities of the Arab would—including its oil power—against Israel and its supporters.[85] In a major policy speech on December 28, Sadat stated that Egypt "realized the limits of Soviet aid" and that Egypt would take "new initiatives to make the battle a pan-Arab one." Replying to Syrian demands that Egypt go to war immediately to relieve the pressure on Syria, which was engaged in almost daily battles with Israel at the time, Sadat remarked, "Egypt could not allow international circumstances to determine the course of events in the Middle East but "had to impose its will on circumstances."[86]

The Soviet Press commented favorably on Sadat's pan-Arab battle plan, and the Russians utilized the opportunity to remind the Arabs that the United States, Israel's main supporter, was becoming very vulnerable to the oil pressure Sadat had recommended. Thus in a *New Times* article in late January, Victor Kudryavtsev, one of the main Soviet commentators on the Middle East, stated:

Egyptian newspapers report that the Cairo government submitted to the [Arab] joint defense council a plan providing for proportional contribution by the Arab countries to the common struggle with the means available to them—military, economic or financial. It is noted that stress is laid in this plan on the need to work out a joint oil policy.

A coordinated Arab policy in this sphere could be especially effective inasmuch as Israel's main backer, the United States, is displaying an increasing interest in the oil deposits of the Persian Gulf and in Libya. Reference is made in Cairo to a survey made by a U.S. Senate committee showing that in the coming years between 20 and 30 per cent of U.S. fuel requirements will be met with Middle East oil. The Egyptian plan, newspapers say, also envisiages an increase in the financial contribution by the oil-rich Arab countries to the common struggle against the aggressor.[87]

Kudryavtsev also warned the Arabs, however, that "[e]xperience has convinced the Arab peoples that they can achieve real unity only on a clearly expressed anti-imperialist basis and by promoting friendship and cooperation with the Soviet Union. . . ."[88]

In the very next issue of *New Times*, Dmitry Volsky, another key Soviet commentator on Middle East affairs, warned against Saudi Arabia's increasingly important role in the Arab world:

What lies behind the activization of Saudi foreign policy? And what is this thing called the "phenomenon of Saudi Arabia" which the Western press is so zealously touting? . . .

The Saudi monarchy . . . is bent on becoming the bulwark of reaction throughout the Arab world generally. Year after year it spends dozens even hundreds of millions of dollars on what it calls "Arab Policy," the aim of which is to thwart social and economic reforms in other Arab states and subvert their cooperation with the socialist countries. Saudi "dollar diplomacy" is out to rally the Arab nations not for struggle against imperialism and Israeli aggression, for stronger national independence and social and economic advancement, but on purely religious foundations. Riyadh endlessly thumps the drum of the "jihad" or "holy war" that King Faisal has declared against "Communism-Zionism," that fantastic invention of present day obscurantists.

And, as if to discredit Faisal even further, Volsky added:

There is no doubt that Saudi oil could effectively influence Israel's American patrons. But here is what King Faisal said in an interview with the Cairo weekly *Al-Mussawar* "It is useless to talk about the use of oil as a tool against the United States. It is dangerous even to think of it." Sheikh Ahmed Yamani, the Royal Minister for Oil and Mineral Wealth, explaining the King's viewpoint says: "It is our opinion that the best way for the Arabs to use their oil is as a basis for closer cooperation with the West, expecially the United States.[89]

The Russians had good grounds for attacking Saudi Arabia on this point, because in late September Sheik Yamani had come to the United States and, in a speech to the Middle East Institute in Washington, stated that Saudi Arabia would raise production from 6 to 20 million barrels of oil per day by 1980 to satisfy the increasing U.S. oil needs, in return for assured entry into the United States market.[90] Nonetheless, less than six months later Saudi Arabia was threatening to cut oil supplies to the United States, and within a year Saudi Arabia had joined in an oil embargo against the United States. The cause for this policy transformation may be found in the two Middle Eastern developments during this period mentioned earlier: the escalation of the Arab-Israeli conflict and the realignment of alliance relationships throughout the Arab world, which saw a weakening in the Egyptian-Libyan union movement, and the creation of an Egyptian-Saudi Arabian axis, which by October was to emerge as the dominant factor in Middle East politics.

As Egypt was seeking to mobilize the other Arab states for a confrontation with Israel, on February 21, 1973, an incident occurred that was to inflame passions throughout the Arab world against Israel to a fever pitch. On edge because of Palestinian guerrilla threats to hijack an airliner and crash it into an Israeli city, Israeli air force pilots shot down a Libyan jet liner en route from Tripoli to Cairo, which had strayed deep into the Israeli-occupied Sinai desert and whose pilot had refused Israeli orders to land.[91] The Soviet Union seized upon this incident to link the United States to the Israeli action in an attempt to discredit the U.S. efforts to mediate the Middle East conflict then in progress and weaken the American position in the Middle East. As *New Times* columnist V. Katin stated:

> The world press directly links this brigand attack in the air with the intrusion of Israeli troops into Lebanon on the same day. These two sallies testify to the dangerous escalation of Israel's aggression in the Middle East. Tel Aviv is in fact extending the geography of its aggressive actions to Arab countries which were not attacked in 1967. There is also this point. These new provocations were staged on the eve of Golda Meir's visit to the United States. By whipping up military tension, the Israeli government seeks to create a situation in which it will be easier to wrest aid from the backers of Zionism in other countries, particularly the United States.
>
> It is now perfectly obvious that the Israeli rulers' patrons share the responsibility for their crimes.[92]

The Middle East situation heated up further at the beginning of March when two American diplomats were murdered by Palestinian Arab terrorists in the Saudi Arabian embassy in Khartoum in the Sudan. A week after this event, and perhaps partially in response to it, the United States announced the sale of 24 more Phantom and 24 Skyhawk bombers to Israel. Following this announcement, from which the Soviet Union again made propaganda capital, Egyptian President Sadat reorganized his cabinet by firing Premier Aziz Sidky and assuming the premiership himself along with the post of military governor. Sadat stated at the time that he "reluctantly decided" to assume the leadership himself when he got word of the U.S. commitment to deliver additional Skyhawk and Phantom jets to Israel—a development that followed closely upon the failure of the visit of Sadat's security adviser, Hafiz Izmail, to Washington. In his speech the Egyptian president also mentioned that war could not be delayed and that Egypt's relations with the USSR had resumed a "correct friendly pattern."[93]

While the Soviet leadership welcomed the further deterioration in Egyptian-American relations, there is some question as to how friendly they felt toward the Sadat regime. In an effort to stabilize his domestic position before the battle with Israel, Sadat had embarked on a wholesale purge of the Arab Socialist Union, expelling a large number of leftist intellectuals including Lufti al-Kholi, the only Marxist on the Arab Socialist Union's central committee and the man who had earlier praised Sadat's national front.[94] This was clearly a reversal of the national front system the Russians had been urging on Syria, Iraq, and Egypt. In addition, Soviet comments on domestic developments in Egypt began to assume an increasingly negative tone as it appeared, through his encouragement of foreign investment and domestic capitalism, that Sadat was embarking on a program to restore Western-style capitalism to Egypt.[95] Nonetheless, the Russians evidently decided not to let these negative factors stand in the way of improved Soviet-Egyptian relations, and by late March arms were again flowing in large quantities to Egypt. Thus, on March 24, Abdul Koddous, the newspaper editor close to Sadat who had been in the forefront of the Egyptian media attack on the lack of sufficient Soviet support the previous summer, could report in an *Al-Akhbar-*

Yom column that Egypt had now secured "a steady flow of arms from the USSR."[96] Interestingly enough, however, the USSR was apparently not yet sending Egypt the kinds of weapons (fighter-bombers and ground-to-ground missiles) that Sadat had called for the previous summer, as Koddous stated:

> The type of arms does not matter so long as we can use them to strike and repel enemy strikes. In other words, I do not believe that Egypt, as it imports arms from the USSR these days is facing a problem of the type of arms now that it has solved the problem of securing a steady flow of arms.[97]

With Egypt now receiving a steady flow of Soviet arms, Sadat turned his attention to developing his relationship with Saudi Arabian King Faisal, whose oil leverage over the United States was a critical factor in the Egyptian strategy against Israel. Faisal's willingness to use the oil weapon may have been partially due to the pressures on him generated by the escalating Arab-Israeli violence in the Middle East, which reached yet another peak on April 9. On that day Israeli commandos raided Beirut and killed the three Palestinian guerrilla leaders thought by the Israelis to be the masterminds behind the terrorist campaign against Israeli citizens in Europe and responsible for the murder of the Israeli athletes in Munich. As might be expected, the Soviet Union seized upon this incident to discredit the United States further by linking it to the Israeli action, and to urge again the Arabs on to "anti-imperialist Arab unity." Writing in *New Times* Dmitry Volsky asserted:

> An examination of the Beirut provocation leads many observers to the conclusion that it was carried out with direct assistance from Western Secret Services. In its statement the Palestine Liberation Organization, for example, accused the CIA of complicity in the murders. . . .
> The need to unite on an anti-imperialist basis is one of the main conclusions of the Beirut events made by all progressive Arab opinion. The importance of unity is being stressed by papers in Cairo, Damascus and Baghdad. Unity is the motto of numerous protest manifestations now sweeping the Arab world. Concerted actions by the Arab peoples, with the support of their friends, can create an insurmountable barrier in the path of Tel Aviv's encroachments.[98]

Still another factor that might have encouraged Faisal to consider using the oil weapon was the rapid deterioration of the position of the Western oil companies in the Middle East and the increasingly acute energy crisis in the United States, which was making front-page headlines in the Arab press. On January 23, 1973, the Shah of Iran dictated to the Western-owned oil companies operating in Iran a choice that amounted to little more than a threat, that if they did not agree to Iranian terms they would lose access to the Iranian oil once their current contracts expired. The oil companies capitulated to the Shah by March 1.[99] The previous day the Western-owned oil companies that formed the Iraqi Petroleum Company signed an agreement with the Iraqi government in which they meekly consented to the nationalization of their Kirkuk fields (which had occurred the previous June) in return for 15 million tons of oil.[100] Meanwhile, Libyan leader Mu'ammar Kaddafi had been cleverly playing off the Western oil companies in his country against each other, thereby securing increasing control over them while at the same time raising the price for Libyan oil, and neither the oil companies nor governments seemed able to do anything about it.[101]

Whatever the cause, by the middle of April Faisal was threatening the United States that Saudi Arabia would not increase its oil production to meet American needs unless the United States modified its stand on Israel.[102] Following this warning, the United States, Britain, and France all scurried to sell Faisal modern weaponry, a development further underlining Saudi Arabia's growing importance in the Middle East and the West's growing vulnerability to the oil weapon.

In his May Day speech, Sadat hailed the Saudi warning to the United States as further proof of growing Arab unity. Sadat claimed in the speech that he now had Syrian, Kuwaiti, Algerian, Saudi, Moroccan, and even Iraqi support for the forthcoming battle with Israel, which he termed necessary to prevent "domestic explosions" in Egypt and elsewhere in the Arab world because of frustration over the "no war-no peace" situation. At the same time he pointedly reminded the Russians:

> Regarding a peaceful solution, our friends in the Soviet Union must know the true feeling of our people. From the first moment we believed that what was taken by force can only be regained by force. Our friends in the USSR must know that the peaceful solution which the US has been talking about is ficti[ti]ous.[103]

At this point, however, although urging the Arabs to use their oil weapon against the United States, and sending a steady supply of weapons to Egypt and Syria, the Russians appeared not yet willing to back Egypt in a war against Israel. Instead, with the Brezhnev visit to Washington approaching, the Soviet leadership limited itself to supplying weaponry and trying to discredit further Israel and its U.S. supporters in the United Nations and other public forums, including those specifically convened for the purpose,[104] as the USSR continued its efforts to stimulate and reinforce anti-Western trends in the Middle East. The outbreak of very serious fighting in Lebanon in early May, which pitted the Palestinian guerrillas and their Lebanese supporters against the Lebanese government, may have been another factor in the Soviet Union's urging of caution on the Arabs.

As Brezhnev prepared to go to Washington, however, criticism of the lack of sufficient Soviet support for the Arab cause again began to rise. The Soviet-American detente had reached the point that on June 11 a Soviet newsman was invited to the U.S. Sixth Fleet change-of-command ceremony aboard the aircraft carrier John F. Kennedy in the Mediterranean.[105] Three days later, the Egyptian newspaper *Al-Gomhouria*, which had been friendly to the USSR in the past, warned that Egypt might still resort to force in the Middle East—even at the expense of Soviet-American detente.[106] On June 22 Mohammed Heikal bitterly criticized the USSR in a column in *Al-Ahram* for cutting aid to Egypt while the United States was doubling aid to Israel (another U.S. arms deal to Israel had just been announced, probably in compensation for the proposed U.S. arms shipment to Saudi Arabia). Heikal also asserted: "The United States knows what it wants in the Middle East while the USSR does not. What Moscow does not want is another Arab defeat that would destroy Soviet residual prestige in the Middle East."[107]

Thus, by the time of the Nixon-Brezhnev summit, the Soviet position was a mixed one. On the one hand, the U.S. position had deteriorated sharply, primarily because of its increasing dependence on Arab oil and the apparent willingness of Saudi Arabia to use the oil weapon. In addition, the increasingly bitter Arab-Israeli conflict had radicalized feeling in the Middle East to the point that Libya shut down its oil fields for a day, and Iraq and even pro-Western Kuwait shut down their oil fields for an hour in mid-May in protest against Western support for Israel. On the other hand, Egyptian-Soviet relations, while improved, remained tense; and Libyan leader Mu'ammar Kaddafi, whose nation was set to enter into union with Egypt, continued to complain as bitterly about Soviet imperialism and aid to Israel (through the emigration of Soviet Jews) as he did about the United States. Finally, the escalation of the conflict between Iran and Iraq in the Persian Gulf region, a conflict exacerbated by Iraq's invasion of Kuwait, continued to pose difficult problems of choice for the Soviet leadership.

FROM THE SUMMIT TO THE OCTOBER WAR

As in the 1972 summit, the leaders of the two superpowers appeared to pay little attention to the Middle East in their June 1973 meeting. Indeed, only 87 words out of a total of 3,200 in the final communique issued on June 24 dealt with the Middle East situation, and it appeared as if Nixon and Brezhnev wanted to downplay the conflict deliberately lest it interfere with their pursuit of detente. Thus, the joint communique failed to mention UN Resolution #242—hitherto the basis of the Soviet policy for a settlement of the Arab-Israeli conflict. The text of the communique stated:

> The parties expressed their deep concern with the situation in the Middle East and exchanged opinions regarding ways of reaching a Middle East settlement. Each of the parties set forth its position on this problem.
>
> Both parties agreed to continue to exert their efforts to promote the quickest possible settlement in the Middle East. This settlement should be in accordance with the interests of all states in the area, be consistent with their independence and sovereignty, and should take into due account the legitimate interests of the Palestinian people.[108]

As might be expected, the Egyptian reaction to the summit communique was swift and bitter. On June 25 *Al-Ahram's* managing editor, Ali Hamadi el Gammal, asserted in a column:

> Although we did not expect the talks between the two leaders to produce a specific position with regard to the crisis, we never thought

that the problem would meet this strongly negative attitude on their part.[109]

The Arab reaction to the summit's treatment of the Arab-Israeli conflict was, in fact, so negative that the Russians felt constrained to publish a special statement on Soviet policy toward the Middle East. Issued by TASS on June 27, it reiterated the main tenets of Soviet policy frequently stated in the past, including the need for total withdrawal of Israeli troops to the 1967 borders, a "peaceful solution" based on UN Resolution #242, recognition of the "legitimate interests and rights of the Palestinians," and Soviet support for the Arab states affected by "Israeli aggression" in 1967.[110]

But bitter Arab reaction to a perceived lack of Soviet support at the summit was not the only Middle East problem the Soviet leaders faced following the Brezhnev-Nixon meeting. The Iran-Iraq conflict heated up even more as the dispute between the Kurds and the Iraqi government moved closer to a full-scale war. To complicate matters even more for the Russians, the United States and China moved even closer to the Iranian side. In the middle of June, China openly came out for Iran. Visiting Foreign Minister Chi Peng-fei stated that Iran was fully justified in its arms buildup because "as the Shah has said, the situation on the eastern and western sides of Iran is a very serious threat to Iran."[111] Then, in late June, the Iranian Foreign Ministry, in its annual report, charged Iraq with numerous frontier violations in Kurdistan and elsewhere. At the same time, Kurdish leader Mullah Mustafa Barzani, in an interview with a Washington *Post* reporter, openly appealed for American aid and held out the prospect of Iraqi oil in return:

> We are ready to do what goes with American policy in this area, if America will protect us from the wolves. If support were strong enough, we could control the Kirkuk oil field and give it to a U.S. company to operate. It is in our area, and the recent nationalization of the Western-owned field was an act against the Kurds.[112]

The most serious problem of all for the Russians, however, was the attempted overthrow of the Al-Bakr regime on June 30, in which the number-three man in the Iraqi regime, Abd Al-Khaliq Al-Samarrai, and the chief of security, Nazim Kazar, were heavily implicated, with Kazar apparently being the mastermind behind the plot.[113] In reporting this development, *New Times* urged the Al-Bakr regime to learn from this experience by finally implementing the "progressive national front" of the Iraqi Ba'ath party, the Iraqi Communist Party, and the Kurdish national party it had long promised.[114] Perhaps because it was severely shaken by the coup d'etat attempt against it, the Al-Bakr regime agreed on July 17 to sign the pact for the national front. While the Iraqi Communists agreed to sign as well, the Kurds refused, and hostility between Kurds and the government degenerated into a situation close to full-scale war.[115]

On the same day as the signing of the national front agreement in Iraq came another event the Russians welcomed—the overthrow of the monarchy in Afghanistan by General Muhammed Daud, who proclaimed Afghanistan to be a republic. Daud, as premier between 1953 and 1963, had established good relations with the USSR, and he was also known for encouraging a "Pashtunistan" separatist movement in Pakistan's Northwest Frontier Province. Were Daud to reactivate this policy, and his speech of July 17 indicated he would do just that,[116] Pakistan's security problems, already complicated by the Baluchistani problem, would become more acute, thereby complicating Iran's security problems as well.

Iran's Premier Abbas Hoveida visited the Soviet Union in early August to discuss the Middle Eastern situation, and *New Times* made it clear, perhaps to reassure the Iraqis, that the broadening of Soviet-Iranian cooperation was "by no means at any third party's expense."[117] Nonetheless, the Iraqi regime, beset by its sharpening internal conflict with the Kurds, who continued to refuse to join the national front, apparently needed more reassuring. By late September the USSR had sent a number of TU-22 Blinder bombers to Iraq.[118] The fact that the number-two man in the Iraqi regime, Saddam Hussein, had openly spoken about improved relations with the United States and Britain to a group of Western correspondents and had declared that Iraq followed a policy of "nonalignment" may have also played a role in the Soviet decision to send the bombers.[119]

As the Iran-Iraq conflict, now exacerbated by strife between the Iraqi government and the Kurds (who were supported by Iran) continued to simmer, the Soviet leadership also had to face the increasingly strident calls by Sadat for war and the Egyptian leader's efforts to unite the Arab states in pursuit of this goal. On July 11, Sadat's national security advisor, Hafiz Izmail, journeyed to Moscow for what were termed "frank and friendly" talks. Upon his return Izmail stated that Egypt and the USSR were in "total accord" on their future relationship and assessment of the Middle East situation.[120] Nevertheless, in a speech following Izmail's return, Sadat stated that he was not fully satisfied with the results of the visit and that the Russians had told Izmail that detente could be expected to last from twenty to thirty years.[121] Sadat then warned the Soviet leaders in a speech on Radio Cairo on July 22 that detente would lead to the isolation of the USSR from the "national liberation movement," a warning certain to anger the USSR, because little more than a month away was the fourth nonaligned nations conference, in Algiers, where the Russians and Chinese would be certain to compete again for the allegiance of the developing nations of the Third World.[122]

While Soviet-Egyptian relations remained strained, despite the steady flow of Soviet armaments, the Soviet leadership could perhaps gain some satisfaction that the Libyan-Egyptian merger project was foundering badly. After visiting Egypt for two weeks in late June and early July, Kaddafi had made little headway in convincing the Egyptians whom he met that the advantages of their union with Libya outweighed the disadvantages. According to Moussa Sabry, writing in *Al-Akhbar* on July 8, "legal, economic and religious differences stood in the way of the union" as did Egyptian misgivings about the Libyan "cultural revolution," Libyan policy regarding Israel, and Kaddafi's disapproval of Egypt's relationship to the Soviet Union, limited as it was.[123]

Stung by the failure of his visit to Egypt, Kaddafi then organized a "peoples march" of 20,000 Libyans to Cairo to force the merger—only to find this tactic fail as well.[124] Finally, an embittered Kaddafi in a speech broadcast on Radio Tripoli on July 23, stated that "only a cultural revolution similar to Libya's could make the Egyptians a fighting people." In an evident response to the increasingly close relations between Faisal and Sadat, Kaddafi added, "there could be no truce with Arab reactionaries in league with the United States."[125]

The Soviet leaders were clearly pleased by the failure of the Egyptian-Libyan union and Libya's increasing isolation in the Arab world, since Kaddafi, with his militant anti-Sovietism, had constantly opposed Soviet policies in the Middle East. While applauding Kaddafi for his policy of nationalizing foreign oil companies, the Russians continually attacked him for his "third international force" theory, which rejected both capitalism and communism and claimed to offer a new socialist ideal based on the Koran. What particularly irked the Soviet leaders was that in many ways Kaddafi's theory, which stressed the need for Third World countries to oppose both NATO and the Warsaw Pact, bore a close relationship to the doctrines of China's Mao Tse-tung.[126]

Although the Russians were pleased with the failure of the Egyptian-Libyan union project, they could not have been too happy with Sadat's subsequent choice of Saudi Arabia to be his principal Middle East ally. Sadat, who recognized the fact that he had to unite as many of the Arab states as possible in a coalition to confront Israel, knew that Kaddafi had alienated too many other Arab leaders, including King Hussein and King Faisal, to make this coalition a viable one.[127] Thus, as Egypt's relations with Libya cooled, they became much closer with Saudi Arabia, culminating in a visit by Sadat to Saudi Arabia on August 23 in which Sadat probably informed Faisal of the coming war with Israel (although it is doubtful that the exact date was set), and he urged Faisal to use the oil weapon against the United States. Arab-Israeli tension had reached yet another peak at the time of Sadat's visit, following Israel's diversion of a Lebanese airliner from a flight between Beirut and Baghdad to an Israeli airbase. The goal of the Israeli action, which the Arabs branded as "air piracy," was to capture Palestinian terrorist leader George Habash. In addition, U.S. vulnerability to Arab oil pressure was becoming increasingly apparent following a series of "energy talks" by President Nixon and statements by presidential assistants on the "energy crisis," many of which were given prominent attention in the Soviet media.[128] Indeed, official American recognition of the U.S. oil vulnerability had reached the point by early August that in an interview on Israeli television on August 7, Joseph Sisco, then Assistant Secretary of State for Near Eastern Affairs, told the Israelis that while U.S. and Israeli interests were parallel in many instances, they were not always parallel, and he cited oil as one of the nonparallel cases.[129] In any case, by the end of August, King Faisal had become convinced that the time had come to unfoil the "oil weapon," and in a speech on NBC-TV the Saudi monarch warned the American people that while he did not want to put restrictions on oil exports to the United States, "America's complete support of Zionism makes it extremely difficult to continue to supply oil to the United States or even to maintain friendly relations with it."[130] Despite Faisal's threats to use the oil weapon, by early September the increasingly close relationship of Egypt and Saudi Arabia became a matter of concern for the Soviet leadership, which had long viewed Saudi Arabia in a very negative way. An article in *New Times* discussing the new trends in inter-Arab politics stated:

> The Press in both Arab and Western countries has of late been focusing on the policy of Saudi Arabia. The reactionary Saudi monarchy, which

receives large revenues from the oil monopolies, holds a conspicuous place in the plans of international imperialism. The imperialists, capitalizing on the difficulties experienced by the Arab countries because the settlement of the Middle East problem is dragging out owing to sabotage by Israel, are using the Saudi monarchy as a tool in their efforts to isolate those countries from the Soviet Union and the rest of the Socialist community, with an eye to abolishing the progressive Arab regimes.... At the same time, the Saudi reaction, stinting no money, is out to attain its own hegemonistic goals in the Middle East, to undermine the positions of the national democratic forces, and to block progressive reform in this area.

... Tripoli Radio, the Libyan station, routinely terms the Saudi King an "imperialist agent" and "traitor" to the Arab cause. The Libyan station has bitterly criticized the Egyptian regime for seeking close contacts with him. King Faisal, Arab diplomats here say, is strongly interested in preventing a merger between Egypt and Libya. It was noted in the foreign press that Kaddafi's unexpected arrival in Cairo late in August came precisely at a time when President Sadat was on a confidential visit to Saudi Arabia and other Arab countries.[131]

As Egypt moved toward Saudi Arabia and what appeared as a right-wing orientation in domestic and international politics (both the Arab Communists and the Soviet Press continued their criticism of Sadat's domestic policies during the summer), the Soviet leadership sought to counter this negative trend by upgrading its relations with the Palestine Liberation Organization, which had become one of the centers of anti-Western influence in the Arab world. In August PLO President Yasir Arafat was invited as an honored guest to the World University Games in Moscow,[132] and the PLO was permitted to open an office in East Berlin.[133] At the same time the Soviet government vehemently denied rumors that it was planning to sell a large quantity of cement to Israel (to be used for immigrant housing),[134] and the Israeli team at the University Games met severe harrassment from Soviet authorities—a marked contrast to the warm reception given to Arafat.[135]

Despite the added Soviet attention given to Arafat and the PLO, Egypt was still the prime mover in Arab politics. In August the Soviets became engaged in a dialogue with Egypt over Sadat's plans to go to war, arguing that war was not necessary to regain the lost Arab lands since time was on the side of the Arabs. The Russians argued that through the judicious use of the oil weapon, the Israelis could be forced to withdraw because of pressure from the United States, and that this process could be achieved without war—thanks to the existence of the Soviet-American detente. This rather intricate reasoning was most fully expressed by Dmitry Volsky, an associate editor of *New Times,* in a major article in early August:

The Arabs know the cost of bloodshed as well as anyone else. And the conditions in the world are increasingly favorable *to paying no such price* for the elimination of the consequences of Israel's aggression. . . .

The new climate developing in world affairs is highly unfavorable to the Israeli militarists, it operates against their annexationist designs.

The world press has noted repeatedly, for example, that with tensions in Europe lessening Israel's stock in Europe has been falling. . . .

Many observers believe, for instance that the energy crisis in the West, notably the United States, whose interest in Arab oil is, in the general view, increasing, will affect American Middle East policy, but more important, to our mind, th[a]n such adventitious factors is the inherent trend of the continuing struggle between the forces of progress and reaction, in which the balance is shifting more and more in favor of the progressive forces. The Middle East is no exception in this respect.

The Progressive Fronts in Iraq, Syria and South Yemen have strengthened. The progressive Arab countries are building up their friendship and cooperation with the Socialist states. . . . The attempts of Right nationalistic quarters parading pseudo-patriotic extremist slogans to impose their own conceptions on leading Arab countries and *steer them into adventurist courses* are meeting with no success.[136] [emphasis added]

The Egyptians, however, were evidently not convinced by these arguments nor by the Soviet decision to allow North Koreans and North Vietnamese to help train the Egyptians and Syrians,[137] and Abdul Kouddous's newspaper, *Al-Akhbar-Yom,* came out with a series of articles attacking detente because it subordinated Arab interests to the interests of the superpowers. The Russians appeared to take this attack quite seriously, as *Pravda* warned on August 28:

It looks as if the political line of this Cairo newspaper is acquiring a rather specific coloration. What purpose do the articles serve? The impression is being created that we are dealing with an attempt to sow distrust toward the Soviet Union among the Egyptian public and to distort the meaning of its support for the just cause of the Arab peoples who are struggling to liquidate the consequences of Israeli aggression.

Such misinformation, of course, cannot harm the time-tested Soviet-Egyptian friendship. It is to be hoped that such attempts to sow seeds of distrust among our people will be properly rebuffed in Egypt itself.[138]

On the eve of the fourth conference of the heads of state of nonaligned countries in Algiers on September 5, Volsky published yet another article in *New Times* describing the benefits of the Third World of Soviet-American detente:

An unbiased examination of the international situation shows that the development of Soviet-U.S. contacts has already had a salutary effect on the third world. Transition from confrontation to stable peaceful coexistence makes it harder for the aggressive neo-colonial quarters to impose their diktat on the newly-emerged national states. In this respect the significance of the Agreement on the Prevention of Nuclear War signed on 22 June this year cannot be overestimated. Recall, for instance, this stipulation of the agreement: Each Party will refrain from the threat or use of force against the other party, against the allies of the other party, and against other countries under circumstances which may endanger international peace and security. The parties agree that they will be guided by these considerations in the formulation of their foreign policies and in their actions in the field of international relations. . . .

. . . Given a different world balance of strength, different international conditions, might the imperialists not have resorted to the most dangerous moves against, say, Iraq when it nationalized Iraq Petroleum, *or against the Popular Unity Government in Chile?* . . .

Such, then, are the facts. They show that with the introduction of peaceful co-existence into Soviet-U.S. relations Soviet support for the national liberation movements will increase rather than diminish, and opportunities for cooperation between the socialist nations and the developing countries will be greater. More, in a climate of detente, when the newly independent states can feel more secure and the system of neo-colonialist blocs is breaking down, these countries gain new opportunities to pursue independent home and foreign policies.[139] [emphasis added]

Volsky must have soon regretted these words because less than a week later, the "Popular Unity" government of Salvador Allende in Chile was overthrown, and Allende, who together with Brezhnev had been the recipient of the Lenin Peace Prize in May, was killed. While it is not in the purview of this study to go into the background and development of the events of Chile, it is very clear that the Soviet leadership was bitterly disappointed over the fall of the Allende government. As shown above, the Allende government was an excellent example proving that the Soviet policy of detente was working, and its overthrow appeared to indicate the opposite, particularly to a number of already suspicious leaders in the Middle East. Indeed, in a *New Times* editorial following the coup in Chile, the Russians acknowledged this effect of the coup on detente:

A concentrated offensive is being waged against detente and its practical achievements. The object is at all costs to impede the progress of this process of such vital importance to the peoples.

Unfortunately, it must be said that the psychological pressure applied by the enemies of international detente is not without effect. One Arab newspaper, for instance, affirmed the other day that the reactionary military coup in Chile was nothing short of a consequence of detente.[140]

Two days after the coup, to which the Soviet media directly linked the United States,[141] came a major air battle in the Middle East between Israel and Syria, which resulted in the Israelis shooting down 13 Syrian planes while losing only 1 of their own. These events may have at least partially undercut the supporters of detente within the Soviet Politburo—perhaps to the point where they agreed to respond by increasing shipments of Soviet weaponry such as tanks and antiaircraft missiles to Syria and Egypt and agreed to Sadat's decision to go to war, although the USSR still refrained from supplying the Arabs either with fighter-bombers or with ground-to-ground missiles. These shipments of weapons, however, were to prove sufficient for the Egyptians—who were to use the antiaircraft missiles as a cover for the crossing of the canal and the tanks to spearhead the breakthrough—to make a final decision for war. The Russians must have learned about Sadat's decision in late September, because they began to withdraw nonessential technicians and other civilians from both Syria and Egypt well before the outbreak of the fighting on October 6.

In thus giving their tacit support for the Egyptian decision to go to war—in the viewpoint of this writer it was clearly an Egyptian and not a Soviet decision[142]—the Soviet leaders may have been motivated by a number of considerations. In the first place, it was conceivable that Sadat was again bluffing, as he had appeared to be many times in the past, and that he needed the additional weapons primarily for domestic considerations. Second, should Sadat go to war and be defeated, and this was the virtually unanimous feeling of the Western intelligence community and probably of a number of Russians as well, the Sadat regime would very likely fall, perhaps to be replaced by a more pro-Soviet Egyptian regime led by Ali Sabry. At the very minimum an outbreak of war would further inflame Arab feelings against the United States, much as the 1967 war had done, thus weakening the U.S. position in the Arab world still further. The Soviet leadership may well have seen the possibility that the war would bring a further nationalization of Western oil companies—the trend was already well underway—and possibly even an oil embargo against the United States and Western Europe, which, unlike the situation in 1967, would be a major blow to the economies of the Western world. Such developments would mean a sharp increase in influence for the USSR in its "zero-sum game" influence competition in the Middle East with the United States and possibly even tip what the Soviet leaders called the "world balance of forces" toward the USSR.[143] Perhaps in an effort to secure such gains the USSR failed to inform the United States of the coming war, despite an explicit agreement to do so reached at the 1972 Brezhnev-Nixon summit, where the two powers pledged to warn each other in the event that a dangerous local conflict threatened to arise, and a similar pledge that they would not seek "unilateral advantage" at the expense of the other."[144] On September 28, a week before the war, Soviet Foreign Minister Andrei Gromyko had visited Nixon and Kissinger (who was now officially Secretary of State) at the White House and told the American leaders nothing about the war, despite his almost certain knowledge about it by that late date.

In giving its support for Sadat's decision to go to war, however, the Soviet leadership took its biggest Middle East gamble since February 1970, when it had agreed to Nasser's request for a Soviet-manned air-defense system. In taking that move in 1970, the Soviet leaders had gambled successfully that the Nixon administration, then still bogged down in Vietnam, would make no equivalent countermove. In 1973 the Soviet leaders may have reasoned that the Nixon administration, although out of Vietnam, was now so burdened with Watergate, an ailing economy, and the "energy crisis" that regardless of Soviet action during the war, Nixon could not afford to jettison his detente policy with the USSR, which had proven to be one of his administration's few successes. However, following revelations over the cost to the American consumer of U.S. wheat sales to the Soviet Union, and attacks on detente by Soviet dissidents Andrei Sakharov and Aleksander Solzhenitsyn, who warned against detente without democratization in the USSR, increasing numbers of Americans, even before the outbreak of the war, were beginning to question both the meaning and value of detente with the Soviet Union.[145] Consequently, the Soviet decision to support the Arabs could only provide ammunition for the enemies of Soviet-American detente; but the Soviet leaders, perhaps still smarting from the defeat in Chile, evidently decided that the benefits of aiding the Arabs outweighed the costs of angering the United States. Nonetheless, Soviet caution in the initial stages of the war indicated that the Soviet leaders were hedging their bets on their support of the Arabs until the Arab forces had secured some military successes.

Ironically, while giving their support to Sadat's decision to go to war, the Soviet leadership remained critical of a number of his policies. An article appearing in *Pravda* on the third anniversary of Nasser's death (only eight days before the outbreak of the war) attacked those who "posed as the defenders of Nasserism and tried to impose upon the masses false interpretations of the views of the late President"—particularly as to relations between Egypt and the socialist states.[146] The Arab Communist parties of Lebanon, Syria, Iraq, Jordan, Algeria, and the Sudan, meeting on the eve of the war, were far more explicit in their criticism of the Egyptian leader, attacking him for his policy of close cooperation with King Faisal "who plays a leading role in Imperialist plans"; for his policy of "weakening the bonds of alliance and friendship" between Egypt and the USSR; and for his encouragement of Egypt's private sector and foreign capital at the expense of the public sector.[147]

Despite these differences with Sadat over both domestic and foreign policies, the Soviet leadership gave him their support during the October war. It is conceivable that the Soviet leaders felt that wartime cooperation would serve to overcome the serious differences between the two countries. In addition, the fact that Sadat had managed by mid-September to effect a reconciliation between Syria and Jordan clearly established him as the leader of an Arab alignment, which now included not only the radical states of Syria and Libya, but also the conservative, pro-Western states of Jordan and Saudi Arabia. This made Egypt once again the fulcrum of Middle East politics, and the Soviet leaders may well have thought that Soviet aid to Egypt during a war that would pit Israel, and most likely the United States (at least in a support capacity), against the Arab world would help create the "Arab unity on the anti-imperialist basis" they had so long desired. If this was indeed the Soviet hope, it was not destined to be fulfilled. For despite extensive cooperation between the USSR and Egypt during the war, once the fighting was over Sadat was to return to his earlier patterns of domestic and foreign policy—much to the consternation of Soviet officials who were to see both the collapse of their long-hoped-for anti-imperialist Arab unity and a major turn by the Egyptian president toward the United States.

NOTES

1. Translated in *Current Digest of the Soviet Press* (hereafter *CDSP*) 24, no. 24: 18.
2. New York *Times,* July 20, 1972.
3. Cited in *Middle East Monitor* 2, no. 15 (August 1, 1974): 6.

4. *Pravda,* July 23, 1972. The statement quoted was in Pavel Demchenko's article on the twentieth anniversary of the Egyptian Revolution.

5. Cited in the report by John Cooley in the *Christian Science Monitor,* August 16, 1972.

6. Cited in the report by John Cooley in the *Christian Science Monitor,* August 21, 1972.

7. Cited in the report by Flora Lewis in the New York *Times,* August 22, 1972.

8. See footnote 5.

9. Translated in *CDSP* 24, no. 35: 5.

10. Y. Potomov, "Middle East Alliance Against Progress," *New Times,* no. 34 (1972): 5.

11. Cited in the New York *Times,* September 4, 1972.

12. The Egyptians even began to charge that there were Israeli spies among the Soviet advisers in Egypt! See the report by John Cooley in the *Christian Science Monitor,* September 15, 1972.

13. For a list of the most important Soviet construction projects in the Arab world, see V. Smirnov and I. Matyukhin, "USSR and the Arab East: Economic Contacts," *International Affairs* (Moscow), no. 9 (September 1972): 83-87.

14. See the report in the New York *Times,* June 21, 1972.

15. *Pravda,* July 9, 1972.

16. *Pravda,* August 11, 1972. Translated in *CDSP* 24, no. 32: 20.

17. Cited in the report by John Cooley in the *Christian Science Monitor,* August 12, 1972.

18. I. Gavrilov, "Arab Press on the Middle East Situation," *New Times,* no. 36 (1972): 8.

19. Translated in *CDSP* 24, no. 30: 17.

20. See the reports by Eric Pace in the New York *Times,* September 18 and 21, 1972.

21. Pavel Demchenko, "The Palestinian Resistance and Reactionaries' Intrigues," *Pravda,* August 29, 1972. Translated in *CDSP* 24, no. 35: 2.

22. Ibid., pp. 3-4. For an Arab Communist view of the Palestinian resistance movement and its problems, see Naim Ashhab, "To Overcome the Crisis of the Palestine Resistance Movement," *World Marxist Review* 15, no. 5 (May 1972): 71-78.

23. Until August 3, Soviet Jews seeking to emigrate had to pay an exit fee of approximately $1,000. The new exit fee structure was determined by the amount of education each individual had and ranged from $5,500 for technical school graduates to $40,000 for a scholar with a doctoral degree.

24. Reuters report from Hamburg, citied in the Jerusalem *Post,* September 22, 1972. West Germany, in addition to reestablishing diplomatic relations with Egypt after the seven-year break, had also been engaged in negotiations with other Arab states with whom diplomatic relations had been broken off since 1965.

25. See the report of John Allen May in the *Christian Science Monitor,* September 21, 1972. According to an AP report from London cited in the

Jerusalem *Post,* September 15, 1972, Egypt was seeking $220 million in arms from England.

26. *Middle East Monitor* 2, no. 19 (October 1, 1972): 3.

27. See the report by Terrence Smith in the *Christian Science Monitor,* September 10, 1972.

28. Cited in the report by Francis Offner in the *Christian Science Monitor,* September 23, 1972.

29. Dmitry Volsky, "A Frank Talk with Some Arab Colleagues," *New Times,* no. 37 (1972): 4.

30. *New Times,* no. 38 (1972): 1.

31. V. Rumyanstev, "Syria on the Alert," *New Times,* no. 40 (1972): 8. For an examination of the "Nile to Euphrates" myth, see Mervyn Harris, "From Nile to Euphrates: The Evolution of a Myth," *New Middle East,* nos. 42-43 (March/April 1972): 46-48.

32. *Pravda,* September 7, 1972.

33. See the report by Eric Pace in the New York *Times,* September 22, 1972.

34. Y. Kornilov, "Meetings with the Fedayeen," *New Times,* no. 42 (1972): 24-25.

35. At the very beginning of an article entitled "The Middle East Situation," written at the time of Al-Bakr's visit, Dmitry Voksky wrote: "In the present complex alignment of forces in the Middle East, a positive role is increasingly being played by Soviet-Iraqi relations." *New Times,* no. 39 (1972): 6.

36. Podgorny's speech, which appeared in *Pravda* on September 15, is translated in *CDSP* 24, no. 38: 22.

37. Ibid.

38. *New Times,* no. 41, 1972, pp. 18-20. A more theoretical treatment of this problem is found in R. Ulianovsky, "O edinom anti-imperialisticheskom fronte progressivnikhsil v osvobodivshikhsia stranakh" (About the unity of the anti-imperialist front of progressive forces in newly independent states), *Mirovaia ekonomika i mezhdunarodnaia otnosheniia,* no. 9 (September 1972): 76-86. See also his book, *Sotsialism i osvobodivshikhsia strany* (Moscow: Nauka, 1972).

39. *New Times,* no. 41 (1972): 18-20.

40. "New Stage in the National Liberation Movement: Problems of Anti-Imperialist Unity" (An International Conference held under the Auspices of the *World Marxist Review*), *World Marxist Review* 15, no. 11 (November 1972): 61.

41. Ibid.

42. Ibid.

43. Ibid., p. 64.

44. Ibid., p. 67.

45. *Pravda,* September 15, 1972. Translated in *CDSP* 24, no. 38: 23.

46. *Pravda,* September 20, 1972. Translated in *CDSP* 24, no. 38: 23.

47. Ibid.

48. See the report by John Cooley in the *Christian Science Monitor,* October 13, 1972.

49. Ibid.

50. *Pravda,* October 22, 1972.

51. The text of the declaration is found in *New Times,* no. 17 (1972): 5.

52. Cited in report by Henry Tanner in the New York *Times,* September 29, 1972.

53. See the report by Henry Tanner in the New York *Times,* October 1, 1972.

54. See the report by Juan De Onis in the New York *Times,* October 6, 1972, and the report in the Jerusalem *Post,* October 6.

55. See the report by Henry Tanner in the New York *Times,* October 8, 1972.

56. *Peking Review* 15, no. 42 (October 20, 1972): 21.

57. For a description of this incident, see the report by John Cooley in the *Christian Science Monitor,* November 7, 1972.

58. Cited in the report by Henry Tanner in the New York *Times,* October 16, 1972.

59. The text of the communique is found in *Pravda,* October 19, 1972.

60. Cited in report by John Cooley in the *Christian Science Monitor,* October 24, 1972.

61. Cited in the report by Henry Tanner in the Jerusalem *Post,* October 27, 1972.

62. For a description of the possible effects of these leadership changes, see the report by John Cooley in the *Christian Science Monitor,* November 10, 1972.

63. See the report by William Beecher in the New York *Times,* November 12, 1972.

64. Cited in the report by William Dullforce in the Washington *Post,* October 30, 1972. *Pravda,* November 1, 1972, in reporting a speech by Egypt's new Defense Minister, Ahmed Ismail, gave the same version.

65. See the report by John Cooley in the *Christian Science Monitor,* October 25, 1972.

66. *Pravda,* November 1, 1972.

67. See the report by John Cooley in the *Christian Science Monitor,* November 13, 1972.

68. New York *Times,* October 27, 1972.

69. For the "declaration" on the Munich massacre by the Black September terrorist movement, see the *Middle East Monitor* 2, no. 18 (September 15, 1972): 4-6.

70. Cited in the New York *Times,* October 7, 1972.

71. AFP report cited in the New York *Times,* November 12, 1972.

72. Yuri Gvozdev, "Democratic Yemen: Problems and Aims," *New Times,* no. 48 (1972): 15.

73. *Pravda,* November 26, 1972. The communique is translated in *CDSP* 24, no. 47: 14.

74. Cited in *Middle East Monitor* 3, no. 1 (January 1, 1973): 3.

75. This incident is described in *Middle East Monitor* 3, no. 5 (March 1, 1973): 1.

76. *New Times,* no. 18 (1973): 11.

77. New York *Times,* February 22, 1973.

78. *Pravda,* March 16, 1973. Speech translated in *CDSP* 25, no. 11: 25.

79. *New Times,* no. 14 (1973): 7.

80. See *Middle East Monitor* 3, no. 11 (June 1, 1973): 2-3; and the report by John Cooley in the *Christian Science Monitor,* May 29, 1973.

81. L. Medvenko, "Subversive Activity of Imperialism and Reaction Against the Arab States' National Interests," *Pravda,* August 19, 1972. Translated in *CDSP* 24, no. 33: 17.

82. *New Times,* no. 47 (1972): 13.

83. See the report by Anan Safadi in the Jerusalem *Post,* December 1, 1972.

84. "Marching Together: The Role of the Communists in Building a Broad Alliance of Democratic Forces," *World Marxist Review* 16, no. 2 (February 1973): 112.

85. There had been serious unrest in the Egyptian armed forces, and it had spread to the normally docile Egyptian Parliament as well as to the universities and to the media.

86. Cited in Reuters report in the New York *Times,* December 29, 1972.

87. Victor Kudryavtsev, "On the Arab Diplomatic Front," *New Times,* no. 4 (1974): 12. The Russians had long been urging the Arabs to use their oil weapon. For an early theoretical treatment of the possible effects of oil pressure, see I. Bronin, "Arabskaia neft—Ssha—zapadnaia Evrope" (Arab oil—USA—West Europe), *Mirovaia, ekonomika i mezhdunarodnaia otnosheniia,* no. 2 (February 1972): 31-42.

88. Kudryavtsev, op. cit., p. 13.

89. Dmitry Volsky, "King Faisal's Holy War," *New Times,* no. 5 (1973): 26-27.

90. Cited in *Middle East Monitor* 2, no. 20 (November 1, 1972): 4-5.

91. The best treatment of this tragedy is found in *Aviation Week and Space Technology* (March 5, 1973), pp. 26-28.

92. V. Katin, "Tel-Aviv's Atrocious Crime," *New Times,* no. 9 (1973): 20-21.

93. Washington *Post,* March 27, 1973.

94. Cited in the report by William Dullforce in the Washington *Post,* February 5, 1973.

95. For a contemporary Soviet view of the USSR's relations with Egypt, see N. A. Ushakova, *Arabskaia respublika Egipet* (Moscow: Nauka, 1974). Chapter 3 of this book indicates Soviet displeasure with Egypt's economic turn to the West after 1970.

96. Cited in *Brief: Middle East Highlights* (Tel Aviv), no. 54: 3 (hereafter *Brief*).

97. Ibid.

98. Dmitry Volsky, "The Beirut Crime," *New Times,* no. 16 (1973): 12-13.

99. For a description of these oil developments, see *Middle East Monitor* 3, no. 6 (March 15, 1973): 1-2.

100. Ibid., p. 1.

101. Interestingly enough, following these events, *Pravda* on March 14, 1973, urged the United States to solve its energy problems by investing in Soviet

oil and natural gas. For an excellent account of the difficulties facing any such U.S. investment, see John P. Hardt, "West Siberia: The Quest for Energy," *Problems of Communism* 22, no. 3 (May-June 1973): 25-36.

102. See report in the Washington *Post,* April 18, 1973, and in the Jerusalem *Post* (AP report), April 20, 1973.

103. Cairo Radio, May 1, 1973, reprinted in *Middle East Monitor* 3, no. 10: 3-4.

104. Cf. the International Conference for Peace and Justice in the Middle East, Bologna, Italy, May 13, 1973. For a description of the results of the conference, see *New Times,* no. 21 (1973): 16-17.

105. New York *Times,* June 14, 1973.

106. Cited in the report by John Cooley in the *Christian Science Monitor,* June 20, 1973.

107. Cited in the report by John Cooley in the *Christian Science Monitor,* June 20, 1973.

108. Text of communique is found in *New Times,* no. 26 (1973): 23.

109. Cited in the New York *Times,* June 26, 1973.

110. Reprinted in *Middle East Monitor* 3, no. 14 (July 15, 1973): 1.

111. Radio Tehran, cited in the *Middle East Monitor* 3, no. 13 (July 1, 1973): 6.

112. Cited in report by Jim Hoagland, Washington *Post* services, in the Milwaukee *Journal,* June 24, 1973.

113. For a Baghdad Radio description of the plot, see *Middle East Monitor* 3, no. 14 (July 15, 1973): 5-6.

114. *New Times,* no. 28 (1973): 17.

115. For a description of the composition of the National Front and of the Kurdish opposition to it, see *Middle East Monitor* 3, no. 18 (October 1, 1973): 1.

116. See the text of his speech in *Middle East Monitor* 3, no. 15 (August 1, 1973): 4-6.

117. *New Times,* no. 33 (1973): 6. The article also cited another Kosygin speech opposing arms races.

118. See the reports in the New York *Times* and *Christian Science Monitor,* October 2, 1973.

119. Cited in the report by Juan De Onis in the New York *Times,* July 15, 1973.

120. *Brief,* no. 62: 1.

121. Ibid.

122. Cairo Radio, July 22, 1973.

123. Cited in *Brief,* no. 61: 2.

124. For a Soviet comment on the march, see *New Times,* no. 30 (1973): 16-17.

125. New York *Times,* July 24, 1973.

126. For a detailed Soviet critique of Kaddafi's theories, see *Liturnaia gazeta,* no. 23, 1973. Translated in *CDSP* 25, no. 28: 13-14.

127. Kaddafi also posed a domestic challenge to Sadat, as he had the potential of becoming a rallying point for the Moslem fundamentalists in Egypt, who were still a powerful political force.

128. Cf. articles in *New Times*, nos. 25 and 27, 1973. See also the article on the Organization of Petroleum Exporting Countries in the September 1973 issue of *Mirovaia ekonomika i mezhdunarodnaia otnosheniia*, pp. 129-133.

129. New York *Times*, August 7, 1973.

130. Cited in *Middle East Monitor* 3, no. 18 (October 1, 1973): 4.

131. Y. Potomov, "The Egypt-Libya Merger Project," *New Times*, no. 36 (1973): 11.

132. See the report of his visit in *New Times*, no. 35 (1973): 2.

133. New York *Times*, August 19, 1973.

134. See the report in the *Christian Science Monitor*, July 25, 1973.

135. See the report in the Jerusalem *Post*, August 31, 1973.

136. Dmitry Volsky, "New Opportunities and Old Obstacles," *New Times*, no. 32 (1973): 15.

137. Cited in the New York *Times*, August 16, 1973.

138. Translated in *CDSP* 25, no. 35: 18.

139. Dmitry Volsky, "Soviet-American Relations and the Third World," *New Times*, no. 36 (1973): 4-6.

140. *New Times*, no. 39 (1973): 1.

141. See, for example, Radio Moscow domestic service September 13 and 14, 1973.

142. For a different view of the Soviet position on the eve of the war, see Uri Ra'anan, "Soviet Policy in the Middle East 1969-73," *Midstream* 30, no. 10 (December 1973): 23-45; and the article by Jon Kimhe, "The Soviet-Arab Scenario," in the same journal (pp. 9-22).

143. On this point, see Foy D. Kohler, Leon Goure, and Mose L. Harvey, *The Soviet Union and the October 1973 Middle East War* (Miami: Center For Advanced International Studies, University of Miami, 1974).

144. See above p. 74.

145. See the Sakharov interview with *Der Spiegel*, September 17, 1973. For a Soviet attack on Sakharov because of the interview, see Moscow Radio, September 20, 1973.

146. *Pravda*, September 28, 1973.

147. Cited in the report in the New York *Times*, October 6, 1973.

CHAPTER

5

THE SOVIET UNION AND
THE OCTOBER WAR

SOVIET POLICY DURING THE WAR

As a well-coordinated Syrian-Egyptian attack struck at Israeli positions in the Sinai desert and the Golan Heights, the initial Soviet reaction to the war was a very hesitant one. This may have been because the Soviet leadership had some doubts as to the capabilities of the Syrian and Egyptian armies to carry out their offensive successfully—even against an overconfident and poorly prepared Israel.[1] Alternatively, the Soviet leaders may have had some second thoughts about the desirability of sacrificing detente for the sake of a rather fickle Arab ally. In any case, if we are to believe Sadat's account of the first day of the war, the Russians tried to get him to accept a cease-fire after only six hours of fighting, by claiming that Syria had requested a cease-fire.[2] Even when Sadat rejected the Soviet ploy, the Soviet media downplayed the war with *Pravda* giving far more space to the events in Chile than to the Middle East conflict.[3] It was only after three days of fighting, when it appeared that the Arab side was in fact winning, that the Russians, perhaps sensing the possibility of finally being able to rally the Arabs into the long advocated "anti-imperialist" alignment and strike a blow at U.S. interests in the Middle East, moved to increase their involvement in the war, yet at the same time keeping their involvement within limited bounds.[4] On October 9 Brezhnev sent the following note to Algerian President Houri Boumadienne and similar notes to other Arab leaders:

Comrade President, I believe that you agree that the struggle waged at present against the Israeli aggressor for the liberation of Arab territories occupied since 1967 and the safeguarding of the legitimate rights of the people of Palestine affect the vital interests of all Arab countries. In our view, there must be fraternal Arab solidarity, today more than ever. Syria and Egypt must not remain alone in their struggle against a treacherous enemy.[5]

128

At the same time Moscow Radio tied Israeli "aggression" to "imperialist support," and the Russians began a massive airlift of weapons to Syria and Egypt, thereby demonstrating that while it was to be the Arabs (and not the Russians) who did the fighting, the USSR would provide the necessary supplies.

By October 12, however, Israel, choosing to deal with one enemy at a time, had repulsed the Syrian attack, and Israeli troops were moving past the 1967 cease-fire lines into Syria while remaining on the defensive in the Sinai.[6] At this point U.S. Secretary of State Henry Kissinger stated that the Middle East war had the potential for getting out of hand and involving the great powers, and while thus far the United States was able to "tolerate" Soviet actions, "if Soviet behavior became irresponsible the United States would not hesitate to take a firm stand."[7]

Interestingly enough, while supplying the Syrians and Egyptians with increasing amounts of weaponry, the Russians made a number of moves to appeal to the Jewish and liberal communities in the United States in an effort to keep the spirit of detente alive. Thus, instead of reducing or cutting off the flow of Soviet Jews to Israel during the war, the emigration actually increased.[8] In addition, Soviet Radio broadcasts to the United States during the war emphasized that the Soviet Union was not against Israel as a state—"only against its conquests."[9] Nonetheless, these Soviet gestures held little weight in American government circles when compared to the huge Soviet arms airlift to Egypt and Syria. The United States announced on October 15 that the "massive airlift of Soviet weaponry to the Arabs threatened to upset the military balance against Israel," and the United States began to airlift weapons to Israel.[10]

Meanwhile, just as in the 1967 war, Algerian President Boumadienne had flown to Moscow asking for more support for the Arab cause. Once again he had not received all the aid he asked. Although following his visit TASS published a Soviet pledge to "help in every way" the Arabs to recapture territory seized by Israel in the 1967 war, the communique reporting Boumadienne's talks with the Soviet leaders stated that the talks had taken place in a "frank atmosphere"—the usual Soviet code word for serious disagreement.[11]

Nonetheless, the aid provided by the Soviet Union to the Arabs was sufficient to evoke increasing American ire, and Kosygin in a speech during the visit of Danish Premier Jorgensen acknowledged this development by stating:

> The opponents of detente are trying to use every pretext to revive the atmosphere of the cold war. . . . They are trying in every way to exploit for these purposes the resumption of hostilities in the Middle East.[12]

One of the leading American opponents of detente was Melvin Laird, once Secretary of Defense and now an adviser to President Nixon. On October 16 he attacked the Russians for disrupting U.S. efforts to achieve a cease-fire (the Russians had opposed a cease-fire as long as the Arabs were winning unless it meant a withdrawal of Israeli forces back to the 1967 borders). In addition, Laird pointedly complained: "We are not getting action to support the concept of detente."[13]

While the Russians were not ready for a cease-fire on October 16, the Israeli crossing of the Suez Canal that day and the subsequent enlargement of their salient on the west bank of the canal quickly changed the Soviet leaders' minds.

On October 16 Kosygin flew to Cairo and met for three days with Sadat,[14] and on the same day, eleven Arab countries meeting in Kuwait announced that Arab oil exports to countries "unfriendly to the Arab cause" would be reduced each month by 5 percent until the Israelis withdrew to the 1967 prewar boundaries.[15] Thus the oil weapon, whose use had been urged by the Soviet leaders both before and during the war, had now been employed. If this action, or the visit of Saudi Arabian Foreign Minister Umar Al-Saqqam and other Arab diplomats to the White House to see President Nixon the same day, was meant to deter the United States from granting further assistance to Israel, the attempt was a failure. On October 19 Nixon asked Congress for $2.2 billion in aid for Israel. Highlighting American support of Israel, Moscow Radio again appealed to the Arabs to cut off the flow of oil to the West:

> Favorable conditions now exist for Arab use of oil as an economic and political weapon against capitalist states which are supporting Israel aggression.[16]

Libya announced it was cutting off all oil exports to the United States that day. Saudi Arabia, once the United States' closest ally in the Arab world, followed suit the next day, with Kuwait, Qatar, Bahrein, and Dubai acting similarly on October 21.

The use of the oil weapon, however, could not stop the rapid deterioration in the position of the Egyptian army—a development that led to Kissinger's flying to the Soviet Union on October 20 at the Soviet leaders' "urgent request."[17] The result of Kissinger's visit was a "cease-fire in place" agreement—a major retreat for the Russians from their previous position calling for a return to the 1967 boundaries as a price for the cease-fire. The Soviet-American cease-fire agreement, which was approved by the Security Council in the early hours of the morning on October 23, did not terminate the fighting; both sides, despite agreeing to the cease-fire, continued fighting to improve their positions. The Israelis got much the better of the fighting, however, and by October 24 Sadat was forced to appeal to both the United States and the USSR to send troops to police the cease-fire.[18]

At this point the Soviet Union's Arab client was about to suffer a major defeat, which would have meant a major defeat for Soviet prestige as well, now that the USSR had openly backed the Arabs. Therefore, the Soviet leaders decided to pressure Israel and the United States by alerting Soviet airborne divisions and dispatching Soviet transport planes to the airborne troops' bases. At the same time Brezhnev sent a stiff note to Nixon that reportedly stated: "I say it straight that if the United States does not find it possible to act together with us in this matter, we should be faced with the necessity urgently to consider the question of taking appropriate steps unilaterally."[19] While the Soviet leader may have been bluffing, Nixon decided not to take any chances and he called a nuclear alert. It now appeared not only that detente had died, but also that the two superpowers were on the verge of a nuclear confrontation.[20] Perhaps because this was the last thing the Soviet leaders wished to see develop out of the Middle East war, Brezhnev quickly backed off from his threat to intervene unilaterally. The United States, equally unwilling to see the conflict develop any further, brought pressure on Israel and stopped the Israeli army before it had destroyed the surrounded Egyptian Third Army and marched on to Cairo, although, as will be shown below, Kissinger had additional motives in doing so. The superpowers then decided to bring the issue back to the United Nations, and a UN emergency force was established to police the cease-fire, although the two superpowers were later to wrangle about the composition of the UN force.

As the war came to a close, Soviet policy-makers who had been hesitant about the war at the start were able to total up a number of significant gains for the Soviet Union's position in the Middle East, although a number of these gains were to turn out to be transient ones. Perhaps the main Soviet gain was the creation of the "anti-imperialist" Arab unity they had advocated for so long and the concomitant apparent isolation of the United States from its erstwhile allies in the region. Not only had Syria, Iraq, Egypt, Jordan, Algeria, Kuwait, and Morocco actually employed their forces against Israel, but even such staunch one-time allies of the United States as the conservative regimes of Kuwait and Saudi Arabia, in addition to sending troops to the front, had declared an oil embargo against the United States, while the tiny Gulf sheikdom of Bahrein had ordered the United States to get out of the naval base it maintained there.[21] Thus, as early as the second week in the war, Dmitry Volsky could exultingly declare in *New Times*:

> It is no secret that Tel-Aviv has always banked—and of late quite openly—on differences between the Arabs. And not without reason, for the relations between some Arab states, including states with progressive orientations, did indeed leave much to be desired. Today, however, in the hour of trial, soldiers of different Arab countries are fighting shoulder to shoulder against Israeli expansionism. . . . This solidarity of the Arab countries which have laid aside their differences, is a new and very important factor in the Middle East situation, the significance of which will evidently grow as time goes on.[22]

Evaluating the lessons of the war six weeks later, Georgi Mirsky, perhaps the dean of Soviet commentators on the Middle East, further emphasized this theme:

> The third myth dispelled [by the war] related to the alleged fragility and illusoriness of Arab solidarity. Today this solidarity, founded on the sense of Arab brotherhood and an awareness of facing a common enemy, is an incontestable fact, one that was confirmed in the course of the October fighting. Iraqi, Moroccan, Jordanian and Saudi troops fought side by side with the Syrian army; the Palestinians, and the Kuwaits also saw action, and Algerian aircraft took part in the air war.
>
> But perhaps even more important is the solidarity of the oil-producing Arab states. Although the Arab press has spoken a great deal in recent months about the oil weapon, not everybody took it seriously and many were astounded when after the outbreak of hostilities in October even such countries as Saudi Arabia and Kuwait announced an oil boycott of countries supporting Israel (including a total embargo on oil exports to the United States.[23]

In addition to the establishment of Arab unity on an anti-American basis, and the consequent sharp deterioration of the U.S. position in the Middle East, the Soviet leaders could draw great satisfaction from the fact that their extensive aid to the Arabs, and the conspicuous lack of anything except verbal support from the Chinese, had greatly reinforced the Soviet position as champion of the Arab cause and the cause of the "national liberation" movement throughout the world, while undercutting that of the Chinese. The Russians claimed that by delaying enactment of the cease-fire by the United Nations, the Chinese had actually hurt the Arab cause by enabling the Israeli army to gain more territory. As an article in *New Times* put it:

> The latest aggravation of the Middle East crisis once again showed the Arabs who their real friends are. No amount of demagogy will conceal the fact that at this critical hour for the Arab peoples Peking played into the hands of Israel. "The policy of the P.R.C.," the Beirut *Al-Shaab* wrote on October 31 "does not accord with the interests of the Arab nation or the revolutionary concept of the national liberation struggle against world imperialism and Zionism." The efforts made by the Chinese leaders to undermine Arab-Soviet friendship, to weaken international solidarity with the struggle of the Arabs to liquidate the consequences of the Israeli aggression, are condemned by public opinion in the Arab countries. "Our people," the Syrian *Al-Thawrah* wrote "are well aware of the purpose of these efforts. They know that the object is to shake the Arabs' faith in their own strength and in our friends in order to impel us towards compromise and capitulation." The Lebanese press has stressed that Maoist slander cannot discredit the Soviet Union in the eyes of the Arab peoples who have seen for themselves that "Phantoms were shot down with weapons supplied in Egypt and Syria by the U.S.S.R. and not with Chinese verbiage."[24]

Yet another important benefit for the Soviet Union from the war was the reconciliation between Iran and Iraq. On October 8 Iraq announced its desire to restore diplomatic relations with Iran, and the Iraqi government asked Iran to accept this gesture so that Iraqi troops could be moved from the border with Iran to Syria to join the fighting against Israel. The Iranian government accepted the offer, perhaps in the expectation that it could later trade on its solidarity with the Arabs to get them to agree to a rise in the price for oil.[25] The Russians also must have been satisfied with the reconciliation between the Ba'athist regimes of Syria and Iraq, who had quarreled bitterly before the war over Iraq's decision to build an oil pipeline through Turkey to enable Iraqi oil to flow to the Mediterranean without the constant threat of the Syrians cutting it off.[26]

On the strategic level, the Soviet world position was greatly enhanced by the war. NATO faced its biggest crisis since the Suez war of 1956 because of West European opposition to the supplying of Israel from U.S. bases in Europe. Differences over policy towards the oil embargo exacerbated the strains within the alliance still further. Meanwhile, the Common Market was split by the failure of Britain, France, Italy, and West Germany to come to the aid of fellow EEC member Holland, which was also hit by a total oil embargo. While the Russians welcomed the conflicts within NATO and EEC, they nonetheless expressed some concern that West Europe might yet adopt a "go it alone" strategy and establish its own defensive alliance.[27]

Thus, the Soviet Union had scored a number of gains as a result of the war, although Soviet-American detente had suffered a major blow, with large numbers of Americans both inside and outside the government now openly opposing Nixon's detente policy toward the Soviet Union and the trade and strategic arms policies that went with it. In addition, the fact that the United States and the Soviet Union experienced a nuclear confrontation during the war could not have been too welcome to the Soviet leaders. On balance, however, the Soviet Union's position in the world, and particularly in the Middle East, had been greatly improved by the war, as the position of their main competitor, the United States, had worsened considerably. It appeared as if the Soviet Union had won a major, if not decisive, victory in the "zero-sum game" competition with the United States for influence in the Middle East. Nonetheless, just as the USSR's position, which had been gravely weakened by its expulsion from Egypt in July 1972, had improved sharply only a few months later as a result of the Munich massacre; so too the United States, at a low point in Middle Eastern prestige at the close of the war, was to improve its position, radically several months later, thanks to the astute diplomacy of Henry Kissinger and a reordering of priorities by Anwar Sadat.

THE ISRAELI-EGYPTIAN DISENGAGEMENT AGREEMENT

After the end of the war, the Soviet leadership faced the choice of either trying to capitalize on the serious rifts in NATO and the EEC and further undermining the U.S. position in the Middle East or trying to improve relations with the United States, thereby demonstrating their primary interest in the long-term benefits of arms limitation and trade. While on the one hand continuing to stress the value of detente, and even claiming that the detente relationship had prevented a nuclear war between the superpowers during the Middle East conflict, the Soviet leaders nonetheless chose to urge the Arabs to maintain their oil embargo against the United States—an act clearly not consistent with the U.S. concept of detente, since the embargo was both weakening the American economy and challenging American leadership of the NATO alliance. If the Soviet leaders felt that their verbal endorsements of detente would appease the American people or their government, they were gravely mistaken. Thus, in early November, President Nixon, long an advocate of increased trade with the Soviet Union, decided to have the congressional leadership postpone consideration of an administration bill giving most-favored-nation trading status to the Soviet Union.[28] A New York *Times* editorial several months later summed up many Americans' feelings on the Soviet endeavor to maintain both detente with the United States and the oil embargo against the United States:

The propaganda campaign by Radio Moscow in Arabic urging the Arabs to continue their oil embargo against the United States . . . has been a useful reminder of the Kremlin's double standard on detente.

The Arab oil embargo was both discriminatory and illegal, a violation of treaty obligations and international trade rules. Yet while Moscow was supporting it, Soviet officials fanning across the United States to promote trade, were vociferously protesting discriminatory—though legal—American tarriffs on Soviet exports. . . . Events in the Middle East make it increasingly clear that, in Moscow's view, detente has very narrow limits.[29]

While Soviet-American relations had clearly suffered as a result of the war, the Arab unity created by the war, which the Soviet leaders had welcomed so warmly, began to disintegrate almost as soon as the war ended. Thus, the Ba'athist regime in Iraq, despite the presence of the Iraqi Communists in a national front, and despite close ties to the USSR, rejected the Soviet-supported cease-fire agreement as being "against the will of the Arab masses," much as it had rejected the Soviet-supported UN Resolution #242.[30] The Al-Bakr regime was, in fact, so opposed to the cease-fire that it refused to attend the Algiers summit conference of Arab leaders, which took place in late November to coordinate Arab strategy. Similarly opposed to the cease-fire was Libyan leader Mu'ammar Kaddafi, who characterized it as "a time bomb offered by the United States and Soviet Union."[31] To make matters worse for the Russians, bloody fighting erupted between the Kurds and the Iraqi Communists from November 7 to 20,[32] and it was followed the next month by renewed frontier clashes between Iraq and Iran, which soon escalated into such severe battles that the Russians had to publicly admonish the Iraqis in a *New Times* report of the clashes.[33] Iraq, whose isolation in both the Arab world and in the region as a whole had impelled the Al-Bakr regime to request an alliance with the Russians in the first place, was thus for all intents and purposes again isolated, except for its somewhat improved—although still tenuous—relationship with Syria, to whom it had sent extensive military aid during the war.

A far more serious problem for the Soviet leaders after the war lay in Egypt, where Soviet influence, partially restored by massive shipments of military equipment, including, at the end of the war, SCUD ground-to-ground missiles,[34] had again begun to erode. By the end of the war the primary alignment in the Arab world was the Egyptian-Saudi Arabian alliance, with the Egyptians supplying the military power and the Saudi Arabians the oil leverage. Kissinger clearly recognized this when he helped negotiate the cease-fire, thereby saving Sadat from probable political ruin as his armies seemed to be on the verge of being overrun by the Israelis. Kissinger also probably remembered Sadat's past efforts to improve relations with the West and his evident dislike for the Russians, whom he had openly opposed on a number of occasions since becoming Egypt's president in October 1970. Thus, Kissinger may have decided that he had a unique opportunity to win over Egypt—and perhaps the rest of the Arab world as well (or at least the oil-rich states)—by forcing the Israelis to accept a cease-fire and then working out an exchange of prisoners (November 7) and finally a complete disengagement agreement (January 18), which resulted in Israel's withdrawal not only from its salient near Cairo, but also from the east bank of the Suez Canal, enabling the Egyptians to control both banks of the canal for the first time since 1967. In the process Kissinger managed to secure the reestablishment of diplomatic relations between the United States and Egypt. In fact, relations between Egypt and the United States warmed up so rapidly that there soon began a steady stream of American businessmen to Egypt, which under Sadat's economic policies provided a warm haven for foreign investments. This process culminated in the visit to Cairo of David Rockefeller, Chairman of the Chase Manhattan Bank, which then announced it was planning to open a string of "full-service banks" in Egypt.[35] Not only had Kissinger managed to do this all by himself—leaving out the Russians who had provided the weaponry to enable the Arabs to go to war in the first place—but he also managed to secure Sadat's help in lifting the Arab oil embargo, thus splitting the "anti-imperialist Arab unity" the Russians had worked so diligently to maintain.

As might be expected, the Soviet leadership was far from happy with these developments. *Pravda* articles on November 10 and 16 implicitly criticized Sadat for accepting the Kissinger-mediated agreement without following the Soviet lead in demanding an Israeli withdrawal to the cease-fire lines of October 22. As American influence in Egypt began to rise despite the Soviet warnings, the Russian leaders sought to counter this by deepening their relationship with the Palestine Liberation Organization—one of the most anti-American forces in the Middle East—by floating a "trial balloon" for the establishment of a Palestinian state. Thus, a joint communique issued with visiting Yugoslav leader Josef Tito that was published on the front page of *Pravda* on November 16, stated: "The lawful *national* rights of the Palestinian Refugees must be implemented as part of a peace settlement."[36] Five days later Canadian Foreign Minister Mitchell Sharp commented in a press conference after conferring with Soviet leaders that the USSR would give the Palestinians strong support.[37] Then, on October 22, Arab diplomats in Moscow stated that a PLO delegation had met with Politburo members "at a very high level."[38] This burst of Soviet activity on behalf of the Palestinians came just before the Arab summit conference in Algiers called by Sadat to coordinate Arab strategy, and helped enhance the stature of the PLO at the conference, which recognized the PLO as the "sole legitimate representative" of the Palestinian people. In thus giving stronger backing to the Palestinians than ever before, it appeared as if the Soviet goal—in addition to countering the Egyptian-American rapprochement—was to establish a Palestinian state on the West Bank of the Jordan river and in the Gaza Strip. These areas were occupied by Israel since the June 1967 war; earlier they had been administered by Jordan (the West Bank) and Egypt (the Gaza Strip) after the two Arab states had occupied the territories during the 1948-49 Arab-Israeli war (instead of allowing them to be the basis of a Palestinian Arab state as the UN Resolution of November 1947 had decreed). It would appear that the Russians worked for the establishment of a Palestinian state (they had to convince many Palestinians as well as the Western powers) not only to defuse the Arab-Israeli conflict (if this was their aim at all), but also to secure another area in the Middle East where they could exercise influence, along with South Yemen, Iraq, Syria, and, to a lesser degree, Egypt, where their influence was declining. It may have also been Soviet reasoning that the emplacement of a pro-Soviet regime in the midst of such pro-Western states as Israel, Jordan, and Lebanon would serve to weaken further the position of the United States in the region, while strengthening that of the USSR.

In addition to consolidating their relations with the Palestinians, the Soviet leaders sought to offset the growing Egyptian-American rapprochement by emphasizing the direct U.S. military threat against the Arabs and continued

American support of Israel, while at the same time urging the Arabs to maintain their "anti-imperialist" unity. Thus, in greeting the Arab summit conference that took place in late November, the Soviet leadership stated:

> At the present time the matter of regulating the Near East conflict is entering a practical and very crucial stage. Now, as never before, the fate of peace in the Near East is largely dependent on the coordinated policy of the Arab states and on the further strengthening of their solidarity and unity of action with other peace-loving forces.[39]

Similarly, *Pravda* on December 4 displayed satisfaction with the results of the Arab summit:

> The conference in Algiers reflected the increased degree of unity which was tempered and passed a rigorous test during the October 1973 war. This unity is founded on anti-imperialism and serves the just cause for which the Arab countries' peoples are fighting. . . .
> The Soviet Union's position received a high evaluation at the conference in Algiers. The participants in the conference expressed profound satisfaction with the political and military assistance that the Soviet Union and the other socialist states have rendered the Arab countries and expressed the desire to develop Arab-Soviet cooperation.[40]

While the Russians were being praised for their support at the Algiers conference, the Egyptians were going ahead with their plan announced on December 9 to give the American Bechtel Company the contract to build the Suez to Mediterranean oil pipeline that had long been under discussion. The investment was to be jointly financed by Kuwait and Saudi Arabia—the very nations that had placed the embargo on oil to the United States.[41] Three days later *Pravda* warned the Arabs that American naval maneuvers in the Indian Ocean were aimed against them:

> The appearance of ships of the US Seventh Fleet off the southern coast of the Arabian Peninsula arouses grave anxiety in a number of Asian countries located in immediate proximity to the Indian Ocean. According to reports from the France-Presse wire services, Israeli troops "based on some islands in the Red Sea" i.e. approximately in the same locality—are also on the move. . . .
> At a time when a tense situation persists in the Near East, the appearance of the Seventh Fleet off the coasts of the Arab states looks like a maneuver having nothing to do with the creation of conditions conducive to a peaceful settlement in the Near East. . . . The Seventh Fleet . . . as is known, took a most active part in the aggressive war against the Vietnamese people.[42]

The Soviet Union continued to urge Arab unity as the first Arab-Israeli peace conference in 24 years opened in Geneva on December 22. The conference, however, was boycotted by the Syrians, who claimed that Israel's interests would be served by the conference and that the United States and Israel were engaged in "maneuvers that would lead us into an endless wilderness."[43] The fact that the USSR had strongly supported the conference—to insure Soviet participation in any peace settlement—made the Syrian remarks take on an anti-Soviet as well as an anti-American character. Nonetheless, despite the lack of Arab unity evidenced by the Syrian boycott, the Soviet Union championed the cause of the Arab states and the Palestinian Arabs at the conference and demanded the total withdrawal of Israeli troops to the 1967 prewar boundaries. Soviet Foreign Minister Gromyko, who represented the USSR at the conference, made a point of stating, however, that "the Soviet Union has no hostility to the state of Israel as such."[44] After several days of meetings, the Geneva conference adjourned for the Israeli elections. In the interim period, there were meetings of the Arab oil-producing countries and the Persian Gulf oil-producing countries, which took measures that the Russians greeted with satisfaction. The Persian Gulf oil-producing states more than doubled the "posted price" per barrel of crude oil—in effect, therefore, quadrupling the price they charged for it. This move was certain to aggravate the balance of payments problems of the West European states, thus further hampering both Common Market and NATO unity, as it appeared that the Western nations might have to engage in a trade war to pay for their oil imports.[45] Indeed, France broke Common Market unity on January 19, 1974, by its unilateral decision to float the franc, to help meet the crisis caused by the rise in oil prices.[46] The Russians also profited from the fact that, as a net exporter of oil, their hard-currency income would rise with the market price of oil they sold to the West European nations and Japan. The decision of the Arab oil producers to maintain their oil embargo against the United States was also warmly welcomed, although the *Izvestia* article discussing these developments urged the Arabs to go one step farther and nationalize the holdings of the Western oil companies, much as Iraq had done.[47]

The Soviet media continued its twin themes of the American threat to the Arab states and continued American support for Israel throughout the first part of January 1974. Israeli Defense Minister Moshe Dayan's visit to the United States in early January was described as a quest for more American arms,[48] while the Soviet media also played up United States Defense Secretary James Schlesinger's warning to the Arabs on January 7 that they risked the use of force against them if they carried their oil embargo too far.[49] Nonetheless, *Pravda* complained on January 6 of "attempts to sow discord between the Arab states and their true friends" while also taking the opportunity to blast Libya for "leaking oil" to the United States.

The Soviet leaders, however, were apparently caught by surprise by the Kissinger-arranged Israeli-Egyptian disengagement agreement on January 18, and the new Egyptian Foreign Minister Ismail Fahmy, who had clashed with the Russians in the past, had to make a hurried visit to Moscow immediately thereafter to explain the Egyptian position. The Russians put into *Pravda*'s description of the talks the assertion:

It was stressed that an important factor in the struggle for a just settlement in the Near East is the close coordination of the actions of the

Soviet Union and Egypt at all stages of this struggle including the work of the Near East Peace Conference and all the working groups which come of it.[50]

The Russians probably put this assertion in the description because Soviet-Egyptian coordination was anything but close. Meanwhile, the Russians were also warning the Arabs about U.S., West European, and Japanese plans to increase their investments in Arab countries, and about the "oil for technology" deals a number of West European states and Japan were in the process of signing with Arab states in an effort to assure themselves of a secure oil supply. As *Pravda* stated on January 20:

As the *Wall Street Journal* frankly writes, "a theory has even cropped up among entrepre[ne]urs which reasons that economic and political changes will come with the industrialization of Arab countries." In other words, economic considerations are interwoven with the hope that the influence of the dollar will lead to an "erosion" of Arab unity and a consolidation of the position of the Western powers clientele in the Near East.[51]

The fact that following the disengagement agreement Sadat began to urge the lifting of the embargo was a further blow to the Russians. *Pravda*, in a feature article by "commentator" on January 30, warned against the disengagement agreement leading to only a partial settlement of the Near East conflict:

It should be emphasized that the agreement on troop disengagement can be a positive step only if it is followed by other fundamental measures aimed at ensuring the withdrawal of Israeli troops from all occupied Arab territories and guaranteeing the legitimate rights of the Arab people of Palestine. Without the solution of these problems, which are cardinal to a Near East settlement, a lasting peace cannot be achieved, and the possibility of new military outbreaks, fraught with serious international convulsions, cannot be ruled out. *It can be said that the positive significance of the concluded agreement depends to a decisive extent on its linkage with other fundamental questions of a settlement. . . .*

. . . The question of the return of Syrian territory is just as acute as the question of the return of all other Arab territories occupied by Israel. The problem of troop disengagement as a first step in resolving the question of the return of these territories directly affects Syria as well. This is especially important in view of the fact that the ruling circles of *Israel and imperialist reaction persistently follow a line aimed at weakening the unity of the Arab countries.*[52] [emphasis added]

Yet this appeared to be the direction in which Middle Eastern events were moving. Even the decision by the United States to host a conference of energy-consuming nations did not serve to arrest the slow splintering of the facade of Arab unity. While the Russians hailed the decision of the mid-February Arab mini-summit meeting not to lift the embargo, an article in *New Times* about the Arab meeting clearly recognized the dilemma:

> In this intricate situation, the Arab press believes joint Arab action and co-ordinated Arab policies are of the utmost importance. All the more so since the Israeli militarists, who still count on being able to avoid withdrawing from occupied Arab territories, are trying to set the Arab countries at loggerheads with one other. . . . Further, the fomenting of Arab differences has a definite place in the designs of the Western oil monopolies, who are out to use the present energy crisis to preserve and even multiply the profits derived from Middle East oil.[53]

By this time, however, it appeared to be only a matter of time until the embargo was lifted, since now Sheikh Yamani as well as Sadat spoke openly about lifting it. In this atmosphere Kissinger made yet another journey to the Middle East at the end of February, this time shuttling back and forth between Damascus and Jerusalem and procuring from the Syrian leaders the list of Israeli prisoners of war the Israelis had demanded as a precondition for talks with Syria. At this point it appeared that once again Kissinger would be able to pull off another diplomatic coup. This, apparently, was too much for the Russians. Having seen the United States replace the USSR as the leading foreign influence in Egypt—however temporarily—the Russian leaders had no desire to see the process repeat itself in Syria. Consequently, Gromyko, who had just paid a surprise visit to Cairo (and the joint communique that followed his visit revealed just how far the Soviet position in Egypt had deteriorated[54]), followed Kissinger to Damascus. The Soviet-Syrian communique issued upon Gromyko's departure was far more bellicose than the Soviet-Egyptian communique and demanded a fixed timetable for Israeli withdrawal from all occupied territory, threatening a "new eruption" of war that would bring about "a threat to peace and security in the Middle East and throughout the world" if Arab demands were not met.[55] Strengthened by new shipments of Soviet arms, and encouraged by Soviet support, the Syrian regime of Hafiz Assad, less willing (or able) to make peace with Israel than Egypt, upon Gromyko's departure began a war of attrition against Israeli positions in the Golan Heights.

Apparently, the Soviet and Syrian leaders hoped that by heating up the conflict in the Golan Heights (the war of attrition included artillery, tank, and air battles) they would be able to prevent the oil-rich states from lifting the oil embargo against the United States. While Syria stepped up its level of fighting, the Soviet Union urged the Arab states in very strong terms to maintain their oil embargo. Thus, on March 12 Radio Moscow broadcast:

> If today some Arab leaders are ready to surrender in the face of American pressure and lift the ban on oil before the demands (for a total Israeli withdrawal) are fulfilled, they are challenging the whole Arab world and the progressive forces of the entire world which insist on the continued use of the oil weapon.[56]

While urging continuation of the oil weapon, the Soviet media also belittled Kissinger's mediation efforts, with *Pravda* on March 17 calling them "a mountain that gave birth to a mouse." Nonetheless, despite Syria's war of attrition and the Soviet campaign to maintain the oil embargo, Kissinger's diplomatic efforts were successful. On March 19 the oil embargo against the United States was lifted by the major-oil-producing Arab states, although as a sop to the Syrians, Algeria stated that it would reexamine its embargo policy on June 1. In any case, Arab unity on the oil embargo was clearly broken as Libya and Syria refused to go along with the majority decision to lift the embargo.

The termination of the oil embargo can be considered a significant defeat for Soviet diplomacy in the Middle East. The Soviet leadership had come out strongly for the maintenance of the oil embargo as a means of keeping the Arab world unified against the United States, and the USSR had greatly profited from the disarray in both NATO and the EEC caused by the embargo.[57] Egypt's decision to support an end to the embargo—despite all the aid the USSR had given Egypt before and during the October war—was yet another indication of the sharp diminution of Soviet influence in Egypt and the corresponding rise in American influence. Consequently, following the termination of the oil embargo, the Soviet leadership once again reconsidered its Middle East policies in an effort to halt the pro-American trend that was emerging in the region.

THE ISRAELI-SYRIAN DISENGAGEMENT AGREEMENT

The Soviet response to the termination of the oil embargo was threefold. In the first place, the Soviet leadership launched a public attack on Sadat in an effort to isolate him both inside Egypt and from other Arab leaders. Second, the USSR stepped up support to both Syria and Iraq lest the two clients of the Soviet Union be attracted to the Egyptian-Saudi Arabian alignment, which, backed by the United States, held out the promise of both economic and technological assistance. Finally, the USSR moved to improve relations with Libya, its erstwhile Middle East enemy, which moved closer to the Soviet Union in response to the Egyptian-American rapprochement. In pursuing these policies, however, the Soviet leadership was careful to maintain contact with the United States while Kissinger was working for a Syrian-Israeli troop disengagement. In pursuing this policy, the Russians sought both to maintain the semblance of detente and also to avoid the repetition of their earlier experience when Kissinger had worked out an Egyptian-Israeli disengagement without the participation of the Soviet Union.

Soviet-Egyptian relations began to deteriorate very rapidly following the end of the oil embargo. Just as in 1971 when Sadat had refused to support Soviet policy in the Sudan, here again he had strongly opposed a major Soviet Middle Eastern policy, despite all the economic and military aid that the Soviet Union had given Egypt. The USSR retaliated against Sadat for his opposition on the embargo issue by branding him a traitor to Nasser's heritage—an obvious attempt to undermine Sadat's position among the Egyptian public and among Egyptian elites who still revered Nasser's memory.[58] At the same time the Soviet leaders voiced a great deal of concern as to the erosion of their position in Egypt. The editor-in-chief of *New Times*, Pavel Naumov, in describing his visit to Egypt in late March, stated: "What is in question is the country's [Egypt's] future."[59]

Sadat, however, was not cowed by the Soviet attacks and replied in kind by charging the Soviet ambassador, Vladimir Vinogradov, with lying to him on the first day of the war about Syria's desire for an immediate cease-fire.[60] He followed up this charge in a major speech on April 3 in which he stated that he had expelled the Russians in July 1972 because they had defaulted on promised arms deliveries to Egypt.[61] Then, on April 18, Soviet-Egyptian relations hit a new low when Sadat announced his decision to cease relying exclusively on the Soviet Union for arms.[62] The Egyptian leader, in a New York *Times* interview three days later, which was widely reprinted in the Egyptian press, asked the United States to supply Egypt with arms because the USSR had used the supply of weapons and ammunition as an "instrument of policy leverage" to influence Egyptian actions."[63] While the United States was not yet willing to commit itself to arms sales to Egypt, U.S. officials had discussed loans of up to $250 million as a means of improving Egyptian-American relations.[64] In pursuing this policy of improving relations with the United States, Sadat was attempting to "drive a wedge" between the United States and Israel, while at the same time aiding the Egyptian economy. For his part, Kissinger, in offering Egypt economic aid, was trying to raise the threshold of any Egyptian decision to support Syria in its war of attrition against Israel.[65] While each side was approaching the improvement in relations from a different perspective and with different goals in mind, to many outside observers (including the Russians) it appeared by the end of April that the Egyptian-American rapprochement was turning into an alignment. Perhaps in an effort to prevent this new alignment from solidifying, Brezhnev sent Sadat what the Egyptian leader termed a "conciliatory note" on April 24, an action that Sadat reciprocated two days later.[66]

Meanwhile, despite two Palestinian terrorist attacks against Israeli settlements at Kiryat Shemona (April 12) and Maalot (May 15), it appeared by the latter part of May that the Israeli-Syrian disengagement negotiations, mediated by Kissinger, might well meet with success. Consequently, the Soviet leadership took a more positive posture toward Egypt, whose prestige in the Arab world was sure to rise if the Syrians followed the Egyptian lead in working out a disengagement settlement. On May 19, with the third anniversary of the Soviet-Egyptian treaty approaching, Brezhnev sent a new ambassador to Egypt bearing a friendly message for Sadat[67], and two days later Arab diplomats announced that the Soviet Union had resumed arms shipments to Egypt.[68] Soviet press comment on the treaty's anniversary was far more limited than in the past two anniversaries, however, and a *New Times* article commemorating the occasion implicitly acknowledged Soviet concern over the deepening American involvement in Egypt:

> The Soviet-Egyptian Treaty of Friendship and Cooperation is subjected to unceasing attacks by forces that would undermine Soviet-Egyptian friendship and thereby deprive the Arabs of support in their just struggle.[69]

While welcoming the limited rapprochement that had occurred with the USSR by the end of May, Sadat was busy seeking other sources of military and economic assistance. In addition to improving relations with the United States,

Egypt hosted a meeting of Arab defense and foreign ministers on May 20 in which a decision was taken to establish a cooperative Arab arms industry with Egypt the site of the initial projects. Significantly, Iraq, the USSR's closest ally in the Arab world, boycotted the conference; Libya, whose premier had just visited the Soviet Union, sent only a low-level delegation.[70] In addition to planning this alternate source of weaponry, in case the USSR should again cut off or limit arms deliveries, or if the desired weapons could not be purchased in the United States or Western Europe, Sadat also acquired an additional source of developmental capital in May when Iran signed a $750-million loan agreement with Egypt.[71] While the arms industry would take years to develop, and the Iranian loan, while highly welcome, could meet only a fraction of Egypt's staggering economic needs, these two actions nonetheless gave Sadat bargaining room in his relations with both the Soviet Union and the United States. By the end of May, the Soviet leaders found Sadat less dependent than before the October war on Soviet military and economic aid.

While Sadat's decision to help end the Arab oil embargo against the United States led to a sharp deterioration in Soviet-Egyptian relations, Libyan leader Mu'ammar Kaddafi, who like the Russians opposed an end to the oil embargo, drew closer to the USSR. In many ways Libya's turn to the Soviet Union resembled that of Iraq in 1972. Isolated regionally, Kaddafi was on poor terms not only with Sadat, who had declined Libya's merger offer and allied with King Faisal, one of Kaddafi's chief Arab enemies,[72] but also with Sudanese Premier Jaafar Nimeri, who accused Kaddafi of a number of subversive plots against his regime.[73] To make matters worse for Kaddafi, even his relations with the leaders of fellow Arab radical Algeria were severely strained. Isolated in North Africa as well as throughout most of the Arab world, and angry at Egypt's move toward the United States, Libya turned to the Soviet Union for support, despite the fact that Kaddafi had earlier attacked the USSR in the strongest terms as an "imperialist power." The rapprochement began on April 7 with a two-hour meeting in Paris between Libya's new premier, Abdul Jalloud (Kaddafi had given up the premiership while retaining overall direction of Libya's foreign and domestic policies), and Soviet President Nikolai Podgorny when the two men were in the French capital to attend French President George Pompidou's funeral.[74] *New Times* correspondent Aleksei Zlatorunsky helped set the tone for an improvement in Soviet-Libyan relations in early May with a generally sympathetic article describing Libya's development since its 1969 revolution. The article praised Libya's "clear-cut anti-imperialist stand" and its "vigorous support for the African forces of National Liberation," although Zlatorunsky also took the Libyan leadership to task for "rash actions" in behalf of Arab unity.[75] Libya's past hostility toward the Soviet Union was not totally overlooked either as Zlatorunsky pointedly stated:

> The fact also remains that Libya's anti-imperialist, and on the whole progressive position has been weakened by occasional anti-communist sallies on the part of certain Libyan leaders and press organs.[76]

In sum, however, the article gave a positive view of Libyan development, and the Soviet correspondent concluded his article by offering Libya Soviet support:

We wish the Libyan people success on the hard road of struggle to strengthen national independence and progress. In this struggle they can rely on the support of the socialist states, the natural allies of all national-democratic forces.[77]

It appears as if the Libyan leaders were eager to take up the Soviet offer of support, because soon after the *New Times* article appeared Libyan Premier Jalloud arrived in Moscow seeking Soviet aid. In welcoming the Libyan leader at a dinner given in his honor, Soviet Premier Kosygin emphasized the Soviet Union's willingness to forget the past differences between the two countries in the interest of working together in the future:

If we were to compare that which unites Libya and the Soviet Union to those things on which our views do not coincide, there would be no doubt that the preponderance would fall on the side of that which unites us. This means, above all, the identity or closeness of our position in the struggle against imperialism and colonialism, for the reconstruction of international relations on a just, democratic basis and for the affirmation of and respect for the right of peoples to independent development, including sovereignty over their own natural resources and the implementation of progressive social and economic transformation. . . . As far as differences in views are concerned, evidently they are largely in the field of ideology. But we have never wanted to impose our ideology on others.[78]

Kosygin went on to emphasize Soviet support of the Arab cause and opposition to United States diplomatic efforts in the Middle East:

The Soviet Union condemns the policy of aggression that Israel is pursuing, with the support of outside imperialist forces, and it believes that there can be no lasting and just peace in the Near East without the withdrawal of Israeli troops from all Arab territory occupied in 1967 and later and without guaranteeing the legitimate national rights of the Arab people of Palestine. Any agreements on troop disengagement must be regarded as preliminary steps on the road to an overall settlement and must be followed by other measures to implement the well-known UN Security Council resolutions.

    We emphasize this aspect of the matter because the plans of the aggressor and its protectors to substitute some sort of half measures that create only a semblance of detente in the Near East for an all-encompassing Near East settlement have come to light recently.[79]

In concluding his discussion of Soviet policy in the Middle East, Kosygin stated that he hoped the development of Soviet-Libyan relations would serve the interest of Arab solidarity in their struggle against Israel "on an anti-Imperialist basis."[80]

    In his speech in reply, Abdul Jalloud, in a manner reminiscent of Iraqi Vice President Saddam Hussein's speech of February 1972, emphasized Libya's isolation and need for Soviet support:

We would like to emphasize, in all sincerity, that we are now under pressure from imperialist and reactionary forces. We would like all forces of progress and truly revolutionary forces to come out against this situation, under cover of which the rights and positions that the progressive forces in our region have won as a result of long struggle are being infringed and nullified.[81]

While the Libyan delegation had come to Moscow primarily for political and military support, the Soviet leaders saw in the visit not only a useful opportunity to counter Sadat's move toward the United States, but also a means of strengthening the Soviet economy. In his speech Kosygin also called for an agreement to arrange Soviet-Libyan trade on a long-term basis, and the final communique issued at the conclusion of Jalloud's visit announced the establishment of a Soviet-Libyan intergovernmental commission for this purpose.[82] In addition, the two sides pledged to develop "the highest possible mutually advantageous trade turnover."[83] In calling for a sharp increase in trade, the Soviet leaders may have hoped to gain access to Libya's large hard-currency reserves—a development that would enable the Soviet Union to step up its purchases on Western markets.[84] In addition, the Russians may have hoped to exchange Soviet technology and equipment for Libyan oil, which could be resold on Western markets or used to fulfill the USSR's own increasing domestic oil needs.[85]

Despite the general cordiality of Jalloud's visit, differences remained, and the final communique reported the talks as having taken place "in a spirit of frankness and mutual understanding."[86] Nonetheless, Soviet-Libyan relations had markedly improved over the prewar period when mutual hostility was their primary characteristic. Soviet-Libyan cooperation on Middle Eastern affairs had reached the point by May that Libyan-financed newspapers in Beirut printed Soviet attacks on Sadat's policies.[87]

While Soviet-Libyan cooperation had now become a factor in Middle East politics, the Soviet leadership did not neglect its ties with Iraq, which had been its leading Middle Eastern partner since 1972. Although weakened by its war with the Kurds and its continual confrontation with Iran, Iraq provided a useful center for anti-Western and anti-Egyptian propaganda.[88] The most pressing issue for the Iraqi leaders at this time was their confrontation with the Kurds. The Soviet leadership, faced by the defection of Egypt, now apparently pledged Soviet military support for a massive Iraqi drive against the Kurds—despite the fact that such a policy might trigger a war between Iraq and Iran—in return for continued Iraqi support of Soviet positions on the larger Middle Eastern issues. A trip to Moscow by Iraqi Vice President Saddam Hussein at the end of February was used by the Soviet leadership to demonstrate Arab cooperation with the USSR, and the communique issued at the end of his visit (and published on *Pravda*'s front page) stated:

The two sides believe that the Arab states' solidarity on an anti-imperialist basis and the consolidation of their cooperation with the Soviet Union and other countries of the socialist commonwealth is a major condition for the success of the Arab peoples' struggle against Israeli aggression and for the strengthening of their national independence and economic and social progress.[89]

On March 14, the date on which the Iraqi government's "autonomy" plan for the Kurds was due to come into effect, *Pravda* came out in full support of the Iraqi government. In describing the autonomy agreement and Kurdish leader Mustafa Barzani's opposition to it, *Pravda* columnist Pavel Demchenko stated:

The obstacles to a resolution of the Kurdish question still have not been overcome. Foreign agents are still interfering in Kurdish affairs. The activity of the rightist elements which have penetrated the Kurdish Democratic Party as a result of its class heterogeneity and which are trying to arouse separatist sentiments, is becoming more evident.[90]

As the Kurdish opposition mounted, the Iraqi leaders decided to mount a major offensive against the Kurds to try to end the Kurdish separatist threat (and the danger to the Kirkuk oil fields claimed by the Kurds) once and for all. Possibly to inspect Iraqi preparations for this offensive, Soviet Defense Minister Grechko paid a visit to Iraq between March 23 and 25 for what *Pravda* reported as "a detailed discussion of questions relating to the present state and future development of Soviet-Iraqi cooperation in the military and other spheres."[91]

As the Iraqi government began to mount its offensive against the Kurds in April, *Pravda* took a harder line than ever before against them, while linking the Kurdish opposition to "imperailist forces":

According to foreign press reports, military operations have begun between the Kurds and government troops in the northern regions of Iraq. The Kurdish leaders have refused to acknowledge the law of autonomy of the Kurds, issued by the Iraqi government in March of this year, although it guarantees the 2,000,000 Kurds in Iraq democratic national and social rights within the framework of the Iraqi Republic.

Reports indicate that in making this decision, the Kurdish leaders were not free from interference by imperialist and other reactionary forces who are trying to sow discord between the Arab and Kurdish populations of Iraq and weaken the progressive regime in that country. For these purposes they are supplying the Kurdish extremists with weapons and ammunition and considerable financial support. The foreign "benefactors" are inciting those elements among the Kurdish leadership that oppose progressive changes in Iraq.[92]

Echoing a similar theme, a *New Times* article on Iraq in the middle of May took the opportunity to tie the Kurdish rebellion to the growing American activity in the Middle East:

While exerting pressure on Egypt, Syria and South Yemen, certain quarters in Washington and the Arab reactionaries are at the same time searching for allies inside the progressive Middle East countries. In Iraq they have pinned their hopes on the right-wing elements among the Kurds.[93]

Thus, the Iraqi government had embarked on a full-scale offensive against the Kurds, supported by the USSR, although the offensive raised the possibility of war between Iraq and Iran—an eventuality clearly not desired by the Soviet leadership.[94]

While the Soviet leaders worked to improve relations with Libya and solidify their ties with Iraq, the central Soviet concern during the postembargo period was on their relations with Syria. The Soviet leaders were clearly concerned that Syria might follow Egypt's example and move toward the West in return for economic and technical aid. The Syrian government's decision on March 13 to lift restrictions on the movement of private capital in and out of Syria and to permit the Syrian private sector to sign loan agreements with foreign investors must have added to the Soviet concern.[95] By supporting Syria in its war of attrition against Israel, the Soviet leaders hoped to avert a Syrian turn to the West while at the same time isolating Sadat as the only Arab leader to have reached an agreement with Israel. In addition, the Soviet leadership may have entertained the hope that should fighting intensify sufficiently, the Arab oil-producing states might be forced by Arab public opinion to reimpose the oil embargo, and Sadat himself might be forced to return to war.[96] Yet in pursuing their policy of encouraging Syrian belligerence, the Soviet leaders had to toe a very narrow diplomatic line. A new summit meeting with the United States was on the horizon, and important strategic arms limitation issues between the two superpowers were under active consideration. In addition, the Soviet Union's relations with China had taken another turn for the worse as the Chinese government refused to return the crew of a Soviet helicopter that had crashed on Chinese territory.[97] Consequently, the Soviet leaders adopted a policy of support for Syrian belligerency while at the same time maintaining close contact with Kissinger's mediation efforts. This dual policy would underscore Soviet support for the Arab cause while also enabling the Soviet leadership to claim a share of the credit should Kissinger succeed in persuading the Syrians and Israelis to accept a disengagement agreement. In addition, a series of meetings between Kissinger and top Soviet leaders would help create a positive atmosphere for the convening of a summit conference between Nixon and Brezhnev.

The first high-level Soviet-American meeting after the lifting of the oil embargo came on March 29 when Kissinger journeyed to Moscow for talks with the Soviet leadership. While strategic arms issues were the main topic of consideration—and Kissinger later reported that no "conceptual breakthroughs" had been reached—the two superpowers also discussed the Middle East situation. The final communique however, stated only that the "two sides would make efforts to promote the solution of the key questions of a Near East settlement."[98] Interestingly enough, while Western press reports of Kissinger's talks in Moscow portrayed them as being relatively unsuccessful, the Soviet media challenged this interpretation. Thus, on March 30, *Izvestia* commented:

The mood and content of the talks did not at all correspond to the pessimistic accompaniment that certain Western media provided for H. Kissinger's mission.[99]

While making this gesture toward Soviet-American relations, the Soviet leaders went out of their way to emphasize their support for Syrian President Hafiz Assad during his visit to Moscow in mid-April. Assad was met at the Moscow airport by all three of the primary Soviet leaders (Brezhnev, Kosygin, and Podgorny), and the Syrian president's visit received major front-page coverage in both *Pravda* and *Izvestia*. In his dinner speech welcoming Assad, Brezhnev pointedly attacked Kissinger's diplomatic efforts in the Middle East:

Against the background of reduced tensions, the aggressors and their protectors may once again attempt to evade a fundamental all-inclusive solution to the [Middle East] problem. It is by no means happenstance that recently "ersatz plans" as I would call them for a Near East settlement have been launched.[100]

Following five days of talks, which the final communique described as taking place in an atmosphere "of frankness and mutual understanding," the Soviet leadership agreed to "further strengthen" Syria's defense capacity and stated once again that Syria had a "lawful inalienable right" to use "all effective means to free its occupied lands." And, to underline the Soviet desire to play a role in the peace talks, the joint communique stated:

The Syrian side reemphasized the importance of the Soviet Union's participation in all stages and in all areas of a settlement aimed at establishing a just and lasting peace in the Near East.[101]

Soviet attention switched back to the United States at the end of April when Gromyko met with Kissinger in Geneva as the American Secretary of State was en route to the Middle East for further negotiations with Syria and Israel. While the main topic of the talks was Nixon's forthcoming visit to Moscow, for which no date had been set, *Pravda* also reported that the two leaders

exchanged opinions concerning the current situation in the talks on the Near East settlement and concerning the next stage of these talks. The two sides agreed to exert their influence in favor of a positive outcome of the talks and to maintain close contact with each other while striving to coordinate their actions in the interests of a peaceful settlement in the region.[102]

Kissinger, however, gave a far less optimistic view of the talks, stating only that in regard to his forthcoming mediation efforts, "I expect we'll have Soviet understanding, and I hope cooperation."[103]

Meanwhile, however, opposition to the proposed Nixon trip to Moscow was growing in the United States. Arguing that the United States had been cheated in its wheat deal with the Soviet Union, that the United States had been placed at a disadvantage by the SALT I agreement, and that the Soviet Union had proven itself an unworthy partner because of its aid to the Arabs during the October war and its support of the oil embargo, a growing number of prominent Americans opposed a new summit. *Pravda*'s political commentator Yuri Zhukov, in acknowledging this opposition, claimed it was organized by a "dirty coalition of reactionary forces made up of imperialist circles, the American military-industrial complex, West German revanchists, NATO generals, and Zionists and adventurers of every stripe."[104] At the same time, Zhukov hailed the forces in the world working for detente, lavishing particular praise on West German Chancellor Willy Brandt, and stating that Kissinger's meetings with Brezhnev and Gromyko "inspired confidence that the forthcoming Soviet-American summit talks will be a new step forward in making the process of detente irreversible."[105]

Gromyko met Kissinger yet another time on May 7 as the Soviet leadership continued to demonstrate its desire to remain closely involved with the disengagement talks while also fostering detente. For his part, Kissinger humored the Soviet desire, evidently hoping that the frequent meetings would serve to limit Soviet obstructionism of a peaceful settlement. Only two days later, however, Soviet concern about detente must have been sharply reinforced when West German Chancellor Brandt was forced to resign over a spy scandal involving East Germany. At this point, with both Pompidou and Brandt having departed from the European political scene, and with a Watergate-weakened Nixon under increasing attack by the opponents of detente in the United States, Brezhnev may have seen the whole structure of his detente policy towards the West in danger of collapse. The Soviet leader may have decided that overt obstructionism to a Syrian-Israeli disengagement agreement on American terms was becoming too great a threat to Soviet-American relations. This feeling may have been reinforced by the fact that despite two bloody Palestinian terrorist attacks on Israeli settlements, the latter killing 24 Israeli school children at Maalot on May 15, Kissinger had nonetheless managed to work out the outlines of an agreement by the latter part of May. Consequently, as the Syrians and Israelis were in the process of ironing out the last details of their agreement on May 29, Gromyko made yet another visit to Damascus, hoping to salvage some prestige for the USSR from the American-mediated agreement. Gromyko received from the Syrian government an acknowledgement of the USSR's right to participate in all stages of a peace settlement, much as Assad had given the Russians during his April visit to Moscow.[106] In addition, perhaps as an additional sop to the Soviet leadership—which in reality had played little role in the negotiations and which could well have been afraid that Syria, tempted by promises of American aid, might follow Egypt into the American camp—the joint communique issued upon the conclusion of Gromyko's visit stated:

> The Soviet Union and the Syrian Arab Republic affirm the durability of the relations that have been established between them and the durability of the friendship between the peoples of the two countries, and they declare that *they will let no one disturb these relations and this friendship.*[107] [emphasis added]

Nonetheless, it is clear that the Soviet leaders were worried about just such an eventuality. *New Times* correspondent Alexander Ignatov, in describing the situation in Syria following the disengagement agreement, used much the same terms Pavel Naumov had used two months before in describing Egypt. The Soviet journalist commented that despite the 1966 Ba'ath revolution, the "internal struggle in Syria" between those advocating the private sector and a Western orientation and those advocating promotion of the state sector and stronger ties with the Soviet Union "is still going on."[108]

In general, Soviet comment on the Syrian-Israeli disengagement agreement, which returned to Syria all the land it had lost in the 1973 war as well as the city of Kuneitra lost in 1967, stressed two main points: that the USSR had played a major role in bringing about the agreement, and that it was only the first step toward a much more comprehensive settlement. *New Times* associate editor Dmitry Volsky, in a review of the agreement, also took the opportunity to warn the Arabs that it was not in their interest to have the USSR excluded from the peace negotiations:

> Certain quarters continue their efforts to discredit the Soviet Union's Middle East policy. There are obviously some who would like nothing better than to "squeeze out" the Soviet Union and leave the Arab countries to face alone the combined forces of Zionism and Imperialism.[109]

The Syrian-Israeli disengagement agreement ended the period of direct military confrontation between Israel and the Arab states dating back to the October war, although Palestinian terrorist attacks continued to plague the Israelis. The threat of renewed warfare, for the time being at least, had receded as both sides began to concentrate on diplomatic preparations for a renewal of the Geneva peace conference. In this atmosphere the United States set the date for Nixon's visit to the USSR—indeed, a Syrian-Israeli disengagement agreement may well have been the price exacted by Kissinger for the visit—and the Soviet leadership could perhaps hope that the momentum toward "irreversible detente," interrupted by the October war, had now been restored. Nevertheless, as a result of the disengagement agreement, American prestige rose sharply in the Arab world, and it appeared to many observers that the United States was in the process of replacing the Soviet Union as the dominant foreign influence among the Arabs, a view that was to be reinforced by Nixon's triumphant tour of the Middle East in mid-June.[110]

SOVIET POLICY UP TO THE VLADIVOSTOK SUMMIT

Before his scheduled visit to the Soviet Union on June 27, U.S. President Richard Nixon set out on a multination tour of the Middle East to reap the political benefits of the disengagement agreement so painfully negotiated by his Secretary of State. Kissinger, before the Nixon trip, in an apparent effort to limit Soviet concern over the rising American prestige in the area, had stated in a press conference: "We have no intention of trying to eliminate Soviet influence in the Middle East. We are not even in a position to do so."[111] However, it is doubtful that the Soviet leaders were persuaded by this statement. In their "zero-sum" view of Middle Eastern influence they were quite concerned that the sharp rise in American prestige in the region meant a concomitant drop in Soviet influence. In addition, they might even have considered Kissinger's statement a bit naive—if they really believed it—since they had long been trying to eliminate Western influence from the Middle East. In any case Nixon received a hero's welcome in Egypt as the man who had forced the Israelis to withdraw from the Suez Canal. And he received a warm welcome in Syria, where American aid in getting Israel to withdraw not only from its gains in the 1973 war but also from the city of Kuneitra, which had been captured in 1967, was highly praised. During Nixon's visit to Damascus, diplomatic relations between Syria and the United States were restored. The Soviet leadership could not have been too happy with Syrian Deputy Premier Muhammed Hazdar's statement on June 20 that Syria was ready for "an open-minded dialogue with any foreign capital that wants to participate in Syria's development."[112]

During his trip Nixon signed a large number of economic and technical agreements with Arab leaders, the most important of which was a pledge of American assistance in the development of atomic energy in Egypt.[113] Following Nixon's visit American prestige rose to a new high in the Arab world and the Soviet leaders were clearly concerned about this unwelcome trend. Soviet reporting of Nixon's Middle East trip, as might be expected, downplayed its significance. Thus, before Nixon's departure, Dmitry Volsky, after taking the New York *Times* to task for "wishful thinking" in its description of the disengagement agreement as leading to "dramatic shifts in the American position in the Arab world," may have engaged in a bit of wishful thinking himself in stating that the Arab states "are sufficiently mature politically to take sober stock of the lessons of the recent past and the modifications the USA is obliged to introduce into its Middle East policy."[114] Volsky also reminded the Arabs that the United States remained Israel's main supporter as well as a direct military threat to the Arabs itself because of its plans to construct a military base on Diego Garcia, which was termed a "spearhead against the southern fringe of the Arab world."[115] *Pravda*, in describing Nixon's trip on June 16, echoed many of the same concerns:

> Reactionary bourgeois propaganda is now trying in every way possible to minimize the role of the Soviet Union in the Near East settlement. The right wing press maintains that the Soviet Union, so they say, does not have anything to do with this settlement, that U.S. policy allegedly will lead to the "elimination of Soviet influence in the Near East." . . .
>
> At the present time U.S. President Richard Nixon is traveling through the Near East. The United States has supported Israel for a long time, and this has undermined its relations with the Arabs. The Arabs have justifiably seen the United States as an accomplice of the Israeli aggressors. The new international climate makes it possible to change the nature of American-Arab relations, however, some "cold-war" advocates would like to place their own interpretation on the U.S. President's trip and use it in a campaign to undermine Arab-Soviet friendship. Such attempts are being suitably rebuffed by the Arabs themselves.[116]

Despite the deprecatory treatment accorded Nixon's visit to the Middle East, the Soviet media hailed the American president's visit to the Soviet Union at the end of June as proof that detente was working. While the primary Soviet interest in the summit was to achieve progress in the areas of strategic arms limitation and Soviet-American trade, Sino-Soviet and Sino-American relations could also not have been too far from the minds of the Soviet leaders. Just as Nixon was arriving in Moscow, U.S. Senator Henry Jackson, long a foe of the USSR and one of the leading Democratic candidates for president in 1976, was on his way to Peking at the invitation of the Chinese, who had timed his visit to coincide with the Nixon-Brezhnev talks.[117] The Moscow summit's emphasis was on trade and strategic arms, and the presence of Henry Jackson in Peking underlined the triangular relationship among the United States, the Soviet Union, and Communist China. However, the Middle East situation was not overlooked. In their final communique Brezhnev and Nixon stated, in regard to the Middle East:

Both sides believe that the removal of the danger of war and tension in the Middle East is a task of paramount importance and urgency, and therefore, the only alternative is the achievement, on the basis of Security Council Revolution 338 [which ended the October war] of a just and lasting peace settlement, in which should be taken into account the *legitimate interests of all peoples in the Middle East, including the Palestinian people*, and the right to existence of all states in the area.

As co-chairmen of the Geneva Peace Conference on the Middle East, the USSR and USA consider it important that the conference resume its work as soon as possible, *with the question of other participants from the Middle East Area* to be discussed at the conference. Both sides see the main purpose of the Geneva Peace Conference, the achievement of which they will promote in every way, as the establishment of a just and stable peace in the Middle East.

They agreed that the USSR and the USA will continue to remain in close touch with a view to coordinating the efforts of both countries toward a peaceful settlement in the Middle East.[118] [emphasis added]

Soviet propaganda highlighted the final communique's emphasis on the role of the Palestinians in a peace settlement in an effort to reinforce the USSR's relations with the Palestine Liberation Organization as a counter to Sadat's Westward move and the possibility of a similar move by Syria. Gromyko had met PLO leader Yasir Arafat on a regular basis during the negotiations for the Syrian-Israeli disengagement agreement, and these meetings had been given prominent attention in the Soviet press. Despite their military weakness, the Palestinian guerrilla organizations still enjoyed a great deal of popularity among the more radical Arab states and among large sectors of the Arab public as well. The Soviet leaders, just as after the October war, hoped that by increasing their ties to the Palestinians they would strengthen a major anti-Western force in the Middle East and reap the benefits of guerrilla popularity in the Arab world. For their part, the Palestinian Arabs were now in greater need of Soviet aid than ever before because the Israeli disengagement with Syria—which Palestinian terrorist groups had tried to prevent with attacks on the Israeli settlements of Kiryat Shemona and

Maalot—had left the Palestinian Arabs alone, at least for the time being, in their confrontation with Israel, despite pledges of support by Arab leaders.

Following the Syrian-Israeli disengagement agreement, the Palestinian National Council convened in Cairo to determine the direction of the Palestinian movement. The council was a quasiparliamentary organization composed of representatives from almost all the varied Palestinian organizations. After a great deal of debate, the Palestinian National Council worked out a ten-point program, not all of which was to the liking of the Soviet leadership.[119] In its first point, the program rejected participation in the Geneva conference under Resolution #242 so long as it dealt with the Palestinian Arabs only as a "refugee problem."[120] The second point stated that the PLO would struggle "by all means, foremost of which is armed struggle, to liberate Palestinian Land," while opposing any agreement with Israel.[121] Although disagreeing with the Palestinians' refusal to come to Geneva or deal with Israel, the Soviet leadership warmly welcomed the ninth point of the program, which stated that the PLO "will struggle to strengthen its solidarity with the socialist countries and the world forces of liberation and progress to foil all Zionist, reactionary and imperialist schemes."[122]

In commenting on the meeting of the Palestinian National Council, *New Times* correspondent Viktor Bukharov, citing Arab newspapers, indirectly rebuked the Palestinian guerrillas for rejecting participation in the Geneva conference and for other "extremist" positions.[123] In addition, Bukharov returned to an earlier Soviet theme, arguing that unity was a vital necessity for the Palestinian guerrilla organizations. While describing the Palestinian movement in generally favorable terms, Bukharov reserved his warmest praise for the decision of the PLO executive to admit representatives of the Palestinian National Front.[124] This was a guerrilla organization made up primarily of West Bank Arab Communists, who, once dormant, were now carrying out acts of sabotage against the Israelis. The admission of the Palestinian National Front into the PLO drew such warm Soviet praise because it served both as an excellent example of the success of the national front strategy the Soviet leaders had been urging on the Arab world and as a way they could influence the PLO from the inside.[125]

While the USSR was exhorting the Palestinian guerrilla organizations to unify, and warning them against "extremist positions," it was simultaneously exploiting the Israeli reprisal raids induced by guerrilla attacks to underline the "aggressive nature" of Israel and its ties to the United States. The Soviet goal in this maneuver was to prove to the Arabs that the Soviet Union was their only true friend. *Pravda*, on June 23, denounced Israeli attacks on the "peaceful inhabitants of Lebanon," comparing it to Nazi attacks during World War II, while branding as "absurd" Israel's justification for the attacks as responses to actions by the Palestinian guerrillas operating from Lebanon. Then, following an attack by Palestinian terrorists operating from the Lebanese port of Tyre against the Israeli coastal town of Nahariyah in late June (the attack was timed to coincide with Nixon's arrival in Moscow), the Israelis retaliated with attacks against three Lebanese ports in an effort to deter the Lebanese government from granting naval staging areas to the terrorists. The Soviet leadership seized upon these Israeli attacks to offer aid to Lebanon against Israeli and to pose again as the champion of the Arabs.[126]

As Arab-Israeli tensions heightened once again following the Palestinian terrorist raids against Israel and Israeli reprisals and preemptive attacks against the Palestinian guerrilla bases in Lebanon, the Soviet leadership may have hoped for the repetition of the situation of September 1972. At that time an anti-Soviet and pro-American trend was reversed by the massacre of Israeli athletes at Munich and the subsequent Israeli attacks on Lebanon and Syria, which made Soviet military aid a vital necessity for the Arab states. In any case, in early July 1974 an Arab League Defense Council meeting was called to deal with Israeli attacks on Lebanon, and Soviet comment on the conference hailed Arab "solidarity" in support of Lebanon while once again stressing Soviet support of the Arab cause.[127]

The Soviet leaders were not content, however, with merely encouraging Arab support of the Palestinians and Lebanese in the face of Israeli reprisal attacks. With the reconvening of the Geneva peace conference under active discussion, the Soviet leaders continued their efforts to persuade the Palestinians to participate in the Geneva conference with the ultimate goal of creating a Palestinian Arab state on the West Bank and in Gaza. *Izvestia* correspondent Igor Belyaev, in a key article on the Middle East on July 9, stated:

Back in November 1947, the 1947 UN General Assembly adopted a resolution on the division of Palestine into two independent states— Jewish and Arab. Israel was created in 1948. The Arab Palestinian state never became a reality. . . .

The Palestinian Arabs must now have the opportunity to decide their own fate. The Geneva Peace Conference on the Near East can and must be the most suitable place for a discussion of their legitimate rights.[128]

While the Soviet leadership thus came out more strongly than ever before in favor of a Palestinian state and tried to win the Palestinian Arabs over to their point of view, the Soviet Union's relations with Egypt again deteriorated and the Soviet leaders utilized the Palestinian issue in an effort to isolate and embarrass Egyptian President Sadat. The effusive Egyptian welcome given to Nixon, far greater than the Egyptian welcomes given to Khrushchev in 1964 or to Podgorny in 1971, together with the numerous Egyptian-American agreements signed during Nixon's visit, clearly angered the Soviet leaders, who saw Egypt moving farther and farther into the American camp, despite all the military and economic aid the USSR had given Egypt and the risks the Russians had taken on Egypt's behalf. Soon after the end of the Soviet-American summit, the Soviet leadership demonstrated its displeasure with Sadat's policies by abruptly postponing the scheduled Moscow visit of Egyptian Foreign Minister Ismail Fahmy, which was supposed to lay the groundwork for a Sadat-Brezhnev "summit."[129] This snub, however, did not deter Sadat, who had just received a $200-million loan from Germany, from improving relations with the United States still further in mid-July. On July 17 and 18, he signed agreements safeguarding American investments in the Egyptian economy and allowing four major American banks

(Chase Manhattan, First National City, American Express, and Bank of America) to begin operations in Egypt.[130] As mentioned above, Sadat's strategy at this time was both to strengthen the Egyptian economy and to use his new economic ties with the United States to "drive a wedge" between the United States and Israel, while playing off the United States against the USSR. The Soviet leaders, however, perceived the United States as the primary "wedge driver" in the relationship, viewing the American goal as splitting Egypt off from the USSR—a process that seemed well on the way to success by mid-July.

Egypt's relations with the Soviet Union deteriorated further on July 18 when Sadat, in an interview with the Lebanese weekly *Al-Hawadess*, accused the Russians of trying to restrict Egypt's freedom in determining its foreign policy. The Egyptian leader also criticized the Russians for delaying Ismail Fahmy's visit to Moscow until October.[131] The Soviet leadership responded to Sadat's attacks and to his turn to the United States in a major *Izvestia* article on the Middle East by its editor, L. Tolkunov, who made a detailed attack on "anti-Sovietism in Egypt." Tolkunov began the article by indicating Soviet concern over both American diplomatic efforts in the Middle East and the Arab leaders who supported them:

> Bilateral contacts through someone else's mediation constrict the possible framework of the Arab states' political activeness. Some of these countries are trying to do a balancing act, to draw dividends from both poles as it were; from the US and Western European countries on the one hand, and from the Soviet Union and the National Liberation movement on the other.[132]

Tolkunov went on to remind the Arabs that "in itself" the establishment of diplomatic relations between the United States and a number of Arab states has in no way affected the "provocative aggressive nature of Israel's course." The Soviet editor then attacked "anti-Sovietism in Egypt" as he commented on the growing economic ties between the United States and Egypt:

> Some people in Egypt want to prepare the ground for the broad penetration of Western capital into the country and the simultaneous "liberation" of Egypt from Soviet "economic dependence." Under the same flag, steps are being taken to strengthen economic ties with Western countries, a subject that Egyptian journalists are writing a great deal about. But the most soper-minded people in Cairo are asking: What will too close ties between the Egyptian economy and Western circles really give the Egyptian people? Can they, these circles, provide effective and disinterested assistance to Egypt? Many people in Cairo are talking about the illusory nature of the idea that the Western countries will show much favor toward Egypt if it retreats further from cooperation with the Soviet Union.[133]

While Tolkunov attacked Sadat's economic policy, *New Times* correspondent Y. Potomov was attacking Sadat for his agreement with Jordan's King Hussein that the Jordanian monarch and not the PLO represented the

Palestinians living in his kingdom—including the West Bank.[134] While Sadat was later to change his position on this, Potomov seized the opportunity to use the PLO and Libyan leader Mu'ammar Kaddafi to demonstrate that Sadat was isolated from the mainstream of Arab thinking on the Palestinian question:

> The leaders of the PLO and several other Arab countries disagree with the proviso contained in the communique on the recent talks between President Anwar Sadat of Egypt and King Hussein of Jordan that "the Palestinian Liberation Organization is the legitimate representative of the Palestinians with the exception of those dwelling in the Hashemite Kingdom of Jordan." The communique has been trenchantly criticized by the press in a number of Arab countries.
>
> On July 23 PLO Executive Chairman Yasir Arafat met Libyan leader Muammar Kaddafi. According to Libyan newspapers, they were of one mind in noting that the Jordanian communique cut across the decisions of last year's Arab summit conference in Algiers which recognized the PLO as the sole legitimate representative of the entire Palestinian people.[135]

In the same article, however, Potomov indicated Soviet concern over current Middle East trends:

> Forces trying to spot a weak link in Arab ranks are . . . stepping up their activities. Cashing in on the difficulties the Arab countries are experiencing due to the protracted Israeli aggression, *these forces are endeavoring with the assistance of local reactionaries, to pluck one state after another out of the united Arab front resisting imperialist aggression.*[136] [emphasis added]

The Soviet embrace of the Palestinian cause, which was part of the overall Soviet strategy of encouraging anti-Western trends in the Middle East, reached a new high at the end of July when the Soviet leadership invited Yasir Arafat to come to Moscow. At the time of Arafat's visit the Soviet press gave unprecedented coverage to the Palestinian question, including a six-page report in *New Times* and a 3,700-word article in *Izvestia*.[137] During the talks with Arafat and his delegation the Soviet leadership again emphasized its recognition of the Palestinians as the "sole legitimate representative of the people of Palestine,"[138] thus indirectly attacking Sadat. According to the description of the talks in *Pravda*, the USSR also expressed its support for the participation of the PLO at the Geneva conference "on an equal basis with the other participants," and agreed to the opening of a PLO mission in Moscow.[139] In return, the PLO delegation, which included a Jordanian Communist (probably as a sop to the Russians), gave its usual lip-service praise of the Soviet Union for its "unvarying support and assistance," and for its "principled policy."[140]

Soon after Arafat's departure, however, the Soviet Union was confronted by a problem far more important to the Soviet leadership than the Palestinians: the sudden resignation of U.S. President Richard Nixon, who had been the architect of the detente policy with the USSR. Gerald Ford, his successor, in his speech to a joint session of Congress after assuming the presidency, pledged continuity in American relations with the Soviet Union—a pledge given wide play by the Soviet press[141]—and also pledged to retain Henry Kissinger as Secretary of State. Nonetheless, the accession to power of a man neither burdened by Watergate nor wedded to the detente policy must have been of great concern to the Soviet leaders. They may well have recalled the changes made by Anwar Sadat in Egypt's relations with the Soviet Union when he acceded to the presidency in October 1970.

Gerald Ford came to power in the United States at a time when politics in the Middle East were in a great state of flux. Alignments among the states in the region and between regional states and extraregional powers were constantly changing. While Egypt had moved toward the United States, Libya had moved toward the USSR; but these alignments were neither stable nor permanent, and the Arab oil-producing states were accumulating huge sums of money, so much that the Western economies were groaning under the strain of paying quadrupled prices for Arab oil—a development that held a number of dangers for the future development of Arab relations with the West. At the same time the Cyprus conflict had broken out anew and the Arab-Israeli conflict, while temporarily defused, remained fundamentally unresolved and the danger of a new outbreak of war loomed on the horizon.

Indeed, despite the Israeli-Egyptian and Israeli-Syrian disengagement agreements worked out so painfully by Kissinger, by the time of Ford's accession to the Presidency there were indications that in the absence of further steps toward an Arab-Israeli peace agreement, another war could erupt in the very near future—possibly upon the November 30th termination of the mandate of the United Nations force stationed between Israel and Syria. The Israeli government was complaining about Syrian violations of the disengagement agreement, and about the huge influx of Soviet arms to Syria. For its part, Syria was protesting what it termed Israeli preparations for a new war, including a one-day mobilization of Israeli reservists.[142]

In an attempt to keep the momentum for peace underway, Kissinger and Ford entertained a parade of Middle East leaders in August and September, as the United States leaders sought to work out the optimum approach for the next stage of the peace talks. Visiting Washington during this period were Egyptian Foreign Minister Ismail Fahmy, Syrian Foreign Minister Abdel Halim Khaddam, Jordan's King Hussein, Saudi Arabian Foreign Minister Omar Saqqaf, and finally, in mid-September, Israel's new Premier, Yitzhak Rabin. The Israeli Premier, under intense domestic pressure not to yield any more land without concrete Arab moves toward peace, had a number of discussions with Ford Kissinger.[143] Following these meetings, he presented a formula for Arab "non-belligerency" which he said would be an acceptable price for another Israeli withdrawal. In return for a further withdrawal in Sinai, Rabin stated, Egypt could demonstrate its good intentions by ending its economic boycott of Israel. Rabin chose Egypt as the target of Israel's diplomacy not only because withdrawal in the Sinai was far more acceptable domestically in Israel than pullbacks on the Golan Heights or on the West Bank, but also because he felt that Egypt held the key to a permanent Arab-Israeli peace. In discussing Egypt on the United States television program *Meet the Press* Rabin stated:

If you looked back through the history of the Arab-Israeli conflict, you would realize that the Arab world didn't do anything without Egypt leading them into it, either to war or out of war. . . .

I think there are hopes—at least I hope there are signs that in Egypt . . . there is some sort of readiness for peace.[144]

While one of the goals of Rabin's trip to Washington was to coordinate strategy in the peace negotiations, a second goal was to acquire sufficient weaponry should the peace negotiations fail. It would appear that Rabin was successful in his quest for arms, because in a news conference at Blair House on September 13th Rabin stated, "We reached an understanding on our on-going military relationship in a concrete way with concrete results."[145]

As might be expected, the Soviet leadership, unhappy that Washington continued to be the center of Middle East diplomacy, seized upon the Rabin visit to underline U.S. support for Israel. An editorial in *New Times* commented:

Israeli Premier Yitzhak Rabin has completed his four-day visit to the United States. Before his departure from Tel-Aviv he declared "Israel needs much more aid from the United States—far more than it was receiving before the Yom Kippur War. . . . "

As former Ambassador to the United States, he knows his way about in Washington. And, as former Chief of General Staff, he is quite at home getting new arms shipments.

According to press reports, the United States has agreed to complete the delivery of 50 Phantom fighter-bombers by next summer. Tel-Aviv will also get from 200-250 M-60 tanks and laser-guided miss[i]les. All this will be part of the United States['] "current aid" to Israel for which Congress has appropriated $2,200 million. American officials say Rabin has also "achieved progress" concerning the long-range programme of American arms shipments to Israel. It is quite possible that it is the promise of these deliveries that has prompted the Premier to take, as he himself has said, a "tough stand" on the Middle East settlement.[146]

While the Arab leaders could not have been too happy with the support secured by Rabin in Washington, less than a week after the Israeli Premier's visit another event occurred to irritate Arab-American relations. President Ford, deciding to try to come to grips with the inflation problem which threatened to undermine the economies of the NATO allies and Japan—a problem exacerbated (although not caused) by the quadrupling of oil prices—issued both an appeal for cooperation between the world's food and energy producers and a veiled threat as to what might happen should cooperation not be forthcoming. Speaking at the United Nations on September 18 Ford stated:

The United States recognizes the special responsibility we bear as the world's largest producer of food. That is why Secretary of State Kissinger proposed from this very podium last year a World Food Conference to define a global food policy. And that is one reason why we have removed domestic restrictions of food production in the United States. *It has not been our policy to use food as a political weapon, despite the oil embargo and recent oil price and production decisions.* . . .

Now is the time for oil producers to define their conception of a global policy on energy to meet the growing need—and to do this without imposing unacceptable burdens on the international monetary and trade system. *A world of economic confrontation cannot be a world of political cooperation.*[147] [emphasis added]

Ford followed up his U.N. speech on food and energy with an even stronger warning at the Ninth World Energy Conference in Detroit five days later:

Sovereign nations cannot allow their policies to be dictated or their fate decided by artificial rigging or distortion of world commodity markets. . . . Exhorbitant prices can only distort the world economy, run the risk of a worldwide depression and threaten the breakdown of world order and world safety. It is difficult to discuss the energy problem without lapsing unfortunately into doomsday language. The danger is clear. It is very severe. . . .[148]

Kissinger echoed a similar warning in his address to the United Nations on September 23 when he said, "The world cannot sustain even the present level of prices, much less continuing increases."[149]

Reaction from the oil-exporting states—most of them Arab—to the United States' demand for a lowering of oil prices was strong and often bitter. The Beirut newspaper, *Al Nahar,* went so far as to claim in a headline "America declares war against oil-rich Arabs."[150] Indeed, fear over possible U.S. military intervention to seize Middle Eastern oil fields had reached the point by September 25 that U.S. Defense Secretary James Schlesinger, stated at a news conference that the United States was not contemplating military action against the oil-producing countries in the Middle East, but rather was trying to find a solution to rising oil prices through "amicable discussions."[151]

As in the case of Rabin's visit to Washington, the Soviet leadership seized upon Ford and Kissinger's warnings at the United Nations in an effort to undermine the United States position in the Middle East. In discussing the U.N. speeches, *Pravda* correspondent Yuly Yakhontov stated:

The oil-producing countries are being accused of having artificially created the economic difficulties of the oil-consuming countries. The U.S.A. even threatened to half economic aid and shipments of food to states who raise oil prices or reduce oil production. . . .

The U.S. statement produced a . . . violent reaction in the Near and Middle East. The Iranian newspaper *Kayhan* termed Washington's action as nothing less than "interference in the internal affairs of sovereign states." "The peoples of Arab countries will not bow to threats of force or tolerate intervention in their internal affairs and economic policies" declared the Beirut newspaper *Ash Sharq.*[152]

It was with this background of Arab irritation over United States policies that Kissinger embarked on yet another trip to the Middle East in early October. The main target of the U.S. Secretary of State's diplomacy was Egypt, as both the United States and Israel felt that another Israeli-Egyptian agreement would be the logical "next step" in the process of securing a final Arab-Israeli peace settlement although Kissinger also held out the hope for an Israeli-Jordan accord. Unfortunately for Kissinger, however, Sadat was not to prove as accomodating to the United States as on previous occasions. The Egyptian leader, unhappy at the very slow pace of promised United States economic and nuclear assistance, and desiring to maintain himself as the leader of the Arab world in the face of challenges from Libya and Iraq, was unwilling to agree to the cessation of the Arab economic boycott against Israel desired by Rabin, or make any other political concession to Israel in return for another Israeli withdrawal. Sadat, however, was too clever a diplomat to reject Kissinger's approaches directly. Instead, he decided to throw his support to the PLO and proclaim that any further Israeli-Egyptian agreements were contingent upon Israeli withdrawals from the Golan Heights and the West Bank, in the latter case ceding the territory to the PLO rather than to King Hussein. In adopting these policies, Sadat abrogated his earlier agreement with Hussein, and made Kissinger's mediation efforts considerably more difficult, given the PLO's continuing terrorist activities against Israel and its professed policy of dismantling the Jewish state. In choosing to support the claim of the PLO to represent all Palestinians, Sadat also adopted a policy favored by the Soviet Union, and the two nations drew closer together as Kissinger's peace-making activities waned.

Sadat's policy shift was first made evident on September 22, one week after Rabin's trip to Washington. At a "coordination conference" in Cairo attended by Egypt, Syria and the PLO, and boycotted by King Hussein, the Arab leaders took two steps of major importance to the Arab-Israeli peace negotiations. First, they agreed "to reject any attempt to carry out partial political settlements, considering the Arab cause as one cause." Second, the participants agreed that the PLO was the "sole legitimate representative of the people of Palestine."[153] In agreeing to these two points, Sadat effectively told the United States that a Jordanian-Israeli agreement could not be sanctioned since only the PLO could speak for the West Bank, and that Egypt could not follow a "go it alone" policy apart from its allies. Three days after this conference, in a taped appearance on the United States television program *The Today Show*, Sadat stated his refusal to personally meet Rabin, and intimated that he was willing to shift Egypt's position back to the Soviet Union by stating that Egypt's Foreign Minister Ismail Fahmy, scheduled to visit Moscow in mid-October, would be discussing Soviet arms supplies to Egypt during his visit.[154]

Given Sadat's unwillingness to come to an agreement with Israel, and Egypt's other policy changes, it is not surprising that Kissinger's diplomatic efforts made little progress during his visit to Cairo in early October. Kissinger did, however, obtain Sadat's willingness to a six-month extension of the United Nations force stationed between the Israeli and Egyptian armies in the Sinai Desert—possibly because, without a resumption of the constant flow of Soviet arms and spare parts he had before the October war, Sadat was unable to demonstrate that he could exercise the option of returning to war, should he so decide.

While the paramount Egyptian interest expressed during Fahmy's visit to Moscow was a need for more Soviet arms, the Soviet leaders had other goals in mind. The Russians were clearly still unhappy at the westward turn in Egypt's economy and a *Pravda* article, published on the eve of Fahmy's visit, continued the Soviet leadership's criticism of the Egyptian government's policies weakening the state sector of the Egyptian economy and fostering foreign investment.[155] In addition, in a major policy speech in Kishinev on October 11, just before Fahmy arrived in Moscow, Soviet Party leader Brezhnev made clear his opposition to the type of personal diplomacy carried on by Kissinger with the Egyptians. The Soviet leader also called for a speedy resumption of the Geneva conference where the USSR would be an equal partner with the United States in overseeing Middle East peace negotiations.[156] Possibly reflecting the still cool nature on Soviet-Egyptian relations, no mention of renewed Soviet arms deliveries to Egypt was made in the joint communique issued at the conclusion of Fahmy's visit. This was in marked contrast to Brezhnev's promises of continued Soviet military aid to Syrian President Hafiz Assad who had stopped off in Moscow September 27 on his way to a state visit to North Korea.[157] Nonetheless, the Soviet leadership did agree to a visit by Brezhnev to Cairo in January 1975, and the Brezhnev visit would clearly facilitate Sadat's policies of playing the two superpowers off against each other. In return, however, the Egyptians agreed that "a complete and final settlement to the Middle East Crisis can be achieved only within the framework of the Geneva Conference,"[158] thus implicitly joining the Russians in their criticism of Kissinger's efforts at personal diplomacy. The two sides also agreed that a final peace settlement could be achieved "only if the legitimate rights of the Arab people of Palestine, including their right to a homeland, are guaranteed," and that the PLO should take part in the Geneva Conference on an equal footing with the other participants.[159]

The Soviet press played up the results of the Egyptian Foreign Minister's visit as the Soviet leadership, despite its disappointment with Sadat in the past, saw an opportunity to demonstrate its ties to the most powerful of the Arab states. An editorial in *New Times* stated:

> It is no secret . . . that those who do not want to see close friendship between the Soviet Union and the Arabs have been working hard to drive a wedge between our country and Egypt. The results of the talks the Egyptian delegation led by Ismail Fahmy had in Moscow show that hopes on this score entertained by the reactionaries are groundless. . . .
>
> Leonid Brezhnev's visit to Cairo next January and his meeting with President Anwar Sadat, agreed upon during the Moscow talks, will undoubtedly be a landmark in the development of Soviet Egyptian relations. The decision concerning the Brezhnev-Sadat meeting, the Cairo *Al-Akhbar* stresses, "is convincing proof of the depth and enduring quality of Soviet-Egyptian relations. These are not transient relations nor are they engendered by some extraordinary circumstances."[160]

Having secured Brezhnev's promise to visit Egypt, thus once again demonstrating his ability to play off the Soviet Union against the United States,

Sadat turned his attention to the summit conference of Arab leaders at Rabat, Morocco where the conflict between Jordan and the PLO threatened to once again split apart the coalition of Arab states headed by Egypt. Sadat's support of the PLO at the Rabat summit was in line with his agreement with Syria and the PLO is late September, and with the Soviet-Egyptian communique of mid-October, although many Western observers seemed shocked by the Egyptian position, which they had erroneously felt would be more "moderate." After several days of intense debate, the other Arab states won King Hussein's agreement to a declaration that the PLO was the "sole and legitimate representative of the Palestinian people and had the right to establish the independent Palestinian authority on any liberated Palestinian territory." Perhaps in return for his agreement to renounce Jordan's claims to the West Bank, Hussein was promised a $300 million grant by the oil-rich Arab states. Other Arab states securing funds at the Rabat summit were Egypt, and Syria, which obtained $1 billion annually over a period of four years, and the PLO, which was awarded $50 million.[161]

The Soviet Press hailed the Rabat decision recognizing the PLO and it may have appeared to the Soviet leadership that the radical, anti-Western position of the PLO had won over a number of moderate and pro-Western Arab leaders. Indeed, Dmitry Volsky, writing in *New Times* claimed that the Rabat conference's decision was proof of the Arab states' growing unity on an anti-imperialist basis—the type of unity the Soviets had so long desired:

> The inten[t]ions of Tel-Aviv and its backers are sufficiently transparent. Their aim is to substitute for the Geneva conference "separate talks" with this or that Arab country with a view to preventing a solution of the cardinal issues involved in a Middle East settlement and reducing matters to "partial measures." Associated with all this are attempts to place the Palestinian movement in isolation within the Arab world itself in order subsequently to deal with it separately.
>
> The Rabat summit clearly demonstrated that the designs the Israeli aggressors have been harboring failed of their object. The Conference showed the Arab countries fully able to embody their resolve for unity in concrete decisions and political practice. . . .
>
> There is of course a long way to go before the decisions taken are translated into reality. *Nevertheless, the important thing is that the process of Arab consolidation is gaining headway. It is gaining headway, moreover, on an anti-imperialist platform* and with the support of all progressive forces, primarily the USSR which, as the Soviet leaders emphasized in their message to the Rabat summit, will continue to "do everything to secure a genuinely just Middle East settlement."[162] [emphasis added]

Arab unity at the Rabat conference was not as strong as the Soviet press made it appear, however. Libyan leader Mu'ammar Kaddafi boycotted the conference, and Iraqi leader Saddam Hussein stated at the end of the conference in a clear disagreement with Sadat: "Should the PLO go to Geneva or become a party to the contacts being held with the United States, Iraq's committment to this draft resolution would be null and void."[193] Hussein's statement also clearly demonstrated that despite extension Soviet military aid, and assistance in the war against the Kurds, on this important Middle East policy the two states were diametrically opposed, since the Soviet Union had long advocated a PLO role at Geneva.

While the Arab world may not have been totally unified in its policies toward the PLO, and while the terrorist organization had itself split with George Habash of the PFLP openly denouncing Arafat and the Rabat decisions, nonetheless the Middle East appeared much closer to war as a result of the Rabat conference. Given Arafat's continuing call for the replacement of Israel by a "democratic secular state," the Israelis began to gird for war as even a leader of Israel's dovish *Mapam* party, Dov Zakin, stated, "If you take the Rabat decisions literally, there is no alternative to war."[164]

In an effort to prevent the outbreak of war, Kissinger made yet another visit to the Middle East in early November. At this point Sadat was able to play the role of a "moderate," telling Kissinger "We shall always be, in Egypt, ready to regain whatever land we can . . . I can't see at all that the Rabat conference has put any block in the step-by-step approach."[165] The Egyptian leader made it be known, however, that while he would agree to another Israeli withdrawal, he couldn't make any political agreements with Israeli to obtain it.[166] In taking this position, Sadat indicated to Kissinger that if he wished to keep the momentum of his personal diplomacy toward peace, Egypt would be happy to cooperate so long as Kissinger could secure another Israeli withdrawal at no political cost to Egypt.[167]

If Sadat had hoped that through this diplomatic maneuvering Kissinger would now be forced to bring pressure on Israel for an unconditional withdrawal in order to recoup his personal prestige and secure a continuation of the American-sponsored peace effort, the American Secretary of State's task was made infinitely more difficult by Arafat's speech at the United Nations on November 13. In his UN address, Arafat repeated the PLO call for the dismantlement of Israel and warned that if his demands were not achieved, the PLO would continue its terrorist attacks.[168] The United States strongly opposed both the PLO's program to dismantle Israel, and its terrorist attacks, one of which occurred during the UN debate. The U.S. ambassador to the United Nations, John Scali, gave a very strong speech in favor of Israel's right to existence as a sovereign state.[169] For its part, the USSR, while hailing Arafat's visit to the United Nation's, was careful to continue to emphasize, as it had done in the past, that while the PLO had a right to a state, Israel also had a right to exist.[170] Indeed, given the strong American support for Israel, and a summit conference between Ford and Brezhnev coming up on November 23, the Soviet leadership clearly had no desire to alienate important segments of American-opinion by supporting the PLO's demands to dismantle Israel, particularly with new agreements of strategic arms limitations to be discussed at the summit, and the USSR's need for American technological inputs and long-term grants for the next Soviet Five Year Plan, then in an advanced stage of preparation.

Despite both Soviet and American statements that Israel had a right to exist, it appeared that after Arafat's visit to the United Nations, war loomed ever closer. Indeed, in mid-November, the Syrian government, long a champion of the PLO, refused to comment on whether it would permit a six month extension of the mandate of the United Nations force between Syrian and Israeli lines on the

Golan Heights which was due to expire at the end of the month. The Israelis, not wishing to be caught by surprise, as they were in October 1973, began to prepare for war. Following a report that 20 Soviet ships were unloading arms at Syrian ports, the Israelis began to mobilize reservists and move them to the Golan Heights. For a while it looked as if war was imminent until the personal intervention of Henry Kissinger succeeded in cooling the situation.[171] Nonetheless, the war scare did serve to remind both Brezhnev and Ford that they would have to deal with the Middle East, as well as with arms control, at their summit in Vladivostok. Although the details of the summit negotiations on the Middle East are not yet known, it is probable that Ford specifically asked Brezhnev to restrain the Syrians and convince them to accept an extention of the UN force. Given Syria's need for a continued supply of Soviet weaponry to fight a new war, the Soviet Union was not without leverage in this situation. In any case, at the end of the month the Syrians did agree to extend the UN force, although to what degree the Syrian decision was due to Soviet pressure, internal politics, or Egypt's unwillingness to support Syria in a new war, is not yet known.

The Middle East occupied a relatively small, although not insignificant, section of the communique issued by the two leaders at the conclusion of their meeting at Vladivostok, which was devoted primarily to working out a new nuclear arms limitation agreement. The section of the communique dealing with the Middle East stated:

> In the course of the exchange of views on the Middle East both sides expressed their concern with regard to the dangerous situation in that region. They reaffirmed their intention to make every effort to promote a solution of the key issues of a just and lasting peace in accordance with United Nations Resolution 338, with due account taken of the legitimate interests of all peoples of the area, including the Palestinian people and respect for the *right of all states of the area to independent existence.*
>
> The sides believe that the Geneva Conference should play an important part in the establishment of a just and lasting peace in the Middle East and *should resume its work as soon as possible.*[172] [emphasis added]

While rather vague as to details, the communique appears to have been a compromise between the two sides. On the one hand the statement supporting all the Middle Eastern states' right to an "independent existence" explicitly repudiated the PLO program of dismantling Israel. Indeed, the Soviet Union's support of the PLO, at least as reflected in the joint communique, was weaker than in the Nixon-Brezhnev communique issued four months earlier.[173] On the other hand, however, by agreeing to a resumption of the Geneva Conference, the United States seemed to be acceding to the Soviet desire to play a more active role in the peace negotiations. Nonetheless, since no date was set for the resumption of the Geneva talks, and since similar language had been used in the July communique, the United States kept alive the possibility of more activity by the peripatetic Kissinger.

The Ford-Brezhnev summit at Vladivostok, which seemed to reduce the danger of war between Israel and its Arab neighbors, although perhaps only temperarily, provides a good point of departure for drawing a number of conclusions about the course of Soviet policy in the Middle East in the four year period since the death of Nasser—four of the most turbulent years the region has ever known.

NOTES

1. For an example of the Israeli leaders' lack of mental preparedness for the war, see Defense Minister Moshe Dayan's lecture to the Israeli Command and Staff College on August 9, 1973. Reprinted in *Brief: Middle East Highlights* (Tel-Aviv) (hereafter *Brief*), no. 63, 1973.

2. Sadat interview in *Al Anwar* (Beirut), March 29, 1974, cited in the report byHenry Tanner in the New York *Times*, March 30, 1974.

3. See *Pravda*, October 7, 8, 9, 1973 and Radio Moscow reports of October 6, 7, 8, 9, 1973.

4. The Soviet Union had placed a number of "spy" satellites into the air over the Middle East before the war, and they were brought down at intervals during the war so that the Soviet leadership could be kept abreast of the military situation.

5. For the text of the message, see Radio Paris (Domestic Service), October 9, 1973.

6. For an analysis of Israeli military strategy during the war, see Walter Laqueur, *Confrontation: The Middle East and World Politics* (New York: Bantam Books, 1974), chapter 3.

7. Cited in the report by Bernard Gwertzman in the New York *Times*, October 13, 1973.

8. Cited in UPI report from Moscow in the New York *Times*, November 2, 1973. See also the New York *Times*, October 19, 1973.

9. Cf. Radio Moscow in English to North America, October 15, 1973.

10. Cited in the report by Bernard Gwertzman in the New York *Times*, October 16, 1973. For a reasoned explanation of the delay in the American decision to send arms to Israel, see Edward Luttwak and Walter Laqueur, "Kissinger and the Yom Kippur War," *Commentary* 58, no. 3 (September 1974): 33-40.

11. *Pravda*, October 16, 1973.

12. *Pravda*, October 15, 1973.

13. Cited in the report by Bernard Gwertzman in the New York *Times*, October 17, 1973.

14. *Pravda*, October 20, 1973.

15. Cited in *Middle East Monitor* 3, no. 20 (November 1, 1973): 3.

16. Radio Moscow, October 18, 1974.

17. Cited in the report by Bernard Gwertzman, in the New York *Times*, October 21, 1973.

18. Cited in *Middle East Monitor* 3, no. 20 (November 1, 1973): 5.

19. This was the text of the note published in the Washington *Post*, November 28, 1973.

20. The American alert and the exact nature of Soviet moves are not yet fully clear. For Kissinger's statement about the alert at a press conference and a description of the alert, see the New York *Times*, October 26, 1973.

21. For a detailed description of the actions of the Arab states during the war, see *Middle East Monitor* 3, nos. 19 and 20 (October 15, 1973 and November 1, 1973).

22. Dmitry Volsky and A. Usvatov, "Israeli Expansionists Miscalculate," *New Times*, no. 42 (1973): 10.

23. Georgi Mirsky, "The Middle East: New Factors," *New Times*, no. 48 (1973): 18-19. The other "myths" that Mirsky claimed were dispelled by the war were: (a) Israel would always enjoy military superiority; (b) Arab weaponry was inferior to that of Israel; and (c) detente had no value (Mirsky said that, thanks to detente, a worse "flare-up" was avoided).

24. G. Apalin, "Peking Prov[o]cations," *New Times,* nos. 45-46 (1973): 29-30. Apalin also claimed, as did much of the Soviet media, that the Chinese attempted to use the Middle East war "to provoke a confrontation" between the United States and USSR.

25. A close study of Radio Tehran's announcement of its agreement with Iraq, however, would probably have convinced the Russians that the Iranians remained deeply suspicious of Iraq and that the agreement would probably not last too long. See Radio Tehran domestic service "Commentary," October 8, 1973. The Shah was quoted in *Al Hayat* (Beirut) on November 22, 1973, as saying he had put some Iranian aircraft at the disposal of Saudi Arabia during the war. See *Middle East Monitor* 3, no. 22 (December 1, 1973): 1.

26. A description of this dispute is in *Middle East Monitor* 3, no. 19 (October 15, 1973): 3.

27. See *Pravda*, November 21, 1973, and December 9, 1973.

28. New York *Times*, November 5, 1973.

29. New York *Times*, March 16, 1974.

30. Cited in *Brief*, no. 68: 2.

31. Ibid.

32. *Middle East Monitor* 3, no. 22 (December 1, 1973): 1. Interestingly enough, in a report on these clashes, *New Times* took a far more moderate position on the Kurds than it was to take only two months later. See Vladimir Shmarov, "The Baghdad Dialogue," *New Times*, no. 5 (1974): 10; compare it to *Pravda*, April 26, and Alexander Ignatov, "Iraq Today," *New Times*, no. 21 (1974): 22-25. For the reason for the Soviet change, see pp. 144-146.

33. *New Times*, no. 8 (1974): 13.

34. See AP report, cited in *Brief*, no. 69: 3.

35. Cited in the report by Theodore Shabad in the New York *Times*, February 5, 1974.

36. *Pravda*, November 16, 1973. The communique also demanded Israeli withdrawal to the October 22 cease-fire lines.

37. Washington *Post*, November 21, 1973.

38. Washington *Post*, November 23, 1973.

39. *Pravda*, November 27, 1973. (Translated in *Current Digest of The Soviet Press* (hereafter *CDSP*) 25, no. 48.

40. Translated in *CDSP* 25, no. 49: 18.

41. Cited in the report by John Cooley in the *Christian Science Monitor.* See also *Middle East Monitor* 4, no. 1 (January 1, 1974): 1-2.

42. *Pravda*, December 12, 1973. Translated in *CDSP* 25, no. 50: 21.

43. See the report by Bernard Gwertzman in the New York *Times*, December 19, 1973.

44. Gromyko's speech (*Pravda,* December 22), translated in *CDSP* 25, no. 51: 1-4.

45. For an excellent analysis of the dangers to the world economy caused by the precipitous rise in oil prices, see Walter J. Levy, "World Oil Cooperation or International Chaos," *Foreign Affairs* 52, no. 4 (July 1974): 690-713.

46. See *Izvestia*, January 23, 1974, for a Soviet view of the French action.

47. *Izvestia*, December 30, 1973.

48. *Izvestia*, January 9, 1974.

49. *New Times*, no. 3 (1974): 13.

50. *Pravda*, January 25, 1974. Translated in *CDSP* 26, no. 4: 25.

51. Translated in *CDSP* 26, no. 3: 14.

52. Translated in *CDSP* 26, no. 5: 11-12.

53. *New Times*, no. 8 (1974): 16.

54. The communique was published in *Pravda*, March 6, 1974, and referred to the talks as having taken place in a "businesslike atmosphere"—the usual Soviet terminology for low-level cooperation.

55. The communique was published in *Pravda*, March 8, 1974.

56. Radio Moscow, March 12, 1974 (cited in the New York *Times*, March 13, 1974). See also Radio Moscow (Peace and Progress), March 13, 1974.

57. For Soviet analyses of the effect of the oil embargo on the United States and Western Europe and its relation to the energy crisis, see E. Primakov, "Energeticheskii krizis v kapitalisticheskikh stranakh" (The energy crisis in capitalist states), *Mirovaia ekonomika i mezhdunarodnaia otnosheniia* (hereafter *MEIMO*), no. 2 (February 1974): 65-72; V. Spichkin, "energeticheskii krizis v Ssha" (Energy crisis in the USA), *MEIMO*, no. 3 (March 1974): 85-98; and V. Cherniavina, "Energeticheskie problemy stran EEC" (Energy problems in EEC countries), *MEIMO*, no. 4 (April 1974): 56-65. See also B. V. Rachkov, "Energeticheskie problemy Soedinenykh Shtatov" (Energy problems in the United States), *Ssha*, no. 3 (March 1974): 29-43.

58. *Pravda*, March 25, 1974. *Pravda* was quoting a group of "prominent" Lebanese "public figures" who appealed to Sadat to stop the attacks on Nasser and his policies. For a description of other anti-Sadat actions taken by the Soviet leaders at the time, see the New York *Times* March 26, 1974.

59. Pavel Naumov, "In Egypt Today," *New Times*, no. 12 (1974): 24.

60. Cited in the New York *Times*, March 29, 1974.

61. Radio Cairo, April 4, 1974.

62. Cited in the New York *Times*, April 19.

63. New York *Times* interview, April 22, 1974.

64. In his foreign assistance message to Congress on April 24, Nixon officially requested $250 million in aid for Egypt along with $350 million for Israel and $207.5 million for Jordan. Interestingly enough, the president also requested $100 million in a "Special Requirements" fund, which many observers saw as earmarked for Syria to help in its postwar reconstruction efforts—if the

Syrians agreed to a disengagement agreement. For the text of Nixon's message, see News Release, Bureau of Public Affairs, Department of States, April 24, 1974. For speculation on U.S. aid to Syria, see the New York *Times,* April 25, 1974.

65. For a further development of this point, see Robert O. Freedman's testimony before the Foreign Affairs Committee, United States House of Representatives, May 14, 1974. U.S.-Egyptian cooperation at the time was highlighted by U.S. assistance in the clearing of the Suez Canal, a project in which U.S. helicopters and a U.S. aircraft carrier participated. *The Middle East, 1974: New Hopes, New Challenges* (U.S. Government Printing Office, Washington, D.C.: 1974.

66. See the reports in the New York *Times,* April 25, 1974, and April 28, 1974.

67. Jean Riollot, "Moscow Cries 'Wolf' in the Middle East," *Radio Liberty Report,* May 21, 1974.

68. New York *Times,* May 25, 1974.

69. "The Foundation of Soviet-Egyptian Relations," *New Times,* no. 22 (1974): 17.

70. *Middle East Monitor* 4, no. 11 (June 1, 1974): 1.

71. See the report in *Middle East Monitor* 4, no. 12 (June 15, 1974): 2-3.

72. On April 24, 1974, Egypt officially charged that Kaddafi had been involved in the attempt to overthrow Sadat's government on April 18.

73. On May 11, 1974, Nimeri accused Kaddafi of trying to overthrow his government. See the report in the New York *Times,* May 12, 1974.

74. New York *Times,* April 8, 1974.

75. Aleksei Zlatorunsky, "Libya and its Problems," *New Times,* nos. 18-19 (1974): 35.

76. Ibid., p. 36.

77. Ibid.

78. *Pravda,* May 15, 1974. Translated in *CDSP* 26, no. 20: 17.

79. Ibid.

80. Ibid., pp. 17-18.

81. Ibid., p. 18.

82. *Pravda,* May 22, 1974. Translated in *CDSP* 26, no. 20: 18.

83. Ibid.

84. For a recent article depicting Soviet interest in Arab states with "spare capital," see R. Klekovsky, "Fruitful Co-operation Between the CMEA States and the Arab Countries," *Foreign Trade* (Vneshniaia torgovlia), no. 8 (August 1974): 16-19.

85. For a discussion of the sharp increase in Soviet imports of oil, natural gas, and other raw materials from developing countries from 1970 to 1973, see A. Ivanov, "Soviet Imports from Developing Countries," *Foreign Trade,* no. 9 (September 1974): 38-43.

86. *Pravda,* May 22, 1974.

87. See the report by Juan De Onis in the New York *Times,* May 5, 1974.

88. Cf. the Afro-Asian Peoples' Solidarity Organization session in Baghdad in late March 1974, which denounced "Imperialism and Maoism." For a report on the AAPSO meeting, see Dmitry Volsky, "Whose Minefields," *New Times,* no. 14 (1974): 8-9.

89. *Pravda*, February 28, 1974. Translated in *CDSP* 26, no. 9: 19.

90. Pavel Demchenko, "Autonomy for Iraq's Kurds," *Pravda*, March 14, 1974. Translated in *CDSP* 26, no. 11: 21.

91. *Pravda*, March 27, 1974. Translated in *CDSP* 26, no. 13: 18. ˎ

92. *Pravda*, April 26, 1974. Translated in *CDSP* 26, no. 17: 17.

93. Alexander Ignatov, "Iraq Today," *New Times*, no. 21 (1974): 24.

94. Chances of Soviet involvement in such a war could rise if, as the Washington *Post* reported in early October, Soviet pilots are flying missions against the Kurds. See the report by Michael Getler in the Washington *Post*, October 5, 1974.

95. See the report in *Middle East Monitor* 4, no. 7. (April 1, 1974): 1.

96. Radio Peace and Progress (Moscow) echoed this theme on May 16, 1974.

97. *Pravda*, March 29, 1974, printed a very stiff Soviet note to the Chinese about this incident.

98. The communique was printed in *Pravda*, March 29, 1974.

99. *Izvestia*, March 30, 1974. Translated in *CDSP* 26, no. 13: 11.

100. *Pravda*, April 12, 1974. Translated in *CDSP* 26, no. 13: 2.

101. *Pravda*, April 17, 1974. Translated in *CDSP* 26, no. 13: 5-6.

102. *Pravda*, April 30, 1974. Translated in *CDSP* 26, no. 17: 14.

103. New York *Times*, April 30, 1974.

104. *Pravda*, May 3, 1974. Translated in *CDSP* 26, no. 18: 9.

105. Ibid.

106. *Pravda*, May 30, 1974.

107. Ibid. Translated in *CDSP* 26, no. 22: 5.

108. Alexander Ignatov, "This Spring in Damascus," *New Times*, no. 24 (1974): 26-27.

109. Dmitry Volsky, "Step Toward Settlement," *New Times*, no. 23 (1974): 9.

110. For an essay developing this viewpoint, see Bernard Gwertzman's "News Analysis" in the New York *Times*, June 1, 1974.

111. Cited in the report of Kissinger's news conference by Leslie Gelb in the New York *Times*, June 7, 1974.

112. Cited in *Middle East Monitor* 4, no. 13 (June 30, 1974): 1.

113. The text of the joint Sadat-Nixon statement titled "Principles of Relations and Cooperation Between Egypt and the United States" outlining nuclear energy cooperation and other areas was published in the New York *Times,* June 15, 1974.

114. Dmitry Volsky, "Arab East: Miracles and Realities," *New Times*, no. 24 (1974): 12.

115. Ibid., p. 13.

116. *Pravda*, June 16, 1974. Translated in *CDSP* 26, no. 24: 21.

117. *Izvestia*, July 7, 1974, carried a negative description of the Jackson visit.

118. This document, along with the other agreements and documents of the summit, may be found in the document section of *New Times*, no. 28 (1974): 21-32. The document pertaining to the Middle East is found on page 23.

119. A description of the meeting, together with the ten-point program, is found in *Middle East Monitor* 4, no. 13 (June 30, 1974): 3-4.

120. Ibid., p. 4.

121. Ibid.

122. Ibid.

123. Victor Bukharov, "Palestinian National Council Session," *New Times*, no. 25 (1974): 12.

124. Ibid., p. 13.

125. For a detailed description of the activities of the Palestinian National Front on the Israeli-occupied West Bank, see the report by Terence Smith in the New York *Times*, August 23, 1974. This was one of the few successes of Soviet policy towards the Arab Communists, however, as Arab Communists had bitterly attacked the Soviet policy of encouraging Arab solidarity with "Arab reactionaries" such as King Faisal. See, for example, Kerim Mroue, "Use the Opportunities of the New Situation in the Middle East," *World Marxist Review* 17, no. 3 (March 1974): 92.

126. See the report by Juan De Onis in the New York *Times*, July 12, 1974.

127. Georgi Shmelyov, "Solidarity the Keynote," *New Times*, no. 28 (1974): 10.

128. *Izvestia*, July 9, 1974. Translated in *CDSP* 26, no. 27: 21.

129. Cited in the report by Henry Tanner in the New York *Times*, July 11, 1974.

130. *Pravda* printed a description of the agreements in its issue of July 18, 1974. The agreements were signed during U.S. Treasury Secretary William Simon's visit to Cairo.

131. New York *Times*, July 19, 1974.

132. *Izvestia*, July 25, 1974. Translated in *CDSP* 26, no. 31: 2.

133. Ibid., p. 4.

134. Sadat was not explicit as to whether Hussein could be considered the representative of the West Bank Palestinians. It appears as if he signed the agreement with Hussein to encourage prospects of a military disengagement agreement between Israel and Jordan that would give Hussein part of the West Bank. Earlier in the month Israeli Information Minister Aharon Yariv had floated a trial balloon (that was quickly shot down) that Israel might negotiate with the Palestinian guerrilla organizations if they would acknowledge the existence of Israel as a Jewish state and agree to cease hostile actions against it. See the reports in the New York *Times*, July 12 and 22, 1974.

135. Y. Potomov, "Middle East Settlement: Urgent Task," *New Times*, no. 31 (1974): 22.

136. Ibid.

137. *New Times*, no. 32 (1974): 26-31. The same issue of the journal carried a front-page editorial supporting the PLO and a two-page interview with Yasir Arafat (pp. 10-11), who hailed the Palestine National Front and warmly praised the Soviet Union for its aid. See also *Izvestia*, July 30, 1974, for the extensive article on the Palestinians.

138. *Pravda*, August 4, 1974. Translated in *CDSP* 26, no. 30: 5.

139. Ibid.

140. The fact that Arafat met with both Ponamarev and Ulianovsky probably indicated that there were discussions about the links between the PLO leadership and the Arab Communists.

141. Cf. Iona Andronov, "The Change-over in the White House," *New Times*, no. 33 (1974): 6; and *Pravda*, August 11, 1974.

142. For a discussion of the renewed threat of war, see the article by Terrence Smith in the August 18, 1974 issue of the New York *Times*.

143. In mid-September, Rabin's government only had a majority of one seat in the Israeli parliament. Rabin had replaced Golda Meir as Premier in early June following conclusion of the Syrian-Israeli disengagement agreement, when Mrs. Meir had retired.

144. Cited in the report by Bernard Gwertzman in the September 16, 1974 issue of the New York *Times*.

145. Cited in the report by Bernard Gwertzman in the September 14, 1974 issue of the New York *Times*.

146. *New Times*, no. 38 (1974): 17.

147. News Release, Bureau of Public Affairs, Department of State, September 18, 1974.

148. News Release, Bureau of Public Affairs, Department of State, September 23, 1974.

149. News Release, Bureau of Public Affairs, Department of State, September 23, 1974.

150. Cited in the report by John Cooley in the September 25, 1974 issue of the *Christian Science Monitor*.

151. Cited in the report by John Finney in the September 26, 1974 issue of the New York *Times*.

152. *Pravda*, September 29, 1974. Translated in *CDSP* 26, no. 39: 21.

153. For the text of the agreement, see the *Middle East Monitor* 4, no. 18 (October 1, 1974): 4.

154. Cited in the report by Wolf Blitzer in the September 27, 1974 issue of the Jerusalem *Post*. Sadat was also negotiating with France and Britain for weapons at this time. France began supplying Mirage jet fight bombers to Egypt in late November, thereby strengthening Sadat's bargaining position with the Soviet Union.

155. *Pravda*, October 10, 1974.

156. *Pravda*, October 12, 1974.

157. *Pravda*, September 28, 1974.

158. "Fruitful Talks," *New Times*, no. 43 (1974): 17.

159. Ibid.

160. Ibid. See also *Pravda*, October 17, 1974.

161. For a description of the results of the Rabat conference, see the *Middle East Monitor*, 4, no. 21 (November 15, 1974): 2-4.

162. Dmitry Volsky, "After the Rabat Meeting," *New Times*, no. 45 (1974): 10-11.

163. Cited in *Middle East Monitor*, 4, no. 21 (November 15, 1974): 4.

164. Cited in the New York *Times*, October 30, 1974.

165. Cited in the report by Bernard Gwertzman in the November 7, 1974 issue of the New York *Times*.

166. Cf. report by Henry Tanner in the November 9, 1974 issue of the New York *Times*.

167. While apparently getting no promises of U.S. pressure on Israel, Sadat did obtain a promise from Kissinger to sell Egypt 200,000 tons of wheat and sorghum at long-term, low interest, reduced price rates. Given the rapid rise in Egypt's population, and its inability to feed its population without outside assistance, the role of food assistance is likely to grow in importance in the Egyptian-American relationship. Interestingly enough, the promise of 200,000 tons of grain was in addition to a 100,000 ton promise made to Ismail Fahmy when he visited Washington in August.

168. For the text of Arafat's speech and the reply by Israel's representative Yosef Tekoah, see the November 14, 1974 issue of the New York *Times*.

169. The text of Scali's speech is in the November 22, 1974 issue of the New York *Times*. A terrorist raid on the Israeli town of Bet Shan on November 19, during the UN debate on Palestine, killed four Israelis and wounded 19. The raid was carried out by the Popular Democratic Front for the Liberation of Palestine, an organization supporting Arafat within the PLO.

170. Cf. Gromyko's speech to the United Nations on September 24, 1974. See also *Pravda*, November 14, and 15, 1974.

171. For an analysis of the war scare, see the report by John Cooley in the November 18, 1974 issue of the *Christian Science Monitor*.

172. The text of the communique is found in the November 25, 1974 issue of the New York *Times*.

173. See page 151 above.

6

In assessing Soviet policy toward the Middle East from the death of Nasser in September 1970 until the Vladivostok summit of November 1974, one may conclude that Soviet policy toward the region was primarily a reaction to a series of regional developments that the Soviet leadership not only had not caused, but that they were also increasingly unable to shape to fit Soviet goals in the region, and that the Soviet position in the Middle East was much weaker in 1974 than it was in 1970. The Russians suffered a major loss to their Middle East position in July 1971 when an abortive Communist-supported coup d'etat in the Sudan triggered a wave of anti-Communism and anti-Sovietism throughout the Arab world. Similarly, a year later, the USSR suffered another blow when Soviet troops were expelled from their air and naval bases in Egypt, thus weakening the Soviet strategic position in the Eastern Mediterranean. While the Soviet leaders were quick to exploit such events as the Munich massacre in September 1972 and the October 1973 Arab-Israeli war, they were outrun by events and found themselves in a worse position in the region following the war than they possessed before it. Throughout this entire period the Arab leaders of the Middle East, whom the Soviet leadership were diligently trying to court, were only too happy to accept Soviet aid, but they insisted on pursuing their own policies—even when these policies conflicted with those of the Soviet Union.

It is clear from these events that Soviet influence in the Middle East is very limited indeed. Despite massive outlays of military assistance as well as considerable economic aid to a number of the states of the region, the Soviet leadership has been unable to influence the elites of the area to adopt policies consistent with Soviet positions in many key situations. This has been most apparent in Egypt where at the time of Nasser's death the USSR had control over a number of air and naval bases while also playing an active, albeit not dominant, role in Egypt's political and economic life. When Sadat took over from Nasser, however, he soon clashed with the Soviet Union. By November 1974 the new Egyptian leader had undermined the Soviet position in Egypt, which, because of its population, geographical location, and military power, is the most important state in the Arab world. Sadat's first conflict with the Russians erupted in the summer of 1971, when he helped Sudanese leader Jaafar Nimeri regain power during the Communist-supported coup d'etat against his regime. Following this event the Sudanese premier proceeded to execute a number of major Sudanese Communist leaders. When the Soviet Union appealed to Sadat to use his influence with Nimeri to save the lives of the Sudanese Communists, Sadat not only failed to help the Soviet leaders, but also came out strongly in support of Nimeri's anti-Communist actions. In doing so Sadat came into direct conflict with the Soviet leadership, which had mounted a major propaganda campaign to save the lives of the Sudanese Communists.

The second serious Egyptian-Soviet clash came a year later when Sadat, dissatisfied with a perceived lack of Soviet support for his confrontation with Israel, expelled the Russians from their bases in Egypt and turned to the United States. Thus, the Russians suffered a double loss—they were deprived of strategically important bases in Egypt, and their erstwhile ally had turned to their main opponent for assistance. While Soviet-Egyptian relations improved following the Israeli retaliatory raids on Lebanon and Syria after the massacre of the Israeli Olympic athletes at Munich, and the USSR proved willing to supply Egypt both with weapons and diplomatic support during the October 1973 Arab-Israeli war, Soviet-Egyptian relations deteriorated again sharply after the war when Sadat, perceiving a chance to advance the Egyptian objective of securing an Israeli withdrawal from the occupied Sinai desert, while also obtaining economic assistance for his lagging economy, turned again to the United States. Indeed, Sadat led the fight to persuade the oil-producing Arab countries to lift their embargo against the United States—a policy that was in direct conflict with the Soviet effort to maintain the embargo, which was causing both economic dislocations with the United States and political conflict within the NATO alliance. Meanwhile, during the entire period of his presidency, Sadat was also encouraging Western investment in Egypt and expanding Egypt's private sector—policies the Soviet leadership found highly objectionable since they seemed to reinforce economically the political turn Egypt was making toward the West.

While the Soviet leadership had its greatest difficulty in influencing the foreign and domestic policies of the Sadat regime in Egypt, Soviet influence was also at a low level in Syria and Iraq, the other two primary recipients of Soviet economic and military aid in the Arab world. In Syria the regime of Hafiz Assad rejected Soviet requests to sign a friendship treaty on the model of the Soviet-Egyptian treaty (innocuous as that turned out to be), while also opposing UN Resolution #242 and refusing to participate in the 1973 Arab-Israeli peace conference at Geneva, which the Soviet Union had cosponsored with the United States. The Iraqi regime of Hassan Al-Bakr also opposed a number of major Soviet policies, including UN Resolution #242 and the Soviet-American ceasefire resolution that ended the October war.

While the Soviet leadership's limited influence in the Arab world was reflected in these policy clashes where the Arab leaders refused to support the Soviet viewpoint, it was also evident in the unwillingness or inability of the Soviet leaders to effect elite changes in the Arab states to bring to power leaders more sympathetic to Soviet policies. Thus, in Egypt, Sadat succeeded in eliminating from power the more pro-Soviet of the Egyptian hierarchy such as Ali Sabri, while in Syria Assad was able to oust the pro-Russian Salah Jedid clique from power. In both major regime changes the Soviet leadership proved unable to affect events. Perhaps only in the case of Sadat's ouster of Marshall Sadek in October 1972 can the Soviet leaders be credited with influencing a regime change—albeit indirectly—but even here their influence may be considered limited since Sadek was a second-rank leader and his ouster seemed more a sop to the Russians following the Munich massacre (and Egypt's need for more weaponry) than a real power realignment in the Egyptian hierarchy.

Given the lack of success on the part of the Soviet leaders in trying to modify the behavior of Arab elites and the Soviet inability to replace the elites with others more favorably inclined to Soviet policies, how then can one explain the continued Soviet aid to these states and the Soviet leadership's willingness to support the Arabs to the point of confrontation with the United States during the October 1973 war? In seeking an answer for this question, one must keep in mind the overall Soviet goal in the Middle East—the elimination of Western influence—and to view Soviet activity as directed in support of that goal. The Soviet leadership, taking a long-term view of Middle Eastern politics, has been willing to pay a substantial price in economic and military aid to often recalcitrant Arab regimes in the hope of stimulating or reinforcing anti-Western trends in the Middle East or, at the very least, reversing anti-Soviet trends such as the one that occurred following the abortive coup d'etat in the Sudan. In particular, the Soviet leadership has utilized its economic and military aid on a number of occasions to reinforce anti-Western behavior that the leaders of an Arab state were already contemplating, behavior also beneficial to the Soviet Union. A case in point is the Iraqi nationalization of the Iraqi Petroleum Company's oil fields at Kirkuk where the Russians promised developmental aid to support the nationalization. While the Russians were undoubtedly happy to see the weakening of the Western-owned oil consortium, the impetus for the nationalization decision lay not in the Soviet Union but in the Iraqi regime, which wanted to gain control over the major source of hard currency on which its economic development plans depended. Similarly, the Soviet leaders strongly encouraged the Arab nations to impose and maintain the oil embargo against the United States, and the Arab states did in fact do so. Nonetheless, the Arabs were clearly acting on their own initiative, as was demonstrated when the embargo was lifted despite Soviet efforts to maintain it. Finally, the USSR provided the weaponry for Egypt to go to war, but the decision for war was an Egyptian one, not a Soviet one.

In their efforts to foster and reinforce anti-Western trends in the Middle East, the Soviet leadership also changed its policy toward the Communist parties of the Arab world following the debacle in the Sudan in July 1971. Before that time the Brezhnev regime had shown its preference for good relations with the one-party regimes of the Arab world and had tried to convince the Arab Communists that they should be satisfied with the basically educational and propagandistic role of teachers of "scientific socialism" to the leaders and masses of the Arab states. In an effort to remove the suspicion and hostility with which the Arab leaders viewed the Communist parties of their states, the Soviet leadership encouraged the Communist party of Egypt to dissolve and join the Arab Socialist Union, thereby to work for socialism (and good Soviet-Egyptian relations) from the inside. Similarly, following the coup d'etat in the Sudan in May 1969 that brought Jaafar Nimeri to power, the Soviet leadership urged the Sudanese Communist Party to dissolve and join Nimeri's one-party regime. However, this request was refused by an important faction of the Sudanese Communist Party, which then supported a coup d'etat against Nimeri in July 1971—an event that was to have a very negative effect on Soviet policy towards the Arab world and result in the decimation of the leadership of the Sudanese Communist Party. Following this event it became apparent to the Soviet leaders that the policy of urging dissolution of Arab Communist parties had failed, and the Brezhnev regime then began to actively encourage "national fronts" in the Arab world where the Communists would participate as parties, although clearly as junior partners. By stressing the fact that the Communists recognized that the Arab nationalist parties were the dominant force in each national front, the CPSU hoped to allay the fears of the Arab nationalists that the Communists would use their positions to overthrow the nationalist regimes. At the same time, however, it was clearly the wish of the Soviet leadership that the presence of Communists within the national front would help steer the Arab nationalist leaders away from the West and counter the wave of anti-Communism and anti-Sovietism that swept through the Middle East as a result of the failure of the Communist-supported coup attempt in the in the Sudan. Interestingly enough, throughout the entire period since the dissolution of the Egyptian Communist Party in early 1965, the CPSU also sought to influence the one-party regimes of the Arab states directly through relations on a party level, and by 1974 the CPSU had established party relations with the Algerian FLN, the Egyptian ASU, and the Ba'ath parties of Iraq and Syria.

These policies, however, were not particularly successful from the point of view of Soviet foreign policy aims in the Arab world—at least not in the short run. For example, while the coup-weakened Iraqi Ba'athist regime, after much Soviet urging, finally established a national front in July 1973, its subsequent behavior, including its rejection of the Soviet-sponsored cease-fire in the October war, clearly did not indicate that the establishment of the national front made the Iraqi regime any more amenable to Soviet demands on issues the Iraqis deemed important. In the short run, the existence of the national front may have turned out to be counterproductive from the Soviet viewpoint since it seems to have exacerbated the Kurdish-Arab conflict, with the Iraqi Communists themselves now engaged in warfare with the Kurds. In addition, the existence of the front does not seem to have moderated Iraqi policy toward Iran, since after a brief period of cooperation during the October war, Iran and Iraq were again engaged in heavy fighting by the end of the year. It appeared as if the Soviet Union had made little progress in trying to contain this conflict, which was a major obstacle to the growth of Soviet influence in the Perisan Gulf. All in all, it appears as if Arab regimes had established party-to-party relations with the CPSU, established national fronts, and allowed Communists into their governments—in nominal positions—primarily as a device to extract more economic and military assistance from the USSR. It appears that Yasir Arafat of the PLO has now begun to follow a similar policy. While a number of Arab regimes have thus been exploiting Soviet desires to establish national fronts, the Arab Communists have not shown much enthusiasm for the new Soviet policy. Indeed, this is one of the issues on which the Syrian Communist Party split, and in the last several years Arab Communists writing in the *World Marxist Review* have openly criticized Soviet policies toward the so-called revolutionary democratic regimes of the Arab world. While the Soviet decision to print these articles may have been merely an attempt to assuage the Arab Communists' anger by giving them a public forum to air their grievances, the articles also would seem to point to an underlying mood among some Arab Communists that seem to indicate that Communist-supported coup d'etat attempts, on the model of the events in the Sudan in July 1971, are not to be ruled out. Any such attempt would, of course, almost totally undermine Soviet relations with the revolutionary democratic leadership of the Arab state involved, much as happened in the Sudan in 1971. Nonetheless, given the unstable politics of the Middle East and the very narrow bases of such Arab regimes as the Syrian and Iraqi Ba'ath, the Arab Communists may well be tempted to ally with a faction in the nation's army, carry out the coup, and then present the Soviet Union with a fait accompli. This would confront the Soviet leadership with the unpleasant choice of either assisting the new Communist regime (and alienating the Arab nationalists) or else watching such a regime turn to China or even be ousted by neighboring Arab states, as occurred in the Sudan in 1971.

It is no doubt because of these very unpleasant alternatives that the Soviet leadership has been urging the Arab Communists to bide their time and to realize that the evolution of the revolutionary democratic regimes to socialism is a very long process. The current turn of the Arab nationalist leaders toward the United States (which of course may only be a temporary one) may, however, convince the Arab Communists that time is not on their side. It is quite possible that some members of the Soviet political leadership, dismayed by the course of events in the Middle East since Nasser's death, and particularly since the October 1973 Arab-Israeli war, may also wish to work more actively for a change in some of the ruling Arab regimes. In any case, the Soviet Union is likely to be blamed for the activities of the Arab Communist parties whether or not it instigates them, and in the near future, at least, the Arab Communists are more likely to cause problems for Soviet policy-makers in the Middle East than to be of help to them.

While the Soviet leadership changed its policy toward the Arab Communist parties in an effort to arrest anti-Soviet trends in the Middle East and encourage anti-Western ones—albeit with only mixed results—the Soviet leaders also began to encourage a closer relationship with a number of Arab states and guerrilla organizations in an effort to counter Egypt's moves toward the United States and Saudi Arabia. Thus, in the 1972-74 period, the USSR strengthened its ties with Iraq, signing a friendship and assistance treaty and supplying military aid for Iraq's confrontation with Iran and for its offensive against the Kurds. Similarly, after a great deal of mutual invective, the USSR also moved to broaden economic and military cooperation with Libya, whose leader, Mu'ammar Kaddafi, shared the Soviet distaste for Egypt's rapprochement with the United States and alignment with Saudi Arabia. However, Libya and Iraq were less than ideal partners for the Soviet Union in its quest for Middle East influence. Both nations were virtually isolated in the Arab world—indeed, their isolation was the cause of their turn toward the USSR. By broadening and deepening relations with the Kaddafi and Al-Bakr regimes, the Soviet leadership was simultaneously generating a great deal of suspicion in the other Arab states, particularly Egypt, the Sudan, Kuwait, the Union of Arab Emirates, and Saudi Arabia, whose leaders were the victims of subversive activities sponsored by Kaddafi or Al-Bakr. The Soviet shift from Egypt, the most prestigious Arab state, to Iraq and Libya, the most isolated, would appear to be yet another indication of the weakening of the Soviet position in the Middle East since the death of Nasser in 1970, although the Soviet economy undoubtedly profited from the shift.

In its effort to foster anti-Western trends in the Middle East, the Soviet leadership also strengthened its ties to the two main Arab guerrilla organizations, the PLO and the PFLOAG, in the period following Nasser's death. Just as in the cases of Iraq and Libya, the two organizations welcomed Soviet support at a time when they were encountering serious difficulties—the PLO after being mauled by Hussein's troops in September 1970 and July 1971, and the PFLOAG after encountering increasing resistance from the new, Sandhurst-trained Sultan of Oman and his British and Iranian troops. Espousing anti-Western slogans, the leaders of both guerrilla organizations became frequent visitors to Moscow after the Soviet debacle in the Sudan, and they were rewarded with economic, military, and medical support in return for advocating the Soviet line on Middle Eastern issues. Yet in following the example set by the leaders of Egypt, Syria, Iraq, and Libya, who espoused anti-Western slogans in return for Soviet support, the guerrilla organizations joined the long list of Arab leaders who were exploiting the Soviet drive for influence in the Middle East while giving little more than lip service to Soviet policies in return.

In an effort both to counter its deteriorating position in the Middle East and to foster anti-Western trends in the region, the Soviet leadership thus forged closer ties with Iraq, Libya, the PLO, and the PFLOAG, while also changing its policy towards the Arab Communist parties. In addition to taking these steps, however, the Russians also sought to achieve their goals by capitalizing opportunistically on the Arab-Israeli conflict. The Israeli attacks on Palestinian guerrilla bases in Lebanon and Syria in September 1972, following the massacre of Israeli athletes at the Olympic games in Munich, gave the Soviet Union an opportunity to underline its support of the Arab cause while simultaneously undermining the position of the United States, which the Soviet leadership sought to link to Israel's policies. The events at Munich set off a wave of terrorism and counterterrorism that inflamed the Arab-Israeli conflict to a fever pitch, thereby making the USSR once again an important factor to the Arab leaders, given the United States support of Israel. Meanwhile, a shortage of oil had become a serious problem in the United States, which for the first time had become vulnerable to Arab oil pressure. Throughout 1973, with Arab-Israeli tensions rising, the Soviet leaders began to urge the Arabs to use their "oil weapon" against the United States. This dual policy of linking the United States to Israeli actions (such as the killing of three PLO leaders in Beirut) and urging the use of the Arab oil weapon against the United States, was also followed during the 1973 Arab-Israeli war, which the Soviet leadership saw not only as an opportunity to regain its lost ground in the Middle East, but also as a chance to strike a potentially decisive blow against United States interests in the region through the establishment of the long-coveted Arab unity on an "anti-imperialist" basis.

In turning to an evaluation of Soviet behavior during the October war, one is struck by the fact that in many ways its opportunism is analogous to the behavior of American oil companies during the American energy crisis. Thus, while the oil companies may not have deliberately planned the energy crisis, they were certainly quick to exploit it for their own benefit—so quick, in fact, that many observers accused them of deliberately plotting the crisis. The situation with regard to the Soviet role in the October war would appear to be similar. While the Russians may not have actively supported Egypt's decision to go to war against Israel—at least until the coup in Chile—and while the Soviet leaders were very hesitant in both their reporting of the war and their support of the Arabs in the first few days of the conflict, they were quick to try to exploit the Arab military success against Israel and the strains in NATO and the EEC caused by the war and the oil embargo. Unfortunately for the Russians, however, their gains from the war were mostly transient ones. Thus, the "anti-imperialist unity" of the Arabs soon dissolved, and the United States emerged several months after the war with a better Middle Eastern position than it possessed before it began—all this despite the massive Soviet military support for the Arabs during the war and United States support for Israel. In addition, the war strengthened the domestic position of Egyptian President Anwar Sadat, who soon reverted to his earlier policy of moving to improve economic and political relations with the West. This, when coupled with his increasingly close ties with oil-rich Saudi Arabia, another nation that moved to restore its relations with the United States after the war, created an Egyptian-Saudi axis in the Middle East that was potentially much more favorably inclined toward the United States than toward the USSR. This alignment possesses the potential of attracting even such countries as Syria, a development that would further erode the Soviet position in the region. In addition, as an oil-hungry West Europe and Japan scurried to make long-range economic and military deals with the oil-producing Arab states (and Iran), further difficulties were created for Soviet policy-makers because the USSR now had to cope with West European and Japanese competition in the region as well as American. The Arab states were thus able to play off all the major powers against each other, thus limiting the amount of influence any one power, including the USSR, could wield.

Should the situation in the Arab world continue to develop in this pattern—and it is far too early to consider these trends to be permanent particularly after the Arab summit at Rabat—the Soviet leaders may be tempted to urge certain Arab states, such as Syria, whose minority Shii Moslem regime gains legitimacy from its largely Sunni Moslem population by fighting against Israel, to again resort to war. The Assad regime may do so, particularly if the Israelis for security reasons do not withdraw from all the Golan Heights. Soviet reasoning might be that the war would spread to other Arab states, whose leaders, impelled by popular opinion and memories of the Arab successes in the early stages of the October war, would then join Syria in its battle with Israel. Assuming the United States would again support Israel, this would make the USSR once again a major factor in the Arab world because of the need for immense supplies of weaponry to fight an October-type war, while at the same time again undermining the American position.

Yet a Soviet policy of urging renewed warfare also has its limitations. In the first place, Egypt, under Sadat at least, may not be willing to go to war at Syrian (or Soviet) behest, much as it refused in December 1972 when Syria and Israel were engaged in major tank and artillery battles. Second, it may be more difficult for Syria (or the USSR) to mobilize the Saudi Arabian oil weapon, just as they were unable to convince Faisal to maintain the oil embargo despite the "war of attrition" in the Golan Heights. Finally, a clear Soviet push for the Arabs to return to war might just about destroy the vestiges of Soviet-American detente, which was gravely weakened by the October war and Soviet efforts to maintain the oil embargo against the United States. With a new American President in the White House, the Soviet leaders may think twice before getting deeply involved in a new war.

Consequently, although it is very difficult to make predictions about such a volatile region as the Middle East, assuming present trends continue, the Soviet leaders may decide to settle for a Middle East peace agreement that would lead to the establishment of a Palestinian Arab state (on the West Bank of the Jordan and the Gaza strip) in which they could expect to exercise influence. Similarly, they may reason that the conservative monarchies of Saudi Arabia, Kuwait, and the Union of Arab Emirates may soon be replaced by radical regimes of the Iraqi and South Yemeni type, which would call upon the USSR for support; and that the Sadat regime, beset by domestic economic problems, may yet fall, to be replaced by a more radical regime; or that Sadat might turn back to the Soviet Union for arms (he made a move in this direction in October 1974) and go to war again in order to regain territory from Israel. The Soviet leadership may also reason that conflict over the high price of oil may split the conservative oil-producing Arab states away from their alignment with the United States, a development that could spur them to turn to the Soviet Union for support and protection. Such a policy of "watchful waiting" and exploiting regional developments, rather than encouraging a new war, is also less damaging to Soviet-American relations. Yet one could also question the value of this type of "watchful waiting" policy since in the past both South Yemen and Iraq have exploited their relationship with the USSR to pursue goals not particularly to the liking of the Soviet leadership. It is also possible that the oil price problem can be solved without causing a rupture in Arab-American relations and that pro-American trends will continue— particularly if an Arab-Israeli peace agreement is achieved. Nonetheless, given the overall Soviet goal of expelling Western influence from the Middle East, the Soviet leadership seems willing to continue to provide large amounts of military and economic aid as well as diplomatic support to Arab regimes that often oppose the USSR, in the hope of spurring anti-Western trends in the region. While the ultimate success of this strategy remains very much in doubt—the Russians were farther from their goal in November 1974 than they were at the time of Nasser's death four years earlier—there is as yet no indication that the Soviet leadership has given up its efforts to increase Soviet influence in the Middle East while diminishing and ultimately eliminating that of the United States and its Western allies.

The Soviet leaders seem willing to pay the costs involved in pursuing such a policy because they have made the basic decision that the Middle East is a region of major importance to the Soviet Union.

BIBLIOGRAPHY

DOCUMENTARY COLLECTIONS AND
STATISTICAL STUDIES

Documents of the 24th Congress of the Communist Party of the Soviet Union.
Moscow: Novosti Press Agency Publishing House, 1971.

SSSR i arabskie strany. Moscow: Government Printing Office of Political
Literature, 1960.

Vneshniaia torgovlia SSSR 1918-1966. Moscow: Mezhdunarodnye otnsoheniia,
1967.

Vneshniaia torgovlia SSSR za 1967; 1968; 1969; 1970; 1971; 1972 (annual).
Moscow: Mezhdunarodnye otnosheniia, 1968-1973.

BOOKS

Abu-Lughod, Ibrahim, ed. *The Arab-Israeli Confrontation of 1967: An Arab
Perspective.* Evanston, Ill.: Northwestern University Press, 1970.

Agwani, M. S. *Communism in the Arab East.* Bombay: Asia Publishing House,
1969.

Al-Marayati, Abid A., ed. *The Middle East: Its Governments and Politics.*
Belmont, Cal.: Duxbury Press, 1972.

Avakov, R. M., E. A. Bragina, and K. L. Maidanik, eds. *Razvivaiushchiesia
strany: zakonomernosti, tendentsii, perspektivy.* Moscow: Mysl', 1974.

Badeau, John. *An American Approach to the Arab World.* New York: Harper
and Row, 1968.

Becker, A. S., and A. L. Horelick. *"Soviet Policy in the Middle East."* Santa
Monica, Cal.: Rand Publication R-504-FF, 1970.

Be'eri, Eliezer. *Army Officers in Arab Politics and Society.* New York: Praeger,
1970.

180

Bodianskii, V. L. *Sovremennyi kuveit.* Moscow: Nauka, 1971.

Cottam, Richard W. *Competitive Interference and Twentieth Century Diplomacy.* Pittsburgh: University of Pittsburgh Press, 1967.

Dagan, Avigdor. *Moscow and Jerusalem.* New York: Abelard-Schuman, 1970.

Dann, Uriel. *Iraq Under Kassem.* New York: Praeger, 1969.

Dolidze, D. I. *Problemy edinstva antiimperialisticheskoi borby.* Moscow: Nauka, 1973.

Evron, Yair. *The Middle East.* New York: Praeger, 1973.

Fairhall, David. *Russian Sea Power.* Boston: Gambit, 1971.

Fedchenko, A. F. *Irak v borbe za nezavisimost'.* Moscow: Nauka, 1970.

Freedman, Robert O. *Economic Warfare in the Communist Bloc: A Study of Soviet Economic Pressure Against Yugoslavia, Albania and Communist China.* New York: Praeger, 1970.

Gafurov, B. G., and G. F. Kim. *Zarybezhnyi vostok i sovremennost'.* Moscow: Nauka, 1974.

Gafurov, B., ed. *Religiia i obshestvennaia misl' narodov vostoka.* Moscow: Nauka, 1971.

Gerasimov, O. *Irakskaia neft'.* Moscow: Nauka, 1969.

Goldman, Marshall. *Soviet Foreign Aid.* New York: Praeger, 1967.

Gorbatov, O. M., and L. I. Cherkasskii. *Sotrudnichestvo SSSR so stranami arabskogo vostoka i Afriki.* Moscow: Nauka, 1973.

Hammond, Paul, and Sidney Alexander, eds. *Political Dynamics in the Middle East.* New York: Elsevier, 1972.

Heikal, Mohammed. *The Cairo Documents.* New York: Doubleday, 1973.

Hurewitz, J. C. *Middle East Politics: The Military Dimension.* New York: Praeger, 1969.

Kerr, Malcolm. *The Arab Cold War.* New York: Oxford University Press, 1970.

_____ . *Regional Arab Politics and the Conflict with Israel.* Santa Monica, Cal.: Rand Publication RM-5966-FF, 1969.

Khadduri, Majid. *Political Trends in the Arab World.* Baltimore: Johns Hopkins Press, 1970.

————. *Republican Iraq.* New York: Oxford University Press, 1969.

Khouri, Fred J. *The Arab-Israeli Dilemma.* Syracuse, N.Y.: Syracuse University Press, 1968.

Kim, G. F., and F. I. Shabshina. *Proletarskii internatsionalizm i revoliutsii v stranakh vostoka.* Moscow: Nauka, 1967.

Kimhe, David, and Dan Bawly. *The Six-Day War: Prologue and Aftermath.* New York: Stein and Day, 1971.

Klieman, Aaron S. *Soviet Russia and the Middle East.* Baltimore: Johns Hopkins Press, 1970.

Kohler, Foy D., Leon Goure, and Mose L. Harvey. *The Soviet Union and the October 1973 Middle East War.* Miami: Center for Advanced International Studies, University of Miami, 1974.

Kotlov, L. I. *Iemenskaia arabskaia respublika.* Moscow: Nauka, 1971.

Kutsenkov, A. A., ed. *Rabochii klass i antiimperialisticheskaia revoliutsia v Azii Afrike i latinskoi Amerike.* Moscow: Nauka, 1969.

Kylagina, L. M., ed. *Arabskie strany: Turtsia; Iran; Afganistan.* Moscow: Nauka, 1973.

Landis, Lincoln. *Politics and Oil: Moscow in the Middle East.* New York: Dunellen, 1973.

Laquer, Walter. *Confrontation: The Middle East in World Politics.* New York: Bantam Books, 1974.

————. *The Road to Jerusalem.* New York: Macmillan, 1968.

————. *The Soviet Union and the Middle East.* New York: Praeger, 1959.

————. *The Struggle for the Middle East.* New York: Macmillan, 1969.

Laron, Ram. *Hamaatzamot V'hamizrah Hatikon.* Tel-Aviv: Bronfman, 1970.

Lederer, Ivo J., and Wayne S. Vucinich, eds. *The Soviet Union and the Middle East.* Stanford, Cal.: Hoover Institution Press, 1973.

Lenczowski, George. *Soviet Advances in the Middle East.* Washington, D.C.: American Enterprise Institute, 1971.

Levkovskii, A. I. *Ekonomicheskaia politika i gosudarstvennyi kapitalizm v stranakh vostoka.* Moscow: Nauka, 1972.

Linden, Carl. *Khrushchev and the Soviet Leadership 1957-1964.* Baltimore: Johns Hopkins Press, 1966.

Lutskia, N. S., ed. *Arabskie strany: istoriia; ekonomika.* Moscow: Nauka, 1974.

Lutsky, V. *Modern History of the Arab Countries.* Moscow: Progress Publishers, 1969.

Mackintosh, J. M. *Strategy and Tactics of Soviet Foreign Policy.* London: Oxford University Press, 1963.

Mansfield, Peter. *The Middle East: A Political and Economic Survey.* London: Oxford University Press, 1973.

Monroe, Elizabeth, ed. *The Changing Balance of Power in the Persian Gulf.* New York: American Universities Field Staff, 1972.

Mueller, Kurt. *The Foreign Aid Programs of the Soviet Bloc and Communist China.* New York: Walker, 1967.

Namir, Mordecai. *Shlihoot B'Moskva.* Tel-Aviv: Am Oved, 1971.

Nielsen, Waldemar A. *The Great Powers and Africa.* New York: Praeger, 1969.

Nukhovich, E. S. *Ekonomicheskoe sotrudnichestvo i manevry anti-kommunistov.* Moscow: Mezhdunarodnye otnosheniia, 1969.

Nutting, Anthony. *Nasser.* New York: Dutton, 1972.

Ottaway, David and Marina. *Algeria: The Politics of a Socialist Revolution.* Berkeley: University of California Press, 1970.

Pennar, Jaan. *The USSR and the Arabs: The Ideological Dimension.* New York: Crane Russak, 1973.

Polk, William. *The United States and the Arab World.* Cambridge, Mass.: Harvard University Press, 1969.

Pranger, Robert J. *American Policy for Peace in the Middle East 1969-1971.* Washington, D.C.: American Enterprise Institute, 1971.

Quandt, William B., Fuad Jabbar, and Ann Lesch. *The Politics of Palestinian Nationalism.* Berkeley: University of California Press, 1973.

Rabinowich, Itamar. *Syria Under the Ba'ath.* Jerusalem: Israel Universities Press, 1972.

Ra'anan, Uri. *The USSR Arms the Third World.* Cambridge, Mass.: M.I.T. Press, 1969.

Sachar, Howard M. *Europe Leaves the Middle East 1936-1954.* New York: Alfred A. Knopf, 1972.

Safran, Nadav. *From War to War.* New York: Pegasus, 1969.

Seale, Patrick. *The Struggle for Syria.* London: Oxford University Press, 1965.

Semin, N. S. *Strany SEV i Afrika.* Moscow: Mezhdunarodnye otnosheniia, 1968.

Sevortian, R. E. *Armiia v politicheskom rezhime stran sovremennogo vostoka.* Moscow: Nauka, 1973.

Shakhbazian, G. S. *Gosudarstvennyi sektor v ekonomike Iraka.* Moscow: Nauka, 1974.

Sharabi, Hisham. *Palestine and Israel.* New York: Pegasus, 1969.

Shiff, Zeev, and Raphael Rothstein. *Fedayeen.* New York: David McKay, 1972.

Singer, Marshall R. *Weak States in a World of Powers.* New York: Free Press, 1972.

Smirnov, S. R., ed. *A History of Africa 1918-1967.* Moscow: Nauka, 1968.

Smolansky, Oles M. *The Soviet Union and the Arab East Under Khrushchev.* Lewisburg, Pa.: Bucknell University Press, 1974.

Spector, Ivan. *The Soviet Union and the Muslim World.* Seattle, Wash.: University of Washington Press, 1956.

Stephens, Robert. *Nasser: A Political Biography.* New York: Simon and Schuster, 1971.

Talbott, Strobe, ed. *Khrushchev Remembers.* Boston: Little, Brown, 1970.

Trevelyan, Humphrey. *The Middle East in Revolution.* Boston: Gambit, 1970.

Ulam, Adam. *Expansion and Coexistence: A History of Soviet Foreign Policy 1917-1967.* New York: Praeger, 1968.

Ulianovsky, R. *Sotsialism i osvobodivshikhsia strany.* Moscow: Nauka, 1972.

Ushakova, N. A. *Arabskaia respublika Egipet.* Moscow: Nauka, 1974.

Wolfe, Thomas W. *Soviet Power and Europe*. Baltimore: Johns Hopkins Press, 1970. .

World Communism 1967-1969: Soviet Efforts to Re-establish Control. Washington: U.S. Government Printing Office, 1971.

Yaari, Ehud. *Fatah*. Tel-Aviv: Levin-Epstein, 1970.

Yodfat, Aryeh. *Arab Politics in the Soviet Mirror*. Jerusalem: Israel Universities Press, 1973.

Zhurkin V. V., and E. Primakov, eds. *Mezhdunarodnye konflikty*. Moscow: Mezhdunarodnye otnosheniia, 1972.

ARTICLES

Adie, W. A. C. "Peking's Revised Line." *Problems of Communism* 21, no. 5 (September-October 1972): 54-68.

Andronov, Iona. "The Change-over in the White House." *New Times* (Moscow), no. 33 (1974): 6-7.

Apalin, G. "Peking Provocations." *New Times* (Moscow), nos. 45-46 (1973): 28-30.

Ashhab, Naim. "To Overcome the Crisis of the Palestine Resistance Movement." *World Marxist Review* 15, no. 5 (May 1972): 71-78.

Barnds, William. "China and America: Limited Partners in the Indian Subcontinent." In *Sino-American Detente and its Policy Implications*, ed. Gene T. Hsiao, pp. 226-248. New York: Praeger, 1974.

Bechtold, Peter K. "New Attempts at Arab Cooperation: The Federation of Arab Republics 1971—?" *Middle East Journal* 27, no. 2 (Spring 1973): 152-172.

Becker, Abraham S. "Oil and the Persian Gulf." In *The USSR and The Middle East*, ed. Michael Confino and Shimon Shamir, pp. 173-214. Jerusalem: Israel Universities Press, 1973.

Bronin, I. "Arabskaia neft—Ssha—zapadnaia Evrope." *Mirovaia ekonomika i mezhdunarodnaia otnosheniia*, no. 2 (February 1972): 31-42.

Bukharov, Victor. "Palestinian National Council Session." *New Times* (Moscow), no. 25 (1974): 12-13.

Campbell, Robert W. "Some Issues in Soviet Energy Policy for the Seventies." *Middle East Information Series,* no. 26-27 (Spring-Summer 1974): 92-100.

Carlson, Sevinc. "China, the Soviet Union and the Middle East." *New Middle East* (London), no. 27 (December 1970): 32-40.

Cherniavina, V. "Energeticheskie problemy stran EEC." *Mirovaia ekonomika i meshdunarodnaia otnosheniia,* no. 4 (April 1974): 56-65.

Choui, Nicholas. "The Middle East Crisis and the Arab Liberation Movement." *World Marxist Review* 14, no. 9 (September 1971): 28-34.

Cooley, John. "Moscow Faces a Palestinian Dilemma." *Mid East* 11, no. 3 (June 1970): 32-35.

Dann, Uriel. "The Communist Movement in Iraq Since 1963." In *The USSR and the Middle East,* ed. Michael Confino and Shimon Shamir, pp. 377-398. Jerusalem: Israel Universities Press, 1972.

Demchenko, Pavel. "Arab Oil for the Arabs." *New Times* (Moscow), no. 25 (1972): 10-11.

Field, Michael. "Iraq-Growing Realism among the Revolutionaries." *New Middle East* (London), no. 29 (February 1971): 27-29.

————. "Foundation of Soviet-Egyptian Relations." *New Times* (Moscow), no. 22 (1974): 17.

Freedman, Robert O. "Soviet Dilemmas in the Middle East." *Problems of Communism* 23, no. 3 (May-June 1972): 71-73.

————. "The Partition of Palestine: Conflicting Nationalism and Power Politics." In *Partition: Peril to World Peace,* ed. Thomas Hachey, pp. 175-212. New York: Rand McNally, 1972.

Gaspard, J. "Damascus After the Coup." *New Middle East* (London), no. 28 (January 1971): 9-11.

Gasteyger, Kurt. "Moscow and the Mediterranean." *Foreign Affiars* 46, no. 4 (July 1968): 676-687.

Gavrilov, I. "Arab Press on the Middle East Situation." *New Times* (Moscow), no. 36 (1972): 8-9.

Ginsburgs, George. "Moscow's Reaction to Nixon's Jaunt to Peking." In *Sino-American Detente and its Policy Implications,* ed. Gene T. Hsiao, pp. 137-159. New York: Praeger, 1974.

Gvozdev, Yuri. "Democratic Yemen: Problems and Aims." *New Times* (Moscow), no. 48 (1972).

Hardt, John P. "West Siberia: The Quest for Energy." *Problems of Communism* 22, no. 3 (May-June 1973): 25-36.

Harris, Mervyn. "From Nile to Euphrates: The Evolution of a Myth." *New Middle East* (London), nos. 42-43 (March-April 1972): 46-48.

Ignatov, Alexander. "Iraq Today." *New Times* (Moscow), no. 21 (1974): 22-25.

_____ . "This Spring in Damascus." *New Times* (Moscow), no. 24 (1974): 26-28.

Ivanov, A. "Soviet Imports from Developing Countries." *Foreign Trade* (Moscow), no. 9 (September 1974): 38-43.

Katin, V. "Tel-Aviv's Atrocious Crime." *New Times* (Moscow), no. 9 (1973): 20-21.

Kerr, Malcom. "The Middle East and China." In *Policies Toward China: Views From Six Continents,* ed. A. M. Halpern, pp. 437-456. New York: McGraw-Hill, 1965.

_____ . "The Covenient Marriage of Egypt and Libya." *New Middle East* (London), no. 48 (September 1972): 4-7.

Kimhe, Jon. "The Soviet-Arab Scenario." *Midstream* 30, no. 10 (December 1973): 9-22.

Klekovsky, R. "Fruitful Cooperation Between CMEA States and the Arab Countries." *Foreign Trade* (Moscow), no. 8 (August 1974): 16-19.

Kornilov, Y. "Meetings with the Fedayeen." *New Times* (Moscow), no. 42 (1972): 23-25.

Kudryavtsev, Viktor. "The Political Consolidation in the UAR." *New Times* (Moscow), no. 43 (1970): 6-7.

_____ . "On the Arab Diplomatic Front." *New Times* (Moscow), no. 4 (1973): 12-13.

Laquer, Walter, and Edward Luttwak. "Kissinger and the Yom Kippur War." *Commentary* 58, no. 3 (September 1974): 33-40.

Levgold, Robert. "The Soviet Union's Changing View of Sub-Saharan Africa." In *Soviet Policy in Developing Countries,* ed. W. Raymond Jackson, pp. 62-82. Waltham, Mass.: Ginn-Blaisdell, 1970.

Levy, Avigdor. "The Syrian Communists and the Ba'ath Power Struggle 1966-1970." In *The USSR and the Middle East,* ed. Michael Confino and Shimon Shamir, pp. 395-417. Jerusalem: Israel Universities Press, 1973.

Levy, Walter J. "World Oil Cooperation or International Chaos." *Foreign Affairs* 52, no. 4 (July 1974): 690-713.

Lowenthal, Richard. "Russia, the One-Party System and the Third World." *Survey,* no. 58 (January 1966): 43-58.

Mansfield, Peter. "After the Purge." *New Middle East* (London), no. 33 (June 1971): 12-15.

"Marching Together: The Role of the Communists in Building a Broad Alliance of Democratic Forces." *World Marxist Review* 16, no. 2 (February 1973): 111-118.

Mirsky, Georgi. "Israeli Aggression and Arab Unity." *New Times* (Moscow), no. 28 (1967): 6-8.

———. "The Path of the Egyptian Revolution." *New Times* (Moscow), no. 30 (1972): 21-24.

———. "The Middle East: New Factors." *New Times* (Moscow), no. 48 (1973): 18-19.

Medzini, R. "China and the Palestinians." *New Middle East* (London), no. 32 (May 1971): 34-40.

Mosley, Phillip. "The Kremlin and the Third World." *Foreign Affairs* 46, no. 1 (October 1967): 64-77.

Mroue, Kerim. "Use the Opportunities of the New Situation in the Middle East." *World Marxist Review* 17, no. 3 (March 1974): 90-97.

Naumov, Pavel. "In Egypt Today." *New Times* (Moscow), no. 12 (1974): 24-26.

"New Stage in the National Liberation Movement." *World Marxist Review* 15, no. 11 (November 1972): 58-82.

Ojha, Ishwer C. "The Kremlin and Third World Leadership: Closing the Circle?" In *Soviet Policy Toward Developing Countries,* ed. W. Raymond Duncan, pp. 9-28. Waltham, Mass.: Ginn-Blaisdell, 1970.

Pennar, Jaan. "The Arabs, Marxism and Moscow: A Historical Survey." *Middle East Journal* 22, no. 3 (September 1968): 433-447.

Perlmutter, Amos. "Big Power Games, Small Power Wars." *Transaction* 7, nos. 9-10 (July-August 1970): 79-83.

Petrov, R. "Steps Toward Arab Unity." *New Times* (Moscow), no. 35 (1971): 20-

Ploss, Sidney. "Politics in the Kremlin." *Problems of Communism* 19, no. 3 (May-June 1970): 1-14.

Ponamarev Boris. "Under the Banner of Marxism-Leninism and Proletarian Internationalism: The 24th Congress of the CPSU." *World Marxist Review* 14, no. 6 (June 1971): 3-19.

Potomov, Y. "A Just Peace for the Middle East." *New Times* (Moscow), no. 24 (1972): 15-16.

_____. "Middle East Alliance Against Progress." *New Times* (Moscow), no. 34 (1972): 4-5.

_____. "The Egypt-Libya Merger Project." *New Times* (Moscow), no. 36 (1973): 10-11.

_____. "Middle East Settlement: Urgent Task." *New Times* (Moscow), no. 31 (1974): 21-22.

Primakov, Y. "Energeticheskii krizis v kapitalisticheskikh stranakh." *Mirovaia ekonomika i mezhdunarodnaia otnosheniia,* no. 2 (February 1974): 65-72.

Ra'anan, Uri. "Soviet Policy in the Middle East 1960-1973." *Midstream* 30, no. 10 (December 1973): 23-45.

Rachkov B. V. "Energeticheskie problemy soedinenykh shtatov." *Ssha,* no. 3 (March 1974): 29-43.

Rumyanstev, V. "Syria on the Alert." *New Times* (Moscow), no. 40 (1972): 8-9.

Safran, Nadav. "The Soviet-Egyptian Treaty." *New Middle East* (London), no. 34 (July 1971): 10-13.

Shaked, Haim, Esther Souery, and Gabriel Warburg. "The Communist Party in the Sudan 1946-1971." In *The USSR and the Middle East,* ed. Michael Confino and Shimon Shamir, pp. 293-319. Jerusalem: Israel Universities Press, 1973.

Shamir, Shimon. "The Marxists in Egypt: The 'Lincensed Inflitration' Doctrine in Practice." In *The USSR and the Middle East,* ed. Michael Confino and Shimon Shamir, pp. 293-319. Jerusalem: Israel Universities Press, 1973.

Shmarov, Vladimir. "The Baghdad Dialogue." *New Times* (Moscow), no. 5 (1974): 10-11.

Shmelyov, Georgi. "Solidarity the Keynote." *New Times* (Moscow), no. 28 (1974): 10.

Shumilin, Boris. "Zionist Fabrications and the Reality." *New Times* (Moscow), no. 16 (1972): 12-13.

Singer, A. David. "Internation Influence: A Formal Model." In *International Politics and Foreign Policy*, ed. James N. Rosenau, pp. 380-391. New York: Macmillan, 1969.

Smirnov, V., and I. Matyukhin. "USSR and the Arab East." *International Affairs* (Moscow), no. 9 (September 1972): 83-87.

Spichkin, V. "Energeticheskii kriziz v Ssha." *Mirovaia ekonomika i mezhdunarodnaia otnosheniia*, no. 3 (March 1974): 85-98.

Sylvester, Anthony. "Mohammed vs. Lenin in Revolutionary Sudan." *New Middle East* (London), no. 34 (July 1971): 26-28.

Thompson, W. Scott. "Parameters on Soviet Policy in Africa: Personal Diplomacy and Economic Interests in Ghana." In *Soviet Policy in Developing Countries*, ed. W. Raymond Jackson, pp. 83-106. Waltham, Mass.: Ginn-Blaisdell, 1970.

Ulianovsky, R. "Nekotorie voprosy nikapitalistichekogo razvitiia." *Kommunist*, no. 4 (1971): 103-112.

_____ . "Marxist and Non-Marxist Socialism." *World Marxist Review* 14, no. 9 (September 1971): 119-127.

_____ . "O edinom anti-imperialisticheskom fronte progressivnikh sil v osvobodivshikhsia stranakh." *Mirovaia ekonomika i mezhdunarodnaia otnosheniia*, no. 9 (September 1972): 76-86.

Vatikiotis, P. J. "Egypt's Politics of Conspiracy." *Survey* 18, no. 2 (Spring 1972): 83-89.

_____ . "Two Years After Nasser: The Chance of a New Beginning." *New Middle East* (London), no. 48 (September 1972): 7-9.

Volsky, Dmitry. "Changes in the Sudan." *New Times* (Moscow), no. 30 (1971): 10-11.

_____ . "A Frank Talk with Some Arab Colleagues." *New Times* (Moscow), no. 37 (1972): 4-5.

_____ . "The Middle East Situation." *New Times* (Moscow), no. 39 (1972): 6-7.

_____ . "King Faisal's Holy War." *New Times* (Moscow), no. 5 (1973): 26-27.

_____ . "The Beirut Crime." *New Times* (Moscow), no. 16 (1973): 12-13.

_____ . "New Opportunities and Old Obstacles." *New Times* (Moscow), no. 32 (1973): 14-15.

_____ . "Soviet-American Relations and the Third World." *New Times* (Moscow), no. 36 (1973): 4-6.

_____ . "Step Toward Settlement." *New Times* (Moscow), no. 23 (1974): 8-9.

_____ . "Arab East: Miracles and Realities." *New Times* (Moscow), no. 24 (1974): 12-13.

Volsky, Dmitry and A. Usvatov. "Israeli Expansionists Miscalculate." *New Times* (Moscow), no. 42 (1973): 10-11.

Whetten, Lawrence J. "Changing Soviet Attitudes Toward Arab Radical Movements." *New Middle East* (London), no. 18 (March 1970): 20-27.

Yellon R. A. "Shifts in Soviet Policies Toward Developing Areas." In *Soviet Policy in Developing Countries,* ed. W. Raymond Duncan, pp. 225-286. Waltham, Mass.: Ginn-Blaisdell, 1970.

Yodfat, A. "Unpredictable Iraq poses a Russian Problem." *New Middle East* (London), no. 13 (October 1969): 17-20.

_____ . "Moscow Reconsiders Fatah." *New Middle East* (London), no. 13 (December 1969): 15-18.

_____ . "The USSR and the Arab Communist Parties." *New Middle East* (London), no. 32 (May 1971): 29-33.

_____ . "Russia's Other Middle East Pasture—Iraq." *New Middle East* (London), no. 38 (November 1971): 26-29.

Yost, Charles. "The Arab-Israeli War: How It Began." *Foreign Affairs* 46, no. 2 (January 1968): 304-320.

Zlatorunsky, Aleksei. "Libya and its Problems." *New Times* (Moscow), nos. 18-19 (1974): 35-36.

PERIODICALS

Christian Science Monitor, 1969-1974

Foreign Trade (Moscow), 1969-1974

International Affairs (Moscow), 1964-1974

Kommunist (Moscow), 1969-1974

Middle East Journal, 1964-1974

Mirovaia ekonomika i mezhdunarodnye otnosheniia (Moscow), 1969-1974

New Middle East (London), 1968-1973

New Times (Moscow), 1964-1964

New York *Times,* 1969-1974

Peking *Review,* 1969-1974

Pravda, 1969-1974

Radio Liberty Reports, 1969-1974

Ssha, 1970-1974

Washington *Post,* 1970-1974

World Marxist Review, 1960-1974

ABOUT THE AUTHOR

ROBERT OWEN FREEDMAN is Associate Professor and Russian and Middle East Area Specialist in Marquette University's Department of Political Science. Until completion of his army service in July 1970, he was Assistant Professor of Russian History and Government in the Department of Social Sciences at the United States Military Academy at West Point. Dr. Freedman has traveled both in the Soviet Union and the Middle East, and he recently testified on Soviet policy toward the Middle East to the Foreign Affairs Committee of the United States House of Representatives. Dr. Freedman has published *Economic Warfare in the Communist Bloc: A Study of Soviet Economic Pressure Against Yugoslavia, Albania and Communist China* (New York: Praeger, 1970) and a number of articles on Soviet foreign policy and Middle Eastern politics.

Dr. Freedman received his B.A. degree in diplomatic history from the University of Pennsylvania. He is a graduate of Columbia University's Russian Institute, and he also received his M.A. and Ph.D. from Columbia University.

RELATED TITLES
Published by
Praeger Special Studies

CRISIS DECISION-MAKING: Israel's Experience in 1967
and 1973
                    Abraham R. Wagner

MIDDLE EAST OIL AND U.S. FOREIGN POLICY
With Special Reference to the U.S. Energy Crisis
                    Shoshana Klebanoff

SOVIET AND CHINESE INFLUENCE IN THE
THIRD WORLD
                    edited by
                    Alvin Z. Rubinstein

SOVIET NAVAL POLICY: Objectives and Constraints
                    edited by Michael McGwire,
                    Ken Booth, and John McDonnell

SOVIET POLICY TOWARD BLACK AFRICA
                    Helen Desfosses Cohn